The Contribu

MARY ROBINSON, President of Ireland, is a native of Ballina, Co Mayo.

NUALA BOURKE is an occasional writer on theological topics from Castlebar.

PADRAIC BRENNAN is from Charlestown and works for Moy Valley Resources in Ballina.

ANNE CHAMBERS is a biographer and writer from Castlebar who lives in Dublin.

EOIN DE BHALDRAITHE is a Cistercian monk at Moone Abbey and a native of Bekan.

EUGENE DUFFY from Ballaghaderreen is a priest of the Achonry diocese and teaches theology at All Hallows College, Dublin.

MARY DURKAN is a theologian in Chicago whose parents came from Mayo.

MARY FAGAN is a Mercy sister from Knock who teaches in Arklow.

BRENDAN FAHEY is a Columban priest who spent twenty years as a missionary in Japan.

PADRAIG FLYNN, from Castlebar, a former TD and government minister, is a member of the European Commission in Brussels.

ANDREW GREELEY, a Chicago priest, is a novelist and sociologist. His grandparents came from Mayo.

KEVIN HEGARTY, a priest of Killala diocese, teaches in Belmullet and is editor of *Intercom*.

ENDA MCDONAGH, a priest of the diocese of Tuam, is a native of Bekan and teaches at Maynooth.

MAIGHREAD MCDONAGH, a nurse from Claremorris, has worked as a volunteer in the Horn of Africa.

CHRISTINA MURPHY, deputy editor of *The Irish Times*, is from Breaffy.

BERNARD O'HARA, lecturer in the RTC in Galway, is from Killasser.

NOLLAIG Ó MURAÍLE lectures at Queen's University, Belfast, and is a native of Knock.

PAT RABBITTE is a Democratic Left TD in Dublin and a native of Ballindine.

SUZANNE RYDER is a Mercy sister from Ballinrobe who has worked as a missionary in Peru.

ETHNA VINEY is a writer and ecologist from Westport.

Survival Or Salvation?

A SECOND MAYO BOOK OF THEOLOGY

Edited by
Enda McDonagh
with a preface by
President Mary Robinson

the columba press

First published in 1994 by
the columba press
93 The Rise, Mount Merrion, Blackrock, Co Dublin

Cover by Bill Bolger
Origination by The Columba Press
Printed in Ireland by
Colour Books Ltd, Dublin

ISBN 1 85607 101 4

Acknowledgements

The cover photograph, by John Searle, is of the OPW Visitors' Centre at the Céide Fields, and is used by kind permission of the Office of Public Works.

Contents

PART IV: MISSIONARIES AND MIGRANTS

PART V: THREATS TO SURVIVAL AND HINTS OF SALVATION

APPENDIX:

Preface

President Mary Robinson

One of the great pleasures for me in this book – as I hope it will be for other readers – is the chorus of Mayo voices it provides. The voices themselves are many and diverse. They range across different viewpoints and provide fresh perspectives. Above all, they combine and contrast with one another so that the effect left by this book is of a sparkling and engaging conversation. It is real conversation about real issues – between men and women, between local and general. Within that debate there are sharply different analyses but, by and large, a shared and fragile hope.

That hope has its roots – as this book does – in the relation between the local and wider community, for which the local is both a focus and a sign. Being from Mayo myself, I might be thought to be especially engaged in the details of one dear and particular place which these voices offer. And of course I am. But what has impressed and persuaded me most is the way in which the concerns of one part of the world are mobilised, by imagination and expression, to reach well beyond it. China and Peru, Somalia and Chicago and Killasser and the Céide Fields are all encompassed within the range of Mayo concerns.

What we see here is the interaction of both secular and religious voices exploring the deepest needs and ultimate possibilities of a single place. But that single place, in the exciting dialogue which develops, can quickly be construed as a metaphor for the needs and possibilities of other places. It is more and more important, in the world we live in now – with all the temptations it offers to nihilism and fatalism – that we understand that the world-wide issue does not erase the parochial one, and that the parochial does not block out the global. They are parts of one another, whose relation needs to be affirmed by imagination and compassion at all times, as it is here.

In a recent address at Harvard University I called for a renewal of
the determination expressed in the preamble to the United
Nations Charter, written in 1945. The values which that address
emphasised – of connectedness, listening, sharing and participation – all emerge in this book, in different and striking ways. The
voices here are deeply rooted in place and community. They
reach beyond them to the many other communities where such
voices may not yet have found their expression and, by so doing,
they affirm them as well as their own reality. These are voices con-
necting with other voices; but also reaching out to engage the
silences which need a voice. And for that reason I welcome this
Second Mayo Book of Theology and wish it well.

Introduction

Reactions to the first Mayo book of theology, *Faith and the Hungry Grass*, ranged from 'What a silly idea' to 'What an interesting collection'. The theologically interested were engaged by this experiment in local theology and impressed that the 'theologians' should come from a single county. The success of the experiment as theology was obviously more important than the unity of origin of the 'theologians', although in local theology the two aspects could not be separated.

The hope was expressed in that volume that other local Irish theologies (county- or province-wide) might emerge. Indeed a serious effort has been made to develop a regional west of Ireland theological enterprise. It held its first Conference in Galway in 1993 and hopes to continue its course in a variety of ways in the coming years (*cf* Appendix). This may be the next appropriate stage in Irish local theology. However, in that first volume the possibility of a second book of Mayo theology was mentioned. This possibility has now been realised with some innovations. The least important, if most obvious, of these innovations is the list of contributors. The decision to invite a whole new set of potential Mayo 'theologians' appeared rash to many. The first book emerged because the contributors invited had already been engaged at a scholarly or popular level in writing theology. This applies to very few of the second team. The reason for the change, however, was not just novelty. Nor was it to show how many theological teams Mayo could field. The reasons were themselves theological. The theology in question had moved beyond the concerns of *Faith and the Hungry Grass*, more an in-house publication of the *Domus Dei*, Mayo Club rooms.

Sacred and secular in dialogue
While the dialogue between sacred and secular, between church

and world, emerged clearly in that first book, it was largely internal to each contributor and so more or less domesticated in that
house of God. This second project is more ambitious. The *Domus
Dei* is not ecclesially defined or confined. Not every contributor
conducts her own internal dialogue. The contributors were invited
to write of the basic theme *Survival or Salvation?* from within their
own experience, expertise and responsibility and in the sacred or
secular terms which each found appropriate. The dialogue would
be carried on by the whole volume, which would respect the
diverse voices with their religious or political or historical or ecological concerns. Mayo theology would be freshly in the making,
not least because some fresh, and in theological circles, entirely
unexpected voices could be heard.

Risks

The risks of misunderstanding, dissonance, even total incoher-
ence were real. They have not been entirely overcome. The simple
defence of having to begin sometime, somewhere would not justify publication. For all the untidiness and disconnectedness, as
editor I believe that this volume, like its predecessor, takes Irish
theologising a step forward. The final proof will be in the reading
of the contributions themselves. Some insight into the book's purpose, and title, its style, structure and content as a whole may help
the reader in the final reading.

Title and Theme

The theme *Survival Or Salvation?* arose out of the chronic crisis
which Mayo, together with similar places, has experienced over
hundreds of years. In the last half-century the crisis, as it sharp-
ened, provoked local reactions both lay and clerical, party political and social voluntary. The emergence of Clann na Talmhan, for
example, as a significant political party in the west and its participation in two governments (1948-51, 1954-57) compelled some
more detailed attention by all politicians to the declining state of
the west. But, like previous and later political efforts, not to the extent of really interrupting the decline. In the fifties more active
voluntary movements and leaders were beginning to stir, of
which the most notable was Father James McDyer. He had a very

different but worthy successor in another priestly James, James Horan. And the prophetic voice of John Healy had taken the cause to the media. As 'Save the West' campaigns came and went, so did many of the emigrants who returned in the 1960s and the 1970s, attracted by the general economic improvement generated by the Lemass-Whittaker economic revival. The 1980s brought another downward cycle and the latest *Saving the West Together* campaign, initiated by the western bishops, reminds us how fragile the community life of the whole western half of the island is. Survival is at considerable risk; salvation, even for the most hopeful, at a considerable remove.

The title, with its question mark, suggests how far this book is from being a 'know-how' book for saving the west or even a rallying cry to those with responsibility and know-how. Elements of rallying and 'know-how' occur but the book is more in search of understanding than of immediate solutions, or seriously confronting the issues within the interchange of secular and religious or sacred language and thought which characterise so much Mayo and Irish life. With its claim to be a book of theology, the inter-action of the secular and sacred is essential, however inadequately it is realised.

Secular and liberation theologies

The dialogue between sacred and secular can take many forms. In Europe and North America this dialogue has tended to focus around the meaning and credibility of the sacred in a secularised, technological, and in some estimates, self-sufficient human world. More recently, in Latin America and other poorer regions, the dialogue has focused on the relevance of the gospel to problems of poverty, oppression and marginalisation. For Mayo, neither of these kinds of theology, in any pure form, is adequate. Secularisation and marginalisation form two challenges to Christian faith and practice. They may also prove twin resources to the growth of Christian faith and practice. The thrust of this book is to invoke secular and religious resources to reflect on the particular problems of Mayo secularisation and marginalisation. In that dialectical interaction between secular and sacred in response to Mayo, its Irish and world parallels (Mayo and Co.), a fuller stage in Mayo theologising emerges.

Reality and symbol

The origins of the contributors and the focus of their reflections make it clear that they are concerned with the real Mayo, the Mayo of geography and history, of beautiful landscape and buoyant people as well as of peripherality and emigration, of depression and depopulation. In Mayo lie their roots. On Mayo, in this volume, their concerns are concentrated.

Their Mayo origin and preoccupation does not exclude the wider world. Mayo they recognise also as symbol, symbol for many rural and urban deprived areas in Ireland and beyond, and indeed for Ireland itself in its peripherality and privations. Many of these have experienced other such areas in Ireland and the Third World at first hand through personal work and professional interest. Mayo shapes their attitudes and interests in relation to its myriad parallels in a broken world. The problems, insights and creative responses provoked by a particular locale have, at their deepest level, a universal significance. Mayo is symbol as well as reality. Mayo theology, if it is a good local theology, is of much wider significance.

Structure

The final structure of this book has a history. The original idea and outline were despatched to an invited group of potential contributors. Many of them very generously came long distances to a meeting to discuss the project. As the contributions came in, amendments to structure and text became increasingly necessary to maintain the coherence of the book and to keep it to a reasonable size. All of which means that there is further Mayo theology awaiting publication.

The sweep of the book, from 'Cherishing the Heritage' to looking for 'Hints of Salvation', finds recurrent expression in the particular sections and in individual chapters. The dialogues between Mayo past, present and future, between Mayo abroad and at home, between fears for survival and hopes for salvation, match the continual dialogue between sacred and secular. Such structured dialogue is only faintly indicated by section and chapter readings. They do however help orientate the reader and provide a basis for the coherent if multifarious dialogue that constitutes the new phase of Mayo theology.

Section by section

'Cherishing the Heritage' seemed the obvious place to start in a book planned and mainly written in the year Mayo 5000. Naming of places moved naturally to treating our ecological endowment as holy, and focusing on a particular case history of remembrance and renewal in Killasser.

Section two, 'Survivors and Saviours' takes a cool look at some dominant people in Mayo's history. Granuaile, folk heroine, may seem irrelevant to a volume of theology, even where theology is defined as involving the fully secular. Yet her leadership qualities, her fierce capacity for survival and her overcoming the gender handicap, continue to make her relevant to Mayo's difficulties, secular and religious. John Patrick Lyons, as a pre-famine proto-liberation theologian, and Mother Arsenius of Foxford, with her splendid capacity to combine economic practicality and religious faith, are more obvious projectors of a Mayo theology.

Mayo's preoccupation with education has had many ironic twists to it. Many of its political, church, media and sporting leaders came from a professional educational background, as this volume confirms. Ireland's earliest church-sponsored co-educational secondary schools began in Mayo in the 1940s. The participation rates of Mayo in third-level education is among the top two or three counties in Ireland for many years. Yet it has had no third level institution within the county. So the best and brightest had to leave the county to further their education, with naturally diminishing likelihood of return. Without third-level institutions there is no employment for people at that professional and intellectual level. So the county is further impoverished. Without involving this book in any particular advocacy, one might say that Mayo has a strong claim to serious third-level development within the county as well as to an educational centre to focus the great educational energies of the county. In passing it might be suggested that the new centre in Castlebar, for example, should be buttressed by smaller, specialised centres in other areas, like one for archaeology at the Céide Fields, others for farming, angling, ecology, drama, literature and painting (in Achill), specialised catering and cooking, sports coaching, even theology. These places would not need large capital investment but imagination, ideas and people with commitment and skill.

All this is building on the very significant second section 'If Only
Education Could Save ...' The wishful thinking or tinge of cynicism, which the section's title could convey, should not distract
the reader from the section's powerful historical and contemporary reflections.

The title 'Missionaries and Migrants' summarises so much of
Mayo's recent history that this section hardly needs comment. Yet
the foundation of the Maynooth Mission to China/Society of St
Columban, by Mayoman John Blowick and his associates, was an
epoch-making event of Irish church history in this century. The
continuance of that missionary tradition, by lay and religious
from Somalia to Peru, expresses this mutual enrichment of the
sacred and secular energies of Mayo – and the migrants, the emigration, which Pádraig Brennan and Andrew Greely examine in
very different ways, is still Mayo's greatest challenge.

The fears and the hopes will continue long after this book is forgotten. An effort to crystalise them comes at the end of the book
with strong pieces from political leaders, Commissioner Pádraig
Flynn of Brussels and Castlebar, and Pat Rabbitte, TD, originally
from Ballindine. A call to renewal through imagination by Mary
Durkin is followed by a theological effort to expose the darkness
and the light involved in daring to hope.

PART I

Cherishing the Heritage

CHAPTER 1

Mayo's Sacred Place Names

Nollaig Ó Muraíle

From historic Killala, from Swinford to Ballagh,
Newport and Cong, and old Castlebar,
Balla, Ballyhaunis, Belmullet in Erris ...

Of the many and varied facets of Ireland's cultural heritage, few can match our placenames in the fascination they hold for the proverbial 'man (and woman) in the street'. We in, or from, Mayo seem especially proud of the names of our towns, villages and townlands: witness the county's 'anthem', dating from the days of the Land War, 'The Boys from the County Mayo', with its proud, defiant enumeration of places (such as those listed above) which are 'famed near and far'. I have myself heard several local renditions of this ballad with additional verses extolling the townland and other names of a specific locality, and these 'local' verses in particular are generally sung with great gusto and received with a special acclamation. (An east Mayo version regularly sung in Carty's Pub in Knock by Eddie Flatley must run to more than thirty verses.)

A poem of 1417 and its background

Such a listing of places dear to the heart of the poet has roots which reach far back into the Gaelic past. An example which springs readily to my own mind – having recently had occasion to study it in some detail – is a great genealogical and topographical poem of more than 220 quatrains dating from the early fifteenth century. It was composed in the year 1417 by Giolla Íosa Mór Mac Fhir Bhisigh to mark the accession to the lordship of Tireragh (an ancient territory on the east side of Killala Bay) of Tadhg Riabhach Ó Dubhda (O'Dowd). The Uí Dhubhda were the royal family of the Uí Fhiachrach dynasty which in early Christian times held the kingship of all Connacht, and the Clann Fhir Bhisigh were their hereditary poets and historians. Admittedly, at the time the poem in question was composed the poet's family had been settled in what is now Co Sligo for perhaps half a century. But their roots, going back several centuries, were in Co Mayo, in the vicinity of Lough Conn.

In all, the poem mentions nearly ninety Mayo placenames and over seventy Mayo families, mainly in the baronies of Carra, Kilmaine, Tirawley and Erris. The majority of these still survive and are readily recognisable, and most of the unidentified placenames can be located, at least approximately, with the aid of seventeenth-century and later maps and surveys. (Giolla Íosa's poem is preserved in the manuscript known as the Book of Lecan which he himself compiled over a period of more than twenty years, beginning about 1397. 'Lecan' is one of two massive and justly celebrated manuscripts – virtual libraries of medieval Irish learning – produced in north Connacht within a few years of one another, the other being the Book of Ballymote.)

Lore of famous places

In medieval times there was a whole genre of Irish literature, the *Dindsenchus* – 'lore of famous places' – devoted to explaining the meaning of well-known Irish placenames. The *Metrical Dindsenchus*, dating from the eleventh century, includes poems purporting to explain the origin and meaning of such Mayo names as Loch Ceara (Lough Carra), Loch Con (Lough Conn), Ard na Riag (Ardnaree), Inber mBuada, or Muaide (the mouth of the river Moy, or perhaps Killala Bay itself), Carn Amalgaid (near Killala), Nemthend (Nephin) and Umall (a name preserved in Burrishoole). Admittedly, such 'explanation' would find little favour among modern scholars, but their very existence reflects the real interest which these important names generated among our ancestors. And from a later period there are innumerable poems and songs, both in Irish and English, extolling or evoking the memory of some place dear to the poet's heart. Mayo seems to have more than its fair share of these: '*Ar an loing seo Pháid Uí Loingsigh donímse an dobrón ...*' (or in George Fox's celebrated translation, 'On the deck of Patrick Lynch's boat I sat in woeful plight ...'), Rafftery's much-loved '*Anois teacht an Earraigh beidh an lá 'dul chun síneadh ...*', 'Far away from the land of the shamrock and heather ...', even 'Tis just a year ago today I left old Erin's isle ...' These songs and poems in praise of some aspect of our county are deserving of detailed study, as indeed are the placenames of Mayo generally. But there is a particular category of Mayo's toponomy which seems to merit particular attention in the present context. This comprises names which reflect the spiritual experience of our people over a couple of millenia – what we might call 'the sacred placenames of Mayo'. While three-quarters of those 'couple of millenia' have been dominated by the Christian religion, there are some names which have their roots in an earlier dispensation, however difficult it is for us at this remove to understand and appreciate it.

'Cultural ecology'

In a sense, all our placenames are sacred. They are part of what we might term our 'cultural ecology' or, to use that rather hackneyed and yet very true slogan about the Irish language, 'part of what we are'. It would accordingly be a veritable act of desecration willingly to let them die, or even not to strive to keep them alive. They are part of a cultural heritage which we are sometimes prone to think of in rather narrow, exclusivist terms when, in fact, we should see it as a coat of many colours. While we must, I believe, be particularly appreciative of the value of our Gaelic/Celtic heritage, we should now also be acutely conscious of the one-time presence of that stone-age society (long predating the Celts) whose five-thousand-year-old traces Séamus Caulfield has so dramatically uncovered on the Céide-Belderg hillsides. These first (known) 'Boys (and girls) from the County Mayo' may or may not have left some descendants among the present population of the county, but their very presence, and precedence, here should effectively smother the temptation to indulge in an intolerant 'Celtomania' – to borrow a term used in the last century by that fine, open-minded scholar John O'Donovan in relation to the amiably eccentric but overzealous eighteenth-century antiquarian General Charles Vallancey. We should therefore see our Gaelic heritage – which for two millenia has been the dominant one in Co Mayo – as warm and benignly inclusive rather than exclusive. Something to love and cherish for its own sake, rather than another stick with which to beat some 'old enemy', however defined or perceived.

The toponomical pyramid

A brief word of explanation may be in order here on the toponomy (placenames) of Ireland in general. The body of Irish placenames – mainly administrative names – may be set out in the
shape of a pyramid. Working downwards, the various levels com-
prise respectively the name of the country, those of the provinces
(at present four but in earlier times ranging from five to seven or
more), the counties (32), baronies (about 300), civil parishes (dating from medieval times and numbering about 2200) and finally
that the most quintessentially Irish of denominations, the townland (of which there are just over 60,000 in the whole island). The
equivalent numbers for Co Mayo are as follows: 11 baronies, 72
civil parishes and about 3200 townlands. Other categories of
name include those of district electoral divisions, urban districts,
streets in urban areas, as well as those of significant physical features – mountains, rivers, lakes, bays, islands, headlands. In addition, there is a wealth of minor names, particularly in Gaeltacht
areas – fields, hills, rocks, streams, hollows, roads, paths, bridges,
crossroads, and a wide variety of coastal features. Many of these
latter have never appeared on maps or even been recorded and
are therefore in particularly acute danger of being lost forever. (A
couple of examples will serve to illustrate just how rich this micro-
toponomy can be in areas where the Irish language survives: two
decades ago Séamas Ó Catháin of the Department of Irish Folklore, University College, Dublin, collected almost 800 minor
names from a single townland of some 850 acres, Kilgalligan/*Cill
Ghallagáin* in the Erris Gaeltacht, while around the same time I recorded about 600 names from the now grievously attenuated
Gaeltacht area around Toormakeady/*Tuar Mhic Éadaigh* on the
western shores of Lough Mask.)

The vast majority of the names in almost all the various categories
listed above are, linguistically, of Irish origin. In only one county,
Dublin, is the majority of townland-names non-Gaelic in origin.
However, despite this overwhelming preponderance of names
with Gaelic roots, there is believed to be a substratum of names
which may ultimately date from pre-Celtic times. The principal
candidates for inclusion in such a category are names of prominent physical features – notably the larger mountains, rivers and
lakes. While any attempt to list such names can lead to vehement
disagreement among scholars, we might suggest – rather tenta-

tively – that the principal element in names such as *Loch Measca/* Lough Mask, *Loch Ceara/*Lough Carra, *Cuan Mó* (earlier *Cuan Modh* – see also *Innse Mod/*Clew Bay (and its myriad islands) and *Buiríos Umhaill/*Burrishoole, to name just a handful, might well be pre-Celtic in origin, but that can be nothing more than a guess.

Some ancient names

One of Mayo's most venerable names is that of the great conical mountain in the north of the county – *Néifinn* in Modern Irish, *Nemthenn* in the older language and anglicised *Nephin*. A former colleague of mine in the Placenames Branch of the Ordnance Survey suggested to me some time ago an imaginative and even ingenious interpretation of the name: it may reflect, he thinks, the name of a Celtic goddess, Nemetona ('Goddess of the sacred grove'), who was honoured in ancient Gaul and had a cult-site at Bath in the south of Roman Britain. The word *nemeton* itself means 'sacred grove' and lies behind numerous placenames in France and elsewhere on the Continent (most notably Nanterre on the western outskirts of Paris). (Incidentally, the medieval Dindsenchus poet sought to explain the name – as a compound of *nem*, 'poison', and *tenn*, 'strong, vigorous' – with the aid of a story of how a wicked witch, Dreco, slew with poison the twenty-four sons of one Fergus Lethderg.)

If the great mountain of Tirawley does indeed preserve the name of a Celtic goddess, it is perhaps fitting that in its shadow, in all probability, lay the ancient wood whose name is the only Irish placename mentioned by St Patrick in his writings – *Silva Vocluti* (or *Focluti*). (It is, indeed, the only Irish placename to occur in any Irish record of the fifth-century or earlier). The name appears in Patrick's account of the dream he had after his escape from captivity in Ireland. Back home in Britain he had a vision of a man named Victoricus coming from Ireland with many letters, one of which is headed 'The voice of the Irish' (*Vox Hiberionacum – Glór na nGael*). As he reads this, he imagines that he hears the voices of those who were 'beside the Wood of Focult which is near the western sea' calling him to return and walk once more among them. From the context, it seems that this place must have been the scene of Patrick's six-year captivity in Ireland. Much scholarly ink has been spilt in trying to locate the place in question, but the weight of opinion now appears to favour acceptance of the statement of Bishop Tírechán, writing towards the end of the seventh century – about two centuries after Patrick's death – that what he referred to as *Silva Fochlithi* (alias *Fochlothi, Fochloth,* and *Fochluth*) was situated in his own home-area of Tirawley. (Tírechán, although writing as a propagandist on behalf of the church of Armagh, was a 'Mayoman'; he is in fact the first indentifiable writer from the west of Ireland – all of 1300 years ago – and deserves to be widely recognised as such.) The name mentioned in latinised form by Patrick and Tírechán occurs in full Irish dress, as *Caill* (and *Caille*) *Fochlad,* in an Old Irish hymn, 'Génair Pátraic í nNemthur', attributed to Fiac of Slébte (Sletty, Co Laois, near Carlow town) but probably dating from about the mid-eighth century. It takes the form *Coill Fhocladh* in the (probably ninth-century) *Tripartite Life of Patrick,* which may owe something to Tírechán's work; there it is clearly stated to lie immediately west of *Cros Phátraic* (the townland of Crosspatrick just south of Killala). What connection, if any, it may have with the present-day townland of Foghill, some miles north of Killala, is a thorny question which may here be left in abeyance.

The *Tripartite Life* lists more than twenty other placenames in the vicinity of Killala which were allegedly linked to Patrick's mission in the area. Many of these are still identifiable. One which merits a brief comment is effectively disguised by its anglicised form, Tawnaghmore; on a superficial examination, this might seem to represent *Tamhnach Mhór,* '(the) big grassy upland or clearing', but in fact its original form – surviving in seventeenth-century English sources – is *Domhnach Mór,* 'the big church'. Here we have an example of a very ancient word for a church (from Latin *Dominicum*) which disappeared from use in the course of the fifth century. The placename, therefore, very probably dates from the time of St Patrick himself. These north Mayo names associated with the cult of the extraordinary British missionary, Patricius son of the deacon Calpurnius and grandson of the priest Potitus, are deserving of much more scrutiny than they have hitherto received. Considerations of space permit me to make just a brief comment on one other name which occurs in the purported 'lives' of the later seventh century (by Tírechán and by another Armagh propagandist named Muirchú). This is Míliuc moccu Bóin, said to

have been St Patrick's master during his captivity. A suggestion
was made more than thirty years ago that this name may well
have originated as a placename, *Míleac* (Meelick), a medieval parish and early church-site near Swinford, but, in fact, a townland of
the same name immediately adjoining Killala and Tawnagh-
more/*Domhnach Mór* would seem a more likely candidate.

The Reek

The Mayo placename which, above all, is associated with the
Patrician cult is of course Croagh Patrick/*Cruach Phádraig*. The
celebrated annual 'Climbing of the Reek' is on record since the
early twelfth century (when on two separate occasions – 1109 and
1113 – pilgrims on it were killed by lightning), but it is interesting
to see in this holy mountain and its annual 'feastday' a pretty clear
link with the older religion. For 'Reek Sunday' coincides with
what was formerly known as *Domhnach Chrom Dubh* – and in English as 'Garland Sunday' – the modern manifestation of the great
Celtic feast of *Lugnasad* (the festive commemoration of the god
Lug). The very name *Cruach Phádraig* is relatively late; the older
name was *Cruachán Oighle* (or in Tírechán's Latin *Mons Egli*).
Indeed *Aigle* appears to have been the name of the surrounding
territory; whether this is linked – or even identical – with the
name of Achill Island/*Acaill* (anciently *Ecaill, Eccuill*, etc.) is a
moot point. The way in which, according to Tírechán, Patrick was
tormented during his forty-day sojurn on 'The Reek' by swarms
of birds would seem to reflect a desire on the writer's part to portray the place as particularly hostile to the saint's message. The
mountain may well have been the centre of a pagan cult – perhaps
involving sun-worship. Indeed it is very likely that the annual
climbing of the Reek has roots reaching back into the dim pagan
past and, like so many other aspects of Ireland's pre-Christian re-
ligion(s), was taken over by the new generation.

Holy Wells

Another instance of the christianisation of a pre-Christian survival which immediately comes to mind is the 'holy well'. This feature of the Irish countryside was obviously associated with some
now obscure aspect of pre-Christian belief. There are several such
ancient sites in Co Mayo, the most famous being that which in later

times came to bear the name of Patrick himself, *Baile Tobair Phádraig*, or in Latin *Villa Fontis Sancti Patricii* (now simply *Baile an Tobair*/Ballintober, 'the townland of the well'); this appears to be the *Fons Stringille* mentioned by Tírechán. Another well with which the saint is associated by Tírechán was at *Ached Fobair*, meaning '(the) field of (the) spring well', and anglicised Aghagower: it is fascinating to look at the text of Tírechán as written into the Book of Armagh in or about the year 807 and recognise without difficulty the name of this west Mayo parish. (The modern form, *Achadh Ghobhair*, can be interpreted variously as '(the) field or (the) goat'; or 'of (the) horse or mare'; it is interesting to note that the initial 'G' in the second element of the name had made its appearance by about the year 800 – presumably because the word *Fobar* had already gone out of normal use.)

'The holy wells of Mayo' (or indeed of any other Irish county) is a topic deserving of detailed in-depth study and it is indeed remarkable that to date nobody has undertaken it. (We have to make do with the late Dr Pat Logan's brief popular survey, *The Holy Wells of Ireland* (1980).) It would appear to be a subject on which practitioners of various disciplines – folklore, local history, early Irish history, hagiography, onomastics, nineteenth-century social and church history, to name but a few – could fruitfully cooperate and help shed some light on this intriguing part of our cultural and religious heritage.

I did some work a few years ago on a holy well which I had come across in the course of researching aspects of the history of my native parish, Knock. Having turned up a reference to a well in the townland of Caldragh, on the Knock-Ballyhaunis road (near the eastern end of the parish), I managed to locate it, with the kind assistance of the landowner, John Rochford. Without his help I would have had difficulty finding it as the well now has a metal and concrete cover to prevent cattle falling in. It looks unprepossessing – for all the world like a manhole, or the entrance to a septic tank, in the middle of a field – and yet here we have the last trace of a saint's cult which goes back well over a thousand years and recalls the very ancient people who once held sway in this area. The people were the *Ciarraige* – 'the folk of the black goddess (Qéra)' – another branch of whom, the *Ciarraige Luachra*, gave name to the County of Kerry. When the staff of the Ordnance Survey visited Knock in the summer of 1838 they also found a well called 'Tober Keelan' (*Tobar Caolainne*) or, in English, 'Keelan's Well' in the townland of Caldragh – the same rather nondescript covered-over well I mentioned above. The Ordnance Survey Letters also report that the stations were performed at the well on Garland Sunday – a nice marriage of an early Christian cult stretching back well over a thousand years with a pre-Christian festival (*Lughnasa*) which may well be at least a thousand years older still.

Mayo's Cill-Names

The ecclesiastical toponomy of Mayo has so many facets that I could not cover even a fraction of them – much less do them justice – in these few pages. So in the space remaining I will go through, at a gallop, some of the more prominent Mayo names with ecclesiastical/hagiographical connotations – in the hope of whetting the reader's appetite, or even perhaps of spurring someone reading this to do further work in a field in which the labourers are indeed all too few, or too ill-equipped. Looking at the names of Mayo's civil parishes, for instance, it is striking that about a third of them – some two dozen – commence with the element *Cill*, a word deriving from the Latin *cella*. The word originally denoted – at least in the Irish context – a monastic cell, and its popularity in this country, and also in Gaelic Scotland, clearly reflects the remarkable flowering of the monastic ideal in the early Irish church. Some of the Cill-names go back a long way. Kilmoremoy and Kilmaine, for instance, are mentioned by Tírechán as Patrician foundations (*Cellola magna Muaide* and *Cellola Media* respectively; the former is also called *Cell Mór Óchtair Muaide* in the ninth-century *Tripartite Life of Patrick*). Kilbride in north Mayo clearly reflects the cult of the shadowy female patron of Ireland, Brigit of *Cill Dara*/Kildare, the 'Mary of the Gaeil'. That cult seems to have become inextricably mixed up with traditions of a Celtic goddess of the same name who was patron-deity of northern Britain and was esteemed also among the Continental Celts, and whose feast was *Imbolc* or *Oímelc* (1 February – *Lá le Bríde*!).

Of many of the other saints to whom *cella* were dedicated little or nothing is known. I am thinking of the two parishes called *Cill Cholmáin*/Kilcolman (from Colmán, the commonest of all early

Irish saints' names, borne by scores of holy men), two called *Cill Chomáin*/Kilcommon (perhaps with the patron of *Ros Comáin*/ Roscommon), one bearing a variant of the latter name, *Cill Chuimín*/Kilcummin, and another a hypocoristic form (or 'pet-form') of it, *Cill Dachomóg*/Kildacommoge.

Due to the pressure of space, I have generally steered clear of townland-names. But I will mention just two: Killunagher/*Cill Luineachair* near Ballyhaunis and Kildaree near Crossmolina. The former appears a rather puzzling name and being a modest and unremarkable place, might seem unlikely to feature in ancient his-torical records. Yet in the Latin life of St Mochua of Balla, pre-served by the seventeenth-century Donegal-born Franciscan hagi-ographer, John Colgan, there is mention of a lady named *Lukencaria*: Colgan emends this to *Lunecharia* and suggests a link with a place which he calls *Kill-Lunechair* and which is clearly the place near Ballyhaunis. The Ordnance Survey map gives no indic-ation of any antiquities in Killunagher but a recent archaeological survey of the area is reported to have revealed traces of an early Christian foundation. Kildaree has traditionally been explained as *Cill Dá Rí*, 'church of the two kings', but in recent years the leading authority on Irish hagiography, Professor Pádraig Ó Riain of University College, Cork, has argued convincingly that the name commemorates instead a female saint named *Dar Í* (a name meaning 'daughter of (the) yew', comparable to *Nath Í*, already mentioned); the same individual also had two *cella* dedi-cated to her in Co Galway.

If space permitted, I would have liked to look in some detail at several other Mayo placenames which reflect aspects of the spirit-ual history of the scores of generations who have lived in this cor-ner of north Connacht, and most particularly our 1500-year-old Christian heritage derived from the British missionary bishop who, as a teenager, had herded sheep on the western shores of Killala Bay. Among such names would be: Aglish and Ballyna-haglish, both involving the word *eaglais* (from Latin *ecclesia*); Bekan, which may represent a truncated version of *Díseart Béacháin*, the hermitage (Latin *desertum*) of a holy man named Béachán; Crossboyne and Crossmolina, both involving the word *crois*, perhaps denoting the presence of ancient high crosses, and commemorating individuals named respectively Baoithín (perhaps the son of Cuana said to have founded Tibohine/*Tigh Baoithín* near Ballaghadreen) and Maol Fíona ('servant of Fíona'); Oughaval, signifying a 'new holding/settlement/foundation (generally ecclesiastical)'; Tagheen, representing *Teach Chaoin*, whose second component is somewhat doubtful but whose initial element frequently denotes an early religious house; Templemore and Templemurry, both involving the term *teampall* (from Latin *templum*), a word for 'church' which only came into use in Irish in the post-Norman period.

The Yew-Plain of the Saxons

In conclusion, I wish to dwell briefly on the most significant early Christian site of all, the one from which our county takes its name. If the county's roots, in terms of attested human habitation, may be said to lie in the Céide Fields, its history is beholden in a special way to the monastery founded by thirty Saxon monks on the lime-stone plain south-east of Castlebar just over 1300 hundred years ago – round about the time that our 'first Mayo writer', Tírechán, was busy penning his account of St Patrick's missionary journeys. The story of that foundation is especially celebrated by reason of its being recorded in the English monk Bede's *Ecclesiastical History of the English People*, penned in the monastery of Jarrow in or about the year 731. This tells us how the Columban or anti-Romanist party in the Paschal Controversy – the dispute about the method of establishing the date of Easter which split the sev-enth-century church in both Ireland and Britain – was defeated at the Synod of Whitby in Yorkshire in 664 and, under its leader, Colmán, bishop of Lindisfarne, withdrew to 'Whitecow Island' (*Inis Bó Finne*/Inishbofin) in 668. Following a dispute between the Irish and Saxon members of the new foundation, the latter moved some time later to the mainland and established themselves on land, called 'Plain of Yews' (*Mag nÉo*), which had been bought from a local chieftan. Within a very short time their monastery be-came renowned not alone in Ireland but also in England and in Celtic Britain as a seat of learning. It retained its Saxon identity well into the ninth century, and down to the latter middle ages it bore the name *Mag nÉo na Sachsan*, 'the yewplain of the Saxons'. About 780 we find the noted English churchman and scholar, Alcuin of York, corresponding with Leuthfrith, bishop of Mayo, and some twenty years later, the same Alcuin in a letter to the church of Mayo commends the community on 'the light of their knowledge which is spread through a wide area of England'. Leuthfrith's successor as bishop of Mayo, Alduulf, was consecrated bishop in Northumbria by, among others, the archbishop of York, and he took part in 786 in a church council held in England which was presided over by a papal nuncio. Leuthfrith's predecessor bore the Saxon name Hadwine or Edwin, which the *Annals of Ulster* gaelicise as Aedan; it is possible that this is the name – whether commemorating that eighth-century bishop or some other members of the community – which lies behind the parish-name Islandeady. (While the latter is rendered *Oileán Éadaí* by nineteenth-century speakers of Irish, we may note such sixteenth and seventeenth-century forms as *Oleayn Edayn* and *Ellaneden*.)

The only detailed scholarly study of this important centre of holiness and learning to be undertaken in recent times appeared almost thirty years ago from the pen of the noted English Celtic scholar, the late Nora K. Chadwick. In an imaginative and stimulating chapter, entitled 'Bede, St Colmán and the Irish Abbey of Mayo' (published in *Celts and Saxons: Studies in the Early British Border*, Cambridge, 1964), she outlines the background to Mayo's foundation and convincingly sets its eighth-century significance in the context of the struggle to convert the church in the northern half of Ireland (which was heavily influenced by the great Columban monastery of Iona) to the Roman view of Easter. She suggests that an English monk of noble birth, Ecgberht (who died in 729 aged about ninety, having spent most of his life in Ireland), may have been largely instrumental in ensuring the triumph of 'orthodoxy' in the Irish church. She thinks he may have been based in Mayo, and may even had a hand in founding this breakaway Saxon monastery. She even appears to hint that he may have been identical with a shadowy saint named Geralt ('Gerald') who features in various traditions relating to Mayo's early story. Also to the forefront of the campaign for the Roman Easter was the great abbot of Iona, Adamnán, biographer of Colm Cille/Columba. Having been converted to the Roman cause in the late 680s but failing to persuade his own monks in Iona to follow his lead, he spent seven years in Ireland, 697-704, campaigning on behalf of the Roman viewpoint. Nora Chadwick suggests that he and Ecgberht campaigned together and that they may well have used

Mayo as their base for the Romanisation of the northern half of Ireland. Its pivotal role in the reform movement is therefore, she suggests, the key to its status in the eighth-century Irish and British churches – a status which is testified to by Bede and, several decades later, by Alcuin.

Some traces of its former glory must still have remained when in the mid-twelfth century the Synod of Kells gave Mayo diocesan status (as *diocaesis de Mageo*) in the ecclesiastical province of Tuam. While the Roman authorities in the early thirteenth century sought to suppress the new diocese, they discovered that Mayo was not easily beaten down. Despite their efforts, the diocese maintained a fitful existence throughout the later middle ages. Indeed, one of the recently canonised Irish martyrs from the unhappy sixteenth century, the Franciscan Pádraig Ó hÉilidhe, executed in Kilmallock in 1579, bore the title 'bishop of Mayo'. The Roman bureaucrats did not finally get their way until about 1630s. But by that time another development had occurred to ensure that the name of the Plain of Yew-trees would not disappear along with the confiscated monastery and the abolished diocese to which it applied. Appropriately enough, the name of this great Saxon foundation was saved from extinction by the action of the English lord deputy, Sir Henry Sidney, when he decreed about the year 1570 that it be used as the name of the county to be carved out of the corner of the western province as part of the process known as 'the shiring of Connacht'. So the name of this county of ours, like that of the monastery from which it derives, may be seen to reflect the centuries of interaction, whether fruitful and benign or, as all too often, alas!, destructive and malign, between the principal peoples of this archipelago off the northwest coast of Europe. As we approach the third millenium of the Christian era, is it too much to hope that we who are so proud of this ancient paradigm of the interplay of Gael and Saxon, *Mag nÉo na Sachsan*/ The Yewplain of the Saxons, might be able to use it as a symbol of future reconciliation, peace and mutual acceptance between our two peoples whom history has fated to be neighbours?

CHAPTER 2

Saving all our Holy Mountains

Ethna Viney

The Symbol of the Reek

If you stand on the Boheh Stone a few miles south of Westport, on 18 April and 24 August at about six o'clock in the evening, you can see the setting sun roll down the northern slope of Croagh Patrick. From the standing stone at Cross, to the west of the mountain, on the same dates in the early morning, you can see the rising sun roll up the same side of the Reek.[1] The Boheh Stone is engraved with cup-and-ring symbols that could be interpreted as astronomical; the Cross stone has a sunburst carving. Although the precise age of the markings on the Boheh Stone has not been determined, they could be either Bronze age or Neolithic, one thing is certain: Croagh Patrick was a holy mountain long before Christianity or St Patrick put their mark on it. And it was holy in the context of the productive earth: the message from the engravers is one of respect for the land in so far as they understood the dynamics of ecology. The dates on which these startling and splendid phenomena take place have a great significance in the lives of an agrarian people. In our latitude, 18 April marks the beginning of the main sowing season, and 24 August the beginning of the harvest.

As *Mons Egli* or *Cruach Aigle* the mountain was associated with the feast of *Lughnasa*[2] which marks the end of summer. Its fame had spread afar; an ancient pilgrimage route to the mountain from the seat of the Kings of Connacht at *Ráth Cruachan*, near Tulsk in Co Roscommon, later became *Tóchar Phádraig* or Patrick's Causeway[3], and can still be followed.

We should be grateful that these records from the past, whether we fully understand them or not, are carved in stone. Future generations will not fare so well with our multifarious memorabilia, most of which are so ephemerally stored that they will disappear in a puff of wind.

The geology books are unanimous: Croagh Patrick is the shapeliest mountain in Ireland. It is also the foremost, the most acknowledged, holy mountain, and no doubt these two distinctions are linked. Over four hundred million years old, it rises tall and geometrical from the sea and from the surrounding landscape. Like a monument, it is a God-made pyramid, flawless in form except from the north where it seems to carry its great age with a slight stoop. Not least, it is manageable in human terms, being climbable in a matter of hours, and one of the few mountains that can be encircled easily in a day's walk. Can we wonder that it has signified something special in both ancient and modern consciousness?

Through the length and breadth of Ireland there are mountains to which varying degrees of official holiness are attributed: Croagh Patrick is but the best known pilgrimage venue. But to those of us who have lived with them, all mountains are special, holy in a more informally spiritual way. It may be something to do with their size or shape, and that they give a feeling of protection; or perhaps that they provide the solitude that is occasionally balm to the spirit. There are, however, practical as well as spiritual reasons why they should be held sacred: mountains nurture the land. They act as collectors and reservoirs for life-giving water and they provide minerals that keep the land fertile. Therefore if life is sacred, then mountains and the land are by extension also sacred.

It is reasonable to suggest that a greater knowledge of the interaction of the forces of nature exists at present than at any previous time in history, and therefore we should have a greater respect for the land and regard for the consequences of our actions upon it. But that is not the case. At no stage in the known history of the world has humankind wrought such lethal havoc and destruction on the life-giving elements of this earth. At no stage until now has humankind had the technology and the knowledge to wreak this destruction. Therefore it is with a great measure of outrage that I set out to write this chapter, and to exhort people to care for our holy mountains, to protect and conserve our sacred land. Their salvation is necessary for our survival.

The reek, as it is familiarly called, has suffered the ravages of time and weather: it is bare of vegetation, and scores of loose stone abrade its flanks. Rain and wind, frost and ice can bear some of the blame for this erosion, but there may have been other causes. Over-grazing by sheep is causing other mountains in the west to lose their vegetation and subsequently their soil: could this have also happened in earlier times? The Burren with its glorious lime-stone terraces, and its holy mountain, the swirling linenfold edifice of Mullaghmore, are the remaining skeleton of what was once a green and fertile landscape. That land was overgrazed by Neolithic farmers, who then moved on.[4]

The bogs that cover the fields of Céide were also the result of human intervention in Neolithic times. Deforestation of the hills, an analogous type of over-grazing, allowed more rain to reach the ground causing water-logging, and hence the rapid growth of peat.[5] The bog encroached on their pastures and the Mayo Neo-lithic farmers, like their Burren counterparts, moved on; their sur-vival depended on it. That they could move on was their salva-tion; there was room on this island for their relatively small population. Their descendants left when they were pushed out by later arrivals, and even later still, in our own times, when they were pushed abroad by economic pressures. Mayo knows well the sad story of emigration. Moving on is nothing new, after all our early ancestors had arrived here from other lands in search of new pastures.

We tend to be philosophical about the movements of people at different times in history, and at the same time we maintain the right of people to a livelihood in the place where they were born. But people have always moved from overcrowded regions and set up new settlements in 'virgin' lands. But the regions like North America that were colonised by population movements from Europe, were not virgin: they had a stable and renewable ecology for millennia, one that gave rise to and was respected by the nomadic lifestyle of the native Americans. The American prairies remained stable until they were despoiled by human greed: the Dust Bowl of North America was caused in the 1930s by over-cultivation of land that could support extensive grazing, but not intensive cultivation or husbandry (of which more later).

It is difficult to believe that a knowledge of nature that was learned the hard way by those who worked the land of Europe in earlier times could be discounted, disregarded in what we believe to be a more enlightened age. But that is happening even here in

Co Mayo. The 'old' ways are being replaced by 'modern' methods of agriculture. Most of our farmers now seem to know only of chemicals and machinery. They have cut loose from the farming lore of their forefathers, disregarded a knowledge that had been compiled over generations of intimacy with the land. Engagement with the soil is now at tractor's length, and land is exploited rather than cared for. This is the age of science and technology, enthusiastically introduced without a thought for the long-term effects.

Destroying our natural heritage

What have we, as a species, done to the earth we inherited from our ancestors? Or, to put it another way, what have we done to the land that we hold in trust for our children? We have robbed the soil, destroyed and wasted resources, poisoned the water, polluted the air, declared war on other species, and in the process endangered the stability of the planet. Indeed what have we done to our own health, for we are a sick species? We have replaced the plagues of previous centuries (the result of a cruder form of pollution, the dirt and ignorance of early urbanisation) with diseases and sickness that result to a large extent from our scientific abuse of the earth and its produce.

This outrageous situation has been achieved in little more than one generation, and we in Ireland, we in Mayo, carry our share of the blame with those who endanger all life on earth by the manufacture of radiation, defoliants and other land and water poisons.

I remember when this country turned its back on the old knowledge of agriculture. It was in the mid fifties, and in North Mayo where I lived at the time, the way forward was 'to grow an acre of barley and feed a pig'. This policy was designed to bring a new prosperity to small-farm Ireland. There was nothing wrong with it except that it did not stop there, or even at twenty acres of barley and twenty pigs. It turned into no barley and thousands of housed pigs. This was a policy that showed a distinct lack of wisdom and foresight: it was not thought through. The pigs were fed on largely imported feedstuffs. Because they were confined in warm housing they became liable to disease, and needed regular dosing with antibiotics. This is now the accepted pattern of pig production.

Apart from the fact that confinement of the pig is cruel, their flesh is not as tasty because the pigs get no exercise. There is no comparison between the flesh of an organically raised pig and the battery house product. Moreover, those who eat them are imbibing regular doses of antibiotic with serious consequences for their health. They develop a tolerance for the drug which means that when they are ill and need it, it does not work for them. More seriously the antibiotic kills off the useful flora in their intestines and allows debilitating fungi to develop. There is even a question mark over the effect of such regular animal doses on the human immune system. Has anyone researched the effects on meat of all the chemicals with which food animals are dosed?

Other food animals are also being divorced from the land. On mainland Europe for many decades cattle have been moved off grass into housing units, to be fed on compounds made from cereals (imported from America), fishmeal (made from overfished stocks), and, as has been scandalously revealed in recent years, animal offal. The dangers inherent in going against nature and feeding flesh to herbivores were dramatically revealed in Britain. In the case of what has become known as 'mad cow' disease, animal offal, some of it diseased, was introduced as a protein additive to cattle compounds, causing a disease once confined to sheep to infect cattle. Nature may be tolerant up to a point, but in the case of mad cow disease it is unforgiving. Recent reports suggest that after crossing from one species of farm animal to another, the disease may also have passed to humans. Mercifully, it has been kept out of this country, as far as we know.

Another serious problem created by rearing animals in buildings is the great quantities of slurry which are generated. When spread on land it is washed into rivers and lakes where it pollutes drinking water and kills fish. Slurry does not fertilise the land in the same way that farmyard manure did in previous generations. The chemicals given to the animals to kill bacteria, lice and ticks persist in the manure and continue to kill similar organisms in the ground. These ground organisms would, if they were spared, break down the slurry into plant food: instead it is washed away into watercourses.

Irish farmers are increasingly adopting these methods of stock raising. I see stock sheds appearing in the landscape even here in

Mayo. This is happening in spite of the fact that grass-fed cattle produce better milk and meat, that Ireland has an advantage over some other European countries in this form of production, and that there is severe over-production of both beef and milk. The argument for cattle and pig units is that they are more economic, the product is cheaper. But it is cheaper only if the costs of cleaning up afterwards are discounted: the cost of bringing lakes back to health and re-stocking them, of cleaning rivers, (there is no way that the ground water can be cleaned); the cost to the public of buying drinking water in bottles, of restoring the health of those made ill. Meanwhile, what happens to the land that could feed these cattle and pigs more healthily?

The chemical frenzy

To go back to the fifties, the new deal for agriculture required that the stocking rate of cattle be improved to one animal per acre. How do you do that on a forty-acre farm in the west which was traditionally four or five cows' place? How do you do it on any farm? By applying so many tons of chemical fertiliser per acre; by force feeding the land with minerals to produce rank grass for the increased numbers of stock. Nobody at the time considered the consequences of these regular applications of chemicals on the natural fertility of the land. Nobody thought about polluted water systems.

Chemical fertilisers are used to increase the productive capacity of the land yet, paradoxically, they destroy its natural fertility in the long run. Of their nature these chemicals are acid and they dissolve the minerals already in the soil, wash them down out of the top soil to form hard or iron pans, locking away nutrients present in the subsoil. They kill beneficial soil organisms – the insects, fungi, rhizopods and bacteria that break down the minerals already in the soil because they destroy the earthworms that fertilise and aerate it. The result is that the soil becomes compacted, its crumbly friable structure is destroyed, and water lodges instead of soaking down and being held for future use. We have only to look around us at the poached fields left by a wet winter. It will take years of patient care to return such land to natural fertility.

Equally alarming is the pollution of rivers, lakes and the unseen aquifers, the precious ground water reservoirs on which we rely for drinking water. In agricultural areas throughout the EU, water has become so contaminated by nitrates that it exceeds the permitted levels laid down by the Union for drinking water.[6] Our neighbouring island, Britain, has serious nitrate pollution of its water supplies. We have no evidence that this is happening here in this country where many of us get our water supplies from our holy mountains, but lowlands may have a hidden problem. Nitrates are converted in the body into nitrites which are suspected of causing cancer.[7] Are we slowly poisoning ourselves?

To return to the Dust Bowl, the farmers of the early twentieth century believed that the soil was indestructible. So did the experts. In 1909 the US Bureau of Soils claimed that, 'the soil is the one resource that cannot be exhausted; that cannot be used up'.[8] Twenty-five years later the first major dust-storms commenced, removing something like 850 million tons of top soil from the Great Plains of America each year and depositing it on the east coast, on cities and many hundreds of miles out to sea. 'By the 1970s a third of the topsoil of the United States had been lost and nearly 200 million acres of cropland lost ... This widespread devastation was the result of agriculture practices such as extensive and continuing monocropping on marginal land, lack of understanding of the processes that create soil, reliance on chemical fertilisers that do not contribute to the maintenance of healthy soil.'[9] Here in Ireland it is more likely that the land will turn into bog.

Food is now grown not with solar energy but with oil from which nitrogenous fertilisers are largely manufactured, and guess who benefits most. The nutritional value (vitamin, mineral and protein content) and flavour of food grown in this manner is inferior to that which is organically grown. Green vegetables, particularly those grown in greenhouses, take up surplus nitrates, with the consequences cited above. The shelf-life of chemically grown fruit and vegetables is shorter because of the greater uptake of water.[10] In large commercial enterprises they are treated with chemicals to prolong this life. This also means that food products can be transported long distances to the final consumer. The repercussions reach far into the economy and the lives of communities: fewer people are employed in agriculture; industry has not been able to employ all those that leave the land; the dole queues lengthen; emigration increases; and those that remain on the land have difficulty making a living. Here is a strong argument in favour of organically growing vegetables and fruit here in Mayo instead of depending on imports.

I have not come to the end of the depredations being visited on the good earth. More than thirty years ago, in 1962, Rachel Carson wrote a book called *Silent Spring*[11] which drew world attention to the poisoning of the planet by the insecticides DDT, aldrein and dieldrin. Rachel Carson suffered for her revelations about these popular organochlorine pesticides. The chemical industry pilloried her; they tried to discredit her in the eyes of the public by saying that she was an unsuitable person, an embittered spinster who had become emotional about nature. Eventually, however, the world was convinced that DDT was harmful and it was banned in most countries. Today there is prolific literature detailing the poisoning of the planet but a dreadful inertia seems to have gripped the populace, and it is left to groups such as Friends of the Earth and Greenpeace (both regarded by many as cranks) to keep reminding us to do something about it. Now, another generation of chemicals has been brought into play to kill weeds and insects, and to protect crops against disease and pests. Although not as persistent in soil as the organochlorines, the newer insecticides, like organophosphates, together with new chemical fungicides, leave residues in food. In 1985 and 1986 two British reports found dangerous pesticide residues in fruit and vegetables yet no routine checks are made in Britain or here. Weed killers also pollute surface and ground water and remain there long enough to be measured by those who test the water. All of them, insecticides, fungicides and weed killers, are dangerous to our health even when consumed in small quantities.[12]

These pesticides make further onslaughts against the beneficial organisms in the soil, against the balance of nature that matches one crop-enemy with an enemy of its own. Instead of using nature to balance itself, as the farmers of old did, chemical farmers use a crude and metaphoric sledgehammer to kill everything in and out of sight, and in the process poison the land and most of the living things contacted. Organophosphates are now used for killing lice on cattle and farmed salmon, and for dipping sheep. It has recently been discovered that they seriously affect the health of those that use them.

An organic garden, where no pesticides are used, has its collection of useful predators including ground beetles, rove beetles, hover-flies, ladybirds, *Anthocris nemorum* (a tiny bug with no popular name that works overtime eating aphids, small caterpillars, mites and other pests that cause problems to crops), numerous other named and unnamed insects, organisms such as nitrogen-fixing bacteria, fungi that break down vegetable matter into plant food, literally millions of earthworms. One such garden, an acre large, has for almost twenty years been virtually pest free, and enjoys a balance of nature. It is full of birds that help keep down the insect population and with whom we share a proportion of the fruit crop.

It may be argued that for a kitchen garden that's fine but that in a commercial situation it is necessary to use chemicals. Yet a grow-ing number of commercial farmers have returned to organic farm-ing. Most notably, here in the west of Ireland, Anthony and Bridie Kilcullen of Enniscrone have been organic since 1984.

If the CAP fits

So why are we degrading and poisoning the land, adulterating our food, polluting our water? Because of a crazy system of econ-omics that nobody has the courage to change. The way the Com-mon Agricultural Policy (CAP) is organised, the way the General Agreement on Tarrifs and Trade (GATT) wants to regulate food production, are all designed to perpetuate these suicidal methods of exploiting the land.

I take issue with the CAP because of what it has done to our land. The original idea, to ensure a fair livelihood for farmers and to in-crease farm productivity, was admirable. Since the Industrial Revolution, the needs of industry strongly influenced national economics in every country of Europe. Industrialists wanted a cheap labour force, and the simplest way to ensure that was to ini-tiate a policy of cheap food. As a result, farmers suffered.

The CAP set out to achieve its aims by means of grants, subsidies and price maintenance, but the process was not thought through. Within the system were the seeds of its own destruction – over-production, the unholy and notorious product-mountains and lakes. It is easy to judge with hindsight, but it was no secret that a guaranteed price for any produce was going to ensure over-production. I did my economics degree in the early sixties and one of my textbooks[13] dealt with precisely that problem: 'A sub-sidy (or guaranteed price) on only a few products will certainly rapidly increase their output at the expense of other farm prod-ucts.' Serious over-production in beef, sheep and milk has result-ed from EU policies; and crop growing has certainly suffered in this country where we now import potatoes and other vegetables to a disgraceful degree. Moreover, Irish farmers were solvent forty years ago and now they owe billions to the banks.

What we are talking about here is economics and power systems, and one particular brand of economics where the return on capi-tal and the manipulation of money take precedence over all other considerations. It is a system which is failing all over the world, in terms of the welfare of people, in terms of natural resources, and even in terms of capital itself. There are two distinct phases of econ-omic action at work in our interaction as humans with the planet, one superimposed on the other:

1. We believe that we have the right and the power to exploit in an unrestricted manner the physical planet and all other spec-ies, for the benefit of the present generations of humankind.

2. The economic system we adopt disregards the welfare of humankind in general and operates for the benefit of capital and the power of the few who control it. (It is an obscene sys-tem that allows one man to aim at a personal wealth of £500 million, as one Irish-born industrialist recently boasted, when so many millions are unemployed.)

I make no apology for my digression into economics, because it is the root cause of the destruction of our holy mountains, our holy land. Indeed when the subsistence farmers of earlier days cared for the land, fed the soil rather than the crops, rested it periodical-ly, they were motivated by economics. This was their only re-source and they looked after it. (I don't mean to say that previous generations were ecological saints. Attacks on the planet did not start in this century; but at no other time that we know of has a species had the power and ability to destroy earth as a habitat.)

The aims of the CAP were laudable, as I said earlier, particularly the desire to give farmers a decent living; but the methods were deplorable. Why should food be subsidised? Why should it not

command its rightful cost of proper production, rather than trying to make it as cheap as possible regardless of the damage done
in the process? What is more important than food? The problem is
that as a commodity it has been reduced in value because in our
economies (not in many Third World countries) there is too much
of it; a surplus is necessary to bring down the price. This over-
production occurs because of increased productivity brought
about at the expense of the land, water, the quality of the food and
the health of all living things.

A higher value on food

If we put more resources into good food production, employment
would increase and there would be a better return to producers at
all levels. If we decide to stop robbing and poisoning the land,
and resolve instead to maintain its fertility, return to it what we
take away, then we will have to put a higher value on food. That
sounds like a simple solution, and it would be so if we were prepared to put the same money value on food production, on the
labour that goes into the growing and processing of what we eat,
as we put on, say, the production of popular music, or the manipulation of money markets. (Indeed why should any sane society
allow the money magicians, who buy and sell the currencies that
were originally established to facilitate trade in the necessities of
life, to corner the wealth of the country by sleight of hand?)

I have briefly described the effects modern agriculture and horti-
culture are having on our life-supporting soil and water. I should
also mention the seas and oceans of the planet which are being
progressively poisoned by radio-active and toxic industrial
wastes. Governments drag their heels for various reasons: employment, cost of clean-up, cost of policing activities. The Irish
Sea is the most radio-active stretch of water in the world;[14] the
North Sea is poisoned by heavy chemicals;[15] the Mediterranean is
virtually an open sewer;[16] almost all coastal regions of the world
are heavily polluted (except perhaps our own west coast), and
radio-active and chemical pollution is transported around and between the oceans of the world by currents.[17] But the seas are also
polluted by the run-off of agricultural chemicals[18] and we in this
country contribute. Healthy seas are vitally necessary to the long-
term health of the planet.

Although there are very active campaigning groups against agricultural chemicals abroad, we hear very little protest in this country. We have, however, even in Mayo, strong and vocal lobbies
drawing attention to the effects of mining and industry on the environment. Few of us have not heard the warnings of concerned
people about the pollution caused by the extraction methods of
mining: poisoning of watercourses, contamination of soil. However, except in the case of slurry spills which pollute rivers and
kill fish, the voices raised in this country against the destruction of
soil and the pollution of water by agriculture chemicals are small
and faint. It is a most unpopular pursuit.

We must stop this outrageous treatment of our natural resources,
if not because such waste is disgraceful, then because we are destroying ourselves. To call for such a halt is not anti-farming; it is
to advocate a healthy form of farming, to stop the aberrations of
this generation from denying health and life to the next. Once
farming was the healthiest of activities, now it is as hazardous as
working in a chemical factory and a threat to the population at
large.

Those farmers who have turned away from chemical agriculture
have found that their income returns have not suffered: the smaller
yield of organic production is more than balanced by the money
saved on chemicals. My voice is not one that is against the chemical industry; chemicals have a place in our civilisation when manufactured and used in a way that is ecologically safe. I have the
highest regard for the products of human knowledge and ingenu-
ity when used in an environment and human-friendly way.

Holy mountains still at risk

Before I finish I must come back again to our holy mountains and
to their erosion, not by mining or industry, but by over-grazing.
The slopes of the mountain ranges all down the west coast are
carrying unbearable numbers of sheep, and vegetation is disap-
pearing causing widespread erosion. There is a disaster in the
making. Dr Frank Mitchell, soils expert and retired Professor of
Quaternary Studies of Trinity College, Dublin, recently stated:
'The process of erosion is already in full cry in the west, and ruin
will face all if it is not stopped ... This practice of keeping sheep
on land where the vegetation has been overgrazed is fatal for soil

erosion.' He places the 'basic blame on the (European) Commission because of its extraordinary programmes of headage subsidies'.[19] I, too, have seen the slippages of soil on the slopes of the Sheffrey and the Maamtrasna Mountains. Soon the soil will be gone and the bare rock will remain.

It will take a rare burst of enlightenment and activity on the part of all of us, but especially on the part of our rulers and policy makers, to reverse the damage which we have done to the earth, water, and air of our planet. But it's a poor thing if we have to be forced to do what is right. It would help if we would re-examine our values and re-state what is most important to us. Culture used to preserve our values, but in times of cultural change such as the present 'urbanisation' of even rural areas, we need to ensure that values which are important to us are safeguarded. In any event, we can all resolve, as independent intelligent beings, to do everything in our power to care for all our holy mountains.

Notes

1. Gerry Bracken of Westport, local historian and aerial photographer, discovered this phenomenon in 1991 after many and patient visits to the Rock.

2. MacNeill, Máire, *The Festival of Lughnasa*, Oxford 1962, quoted in *Pilgrimage in Ireland*, Harbison, Peter, Barrie & Jenkins, 1991.

3. *Tóchar Phádraig*, *A Pilgrim's Progress*, Ballintubber Teamwork, Ballintubber Abbey Publications, 1989.

4. Waddell, John, 'The First People, The Prehistoric Burren', in J W O'Connell and A Korff, eds., *The Book of the Burren*, Tír Eolas, Kinvara, 1991.

5. Lecture given by Professor Martin Downes at Céide Fields Interpretative Centre, 17 June 1993.

6. Rose, Chris, *The Dirty Man of Europe, The Great British Pollution Scandal*, Simon & Shuster, 1990.

7. Ibid.

8. Ponting, Clive, *A Green History of the World*, Sinclair Stevens, 1991.

9. Ibid.

10. Seymour, John and Girardet, Herbert, *Far From Paradise, The Story of Man's Impact on the Environment*, BBC, 1986.

11. Carson, Rachel, *Silent Spring*, Penguin Books, 1982.

12. Rose, Chris, op. cit.

13. Cohen, R. L., *The Economics of Agriculture*, Cambridge Economic Handbooks, 1949.

14. Cutler, James and Edwards, Rob, *Britain's Nuclear Nightmare: The Shocking Truth Behind the Dangers of Nuclear Power*, Sphere Books, 1988. (Quoted in Chris Rose, op. cit.)

15. Rose, Chris, op. cit.

16. Hinrichsen, Don, *Our Common Seas*, Earthscan Publications, 1990.

17. Ibid.

18. Ibid.

19. Mitchell, Frank, 'Who Is Going To Shout Stop?', *Living Heritage*, Vol 10, No 1.

CHAPTER 3

Killasser: A Case History

Bernard O'Hara

Killasser is a rural parish of eighty square kilometres, situated between Swinford and Foxford at the south-west end of the Ox mountains. The placename is ecclesiastical in origin, an anglicised version of the Irish, *Cill Lasrach*, which means 'the Church of Lasair'. According to a medieval Gaelic source, the eponymous Lasair was ninth in descent from Niall of the Nine Hostages, High King of Ireland from AD 379 to 405, and the daughter of Rónán Mac Ninneadha, who gave his name to the parish of Kilronan in North Roscommon. If St Lasair's genealogy is correct, her *floruit* cannot have been earlier than the eighth century.

Archaeological heritage

There is a tablet over the tomb of Sir Christopher Wren in the crypt of St Paul's Cathedral in London bearing the words '*Si Monumentum Requiris Circumspice*' ('If you seek his monument, look around'). If you seek monuments to previous generations of Killasser people, all you have to do is look around the parish, for it contains evidence of human habitation for about five thousand years. The wealth of its antiquities is by any standards remarkable and represent all periods from the Neolithic Age (c. 3,500 to 2,000 BC) to the present.

Our first farmers arrived in Ireland about five and a half thousand years ago, long before the dawn of recorded history, and some of them settled in Killasser. We know this because they introduced a custom of burying their dead collectively (usually cremated) in tombs made with large stones, known as megalithic tombs, the earliest surviving architectural structures in the country. In the literature on archaeology, Irish megalithic tombs are divided into four classes: court-tombs, portal-tombs, passage-tombs and wedge-tombs, each type named after its chief diagnostic feature. The remains of some such tombs are at present so badly damaged, overgrown, or full of debris, that they cannot be accurately identified from observation, and are consequently recorded as unclassified megalithic tombs. There are eleven megalithic tombs in Killasser: three court tombs (Cartronmacmanus, Coollagagh and Knockfadda); one portal (Prebaun); three wedge (Callow, Doonty and Cullin); four unclassified ones (Cartronmacmanus, Creggaun, Doonty and Prebaun), with five others just outside the boundary of the parish. The Bronze Age (c. 2,000 to 400 BC) is represented by wedge-tombs, mounds (circular earthen structures with rounded profiles, often containing burials), cairns (similar structures made with stones), standing-stones (stones set upright in the ground, often marking burials), stone alignments (straight lines of three or more standing-stones) and cooking-sites known as *fulachta fiadh*. There are also pre-bog walls and enclosures as well as prehistoric house-sites, some of which could date from the Neolithic period. The Early Iron Age (c. 400 BC-AD 400) is represented by four crannogs (dwelling-sites on artificial islands built in lakes), over 130 ringforts (enclosed habitation-sites), and about eighty souterrains (underground chambers), which were in use up to the sixteenth and seventeenth centuries in some cases. There are ecclesiastical sites from the Early Christian Period (AD 400-1100), the late medieval period and modern times, as well as associated sites like bullaun-stones (boulders with artificial basins or hollows), children's burial grounds (unconsecrated places used primarily for the burial of unbaptised children from the Early Christian Period up to this century), crosses and shrines. There are also many sites and artefacts from the nineteenth and twentieth centuries to be seen.

Few parishes can boast of an archaeological heritage like that of Killasser, with over 300 monuments identified in a recent survey. It is really an open air archaeological museum. Many activities of humans can be traced from prehistoric times to the present in the parish: housing from possible Neolithic sites, crannogs, ringforts and thatched houses to the modern bungalows; burial-sites from the megalithic tombs to the cemetery now in use; pre-historic standing stones to mark the sites of burials to the present tombstones; corn grinding devices from the saddle-quern, rotary-quern, horizontal and vertical mills, to the threshing-machine of recent times, while ecclesiastical sites from the original one to the present churches at Killasser and Callow are evidence of a strong spiritual faith over many centuries. This evidence of continuity over time, so evident on the Killasser landscape, is the essence of heritage and roots.

A struggle to survive

During the early nineteenth century, there was a rapid rise in the population of the parish with a concomitant increase in poverty. The population increased by 1,693 between 1821 and 1831 and by a further 381 to 1841 (see table). The deteriorating social conditions were aggravated by the Great Famine from 1845 to 1849, during which many people died from starvation-related diseases and emigration to England and the USA commenced on a big scale, a phenomenon which continues to the present day. Between 1841 and 1851, the population of the parish fell by 2,110 or thirty per cent. It was a sense of social justice which inspired many parishioners to support the Land League, when it was inaugurated in 1879 by Michael Davitt. A branch was established in the parish, and it erected huts to provide temporary accommodation for families who were evicted. Nearly half the population of the parish, led by the Killasser Land League Band, were in Straide on 1 February 1880 to hear Michael Davitt address a monster meeting from a platform erected over the site of the house from which he and his family were evicted in 1850. The Land League campaign led to a series of land purchase legislation from 1885 to 1923, which brought about the greatest social revolution ever seen in this country and transformed tenant-farmers into owner-occupiers by constitutional means. Michael Davitt was revered in Killasser and his framed photograph had a place of honour in many homes until as late as the 1960s, when it was replaced by President John F. Kennedy, Pope John XXIII and the Sacred Heart, a unique Irish holy trinity.

Social conditions were bad at the start of the twentieth century, with large families the norm, most of whom ended up in exile. A number of men from the parish fought in the first world war and some of them never returned. Their sentiments on leaving home were no doubt encapsulated by the poet, William Butler Yeats, when he wrote:

Those that I fight I do not hate,
those that I guard I do not love;
My country is Kiltartan Cross
My countrymen Kiltartan's poor ...

After 1921/22, the rights and wrongs of the Civil War dominated
Irish political life for a generation and relegated economic and
social development to second place, exemplified in Killasser with
massive emigration. The low farm incomes were supplemented in
many cases either by emigrants' remittances or savings from seasonal migratory work in England. In the latter case, many migrants
had not completed their national school education when they
were forced by economic necessity to supplement the family
income. The prevailing economic situation in Ireland was aggravated by 'the economic war' (1933-38) and later by the second
world war. In that environment, small farmers sought the highest
possible level of self-sufficiency in order to survive, and it was
common for housewives to barter baskets of eggs for some essential purchases at the travelling shops which then served the parish.
In that context, the borrowing of money was an anathema, but
several shops did give extended credit, which was repaid in most
cases when the migrants returned at Christmas. It was the worst
of times. The social scene in Killasser then, as in most rural parishes
in Mayo, was no different from Inniskeen in County Monaghan,
as recorded so vividly and poignantly by Patrick Kavanagh, especially in that long sad despairing poem *The Great Hunger*. Like
John Healy's mother's family, as recorded in his book *Nineteen
Acres*, it was a struggle to survive.

The nineteen-fifties in Ireland was a period of economic stagnation, with continual balance of payments crises, rising unemployment, high emigration and a declining population. Profit from
farming was low, with few opportunities to earn supplementary
income, and small farmers did not receive any dole, subsidies or
headage payments. Killasser, like most rural parishes in the west
at the time, was a place of apathy, cynicism and despair. The
social fabric of the parish was on the verge of collapse. During the
1950s, the Killasser GAA Club ceased (the parish had won the
Mayo 1935 junior and the 1937 minor championships), the annual
sports which were organised since the early 1930s came to an end,
Callow Dramatic Society lapsed and the Killasser band (founded

in 1879) disbanded. The reason in each case was emigration. In addition, sixteen families left Killasser under the Irish Land Commission programme introduced to relieve congestion in the west by transferring some families to new holdings in Meath and Westmeath.

However, some improvements did take place in the late fifties: electricity came to the parish in 1956 and, in the same year, Patrick Bolger established a prototype agricultural pilot area which revolutionised farming methods and left an indelible mark on subsequent developments in agriculture.

'The Defence of the West' movement was launched in Charlestown in June 1963 by Reverend James McDyer from Glencolmcille, County Donegal, to highlight the plight of people on the western seaboard and to campaign for new policies. There was considerable support for the movement in Killasser, once again inspired by a sense of social justice and the fact that local schoolteacher, Seán McEvoy, became its secretary. Reverend James McDyer addressed a big enthusiastic meeting in Killasser on 29 September 1966. The movement did get the government to take more interest in the special problems of the west, which resulted in the introduction of the small holders' assistance ('the dole') in 1966 but not in the form advocated by Reverend James McDyer. Economic conditions improved slowly in the parish during the 1960s, with more farmers sending milk to the creamery and other initiatives.

Following the publication of the First Programme for Economic Expansion in November 1958, industrial policy was changed from protectionism to free trade with the objective of establishing an export-orientated manufacturing sector in Ireland by attracting foreign investment and stimulating private enterprise. Many multinational corporations began operations in the country and new employment opportunities were created in industry and services, while the agricultural labour force continued to decline. In the 1970s, the Industrial Development Authority (IDA) began a policy of balanced regional dispersal of industry. Travenol Laboratories (later Baxter Healthcare) was established in Castlebar (1972) and Swinford (1977), while Asahi started operations in Killala during 1977. These developments led to considerable improvements in Killasser, with many parishioners securing off-

farm employment locally. After Ireland joined the European
Community on 1 January 1973, agricultural earnings began to increase. A number of families returned to the parish from England
and the USA and an air of optimism and confidence emerged. The
Killasser Group Water Scheme, organised by local enterprise,
came into operation on 9 May 1976, followed by the Callow
Scheme in August 1980. A community centre was erected, and
various sporting, cultural and social events were organised. In
1980, Killasser won the Mayo Meitheal Award, which is awarded
annually by the Mayo Association in Dublin to honour community
endeavour.

This progress was not maintained during the 1980s, which became a bad decade for general economic management in Ireland,
and the chief victims were school leavers who had to seek their
livelihoods in exile or join the ranks of the unemployed at home.
Few, if any, new employment opportunities arose locally for Killasser people, while EC food surpluses resulted in the curtailment
of agricultural production.

Table: Population of the Civil Parish of Killasser 1821-1991	
Year	Persons
1821	4,888
1831	6,581
1841	6,962
1851	4,852
1861	5,682
1871	5,404
1881	5,547
1891	4,839
1911	4,213
1936	3,148
1946	2,607
1951	2,445
1961	1,955
1971	1,525
1981	1,467
1991	1,186

During the 1980s, the dependence on agriculture and lack of new employment opportunities locally resulted in high out-migration.

Between 1911 and 1991, the number of households in the civil parish fell from 910 to 394 and in the Catholic Church parish (a slightly smaller area) from 784 to 350. The population of the civil parish dropped to 1,186 in 1991 (1,058 in the Catholic Church parish), but that figure included very few between the ages of 20 and 35. This big population decline is also evident in most rural parishes in Co Mayo.

Causes

There are two main causes for the current situation: market forces and a lack of employment opportunities. Market forces are exerting pressures for centralisation and the development of urban centres at the expense of rural areas. It is part of an ongoing process of urbanisation across the developed world, resulting in the outflow of labour and capital from rural to urban areas. This process, if allowed to continue, creates a cumulative decline in rural areas. The effects of market forces are often aided by Government policies. The urban renewal tax concessions introduced in the 1986 Finance Act led to the development of attractive shopping centres and arcades in many of the designated areas in the chosen cities and towns (Ballina and Castlebar are the only Mayo towns included), which attract customers from the smaller towns and rural shops. A declining population creates economic pressure for retrenchment and the centralisation of various services like post offices, schools, garda stations and medical services, and in the process facilitates the disintegration of the local economy. It makes life much more demanding for the people who most require these services at a difficult stage in their lives. We are great advocates of social cohesion within the European Union, but perhaps we should begin by practising in our own state what we preach to others.

The second reason is a scarcity of employment opportunities. Since the 1960s, government policies have addressed the symptom of the problem but not the cause. Schemes like the small holders' assistance and headage payments provide essential income support for the recipients, but they are fostering a dependency culture and ignoring the fundamental cause of the problem: a scarcity of employment opportunities. Pope John Paul II, in his encyclical letter *Centesimus Annus* (1991) wrote: 'The obligation to earn one's bread by the sweat of one's brow also presumes the right to do so. A society where this right is systematically denied … cannot be justified from an ethical point of view, nor can that society attain social peace.' The Irish Episcopal Conference in an excellent Pastoral, *Work is the Key: Towards an Economy That Needs Everyone*, published in 1992, (which has not received the national attention it deserves) addressed the problem succinctly in its introduction: 'The unsatisfied hunger for jobs, with the unemployment and enforced emigration to which it gives rise, is the greatest single social issue confronting Ireland today. The current levels of unemployment, North and South – with their extraordinarily high incidence among some social groups and in some geographic areas – are causing suffering to an extent which is wholly unacceptable. More can be done to bring these levels down, and more must be done. We are aware of other terrible ills which scar the face of our society, especially poverty. However, unemployment is exacerbating these ills and making them more difficult to resolve. Only when we improve our record in job creation shall we also make lasting progress in other areas of pressing social need.' It went on to state: 'While we recognise that factors outside Irish control can work against the creation of jobs here, sometimes very strongly, we regret nothing so much as a growing fatalism about the supposed inevitability of high unemployment and emigration for the rest of this decade.' The bishops of the west of Ireland organised a conference in November 1991 to publicise the affects of the declining population in the region and to shout 'stop'. Most Reverend Dr John Kirby, Bishop of Clonfert, told the conference, 'Developing the West Together': 'We see ourselves as facilitators of a process which we hope will lead to constructive changes in the lives of our peoples. We are not experts in any of the relevant areas; we have not got executive power; we are not trying to tell others their business; quite simply we are using our collective voice to highlight a growing social problem …' Arising from the success of the conference, and subsequent smaller ones around the west, the bishops secured the support of the government for an EU-sponsored study of the causes of rural decline in the region and recommendations for new development initiatives.

New strategies

Any new strategies must include a coherent policy for rural development as part of an integrated development plan, the promotion of a better dispersal of economic activity, the creation of 'growth centres', the fostering of local initiative and education and training. According to the National Development Plan 1989-93 and the Programme for Economic and Social Progress (1991), government policy for rural development is directed towards 'the stabilisation of the rural population through the promotion of the viability of the maximum number of farms and through the diversification of the rural economy by integrated regional development plans for the whole country, increasing income and employment opportunities in rural areas, and integrating agricultural, industrial and other policies'. It is inevitable that the number employed in agriculture will decline further. Consequently, if the objective of stabilising the rural population is to be attained, it will require new off-farm employment opportunities and initiatives to generate income from alternative enterprises. This requires the formulation and implementation of integrated multi-sectoral regional development plans for the whole country and not the hit-and-miss sectoral approaches of the past or treating the country as one region.

In 1926, about seventeen per cent of the population of this state lived in and around Dublin, a figure which is now over a third. This rapid centralisation has created many social problems in Dublin and bled the rest of the country of talent and energy. There are probably too few industrial jobs in Dublin today and too many service jobs, having regard to the needs of the whole country. Why has the head office of almost all semi-state bodies, banks, insurance companies and most other service organisations to be located in Dublin? The way Dublin was allowed to develop at the expense of the rest of the country was one of the biggest mistakes made since independence. These are not anti-Dublin comments; the big expansion which has taken place in our capital city has created many unnecessary social problems there and caused a big deterioration in the quality of life. A better regional dispersal of economic activity and population would benefit the whole country, and public policy should address this objective with imagination and sensitivity.

Many small rural towns are in decline as a consequence of the population decease in the surrounding areas. As we approach the end of the second millennium AD, some towns have no aspirations beyond their original role as service centres for local communities. Such inertia is a recipe for stagnation and further decline. All towns must actively promote development and generate economic activities in every way possible. The selection of a number of growth centres in the county could become the catalyst for such development. Dynamic and expanding local towns would help the surrounding countryside.

Local enterprise, initiative and leadership have big roles to play in promoting rural development. In addition to agriculture, every support has to be given to the creation of alternative enterprises: specialised production for niche markets, tourism, forestry and various services. Any business to be successful has to be market-led, creating customers, leading to an increase in income, which in turn can generate new employment. Mayo has enormous potential in tourism. Few counties have more to offer visitors, with some of the most magnificent scenery in the country and attractions to cater for all tastes, be they geology, archaeology, botany, historical sites, religious sites, angling and opportunities for all kinds of activity-holidays. You name it, Mayo has it naturally! However, the promotion of the county as an important tourist destination is only beginning. Already the Céide Fields Visitors' Centre and the Foxford Mills Centre have attracted a large number of visitors to the county and this extra tourist traffic will benefit many other areas. No one is suggesting that tourism is the panacea for all economic problems in Mayo, but, even allowing for seasonality and the weather, it can generate valuable supplementary income for many people.

The Irish educational system is generally lauded for the quality of the work done at all levels, and compares favourably with other countries. However, it is inadvertently aiding out-migration and providing inadequately for those who remain and want to develop their local communities. In other words, the system is educating young people to leave their communities rather than to stay in their communities. Education and training have big roles to play in helping to preserve the fabric of rural life. In the future, knowledge will expand at an increasing rate, technological advances will accelerate, and the demands of work will constantly change.

In this context, it is important that people develop the capacity to go on learning, to constantly update their knowledge and skills so that they can cope with new developments. This will involve many becoming self-employed and marketing their services rather than the traditional employer/employee relationship. As the pace of change accelerates, the opportunities for many people to earn their livelihoods will depend on their imagination, creativity, flexibility, personal development, innovation and enterprise. Changes will create opportunities for innovation and the provision of new products and services, many of which can be provided from rural areas using modern technology. In this context, family incomes may come from a number of sources. Initiatives like the Integrated Rural Development (IRD) companies, the EU Leader Programme and the Operational Programme for Rural Development in the Community Support Framework, with their 'bottom-up' multi-sectoral approach, are steps in the right direction, but the scale of the problem requires far more dynamic and imaginative initiatives.

PART II

Survivors and Saviours

CHAPTER 4

Granuaile: A Study in Survival

Anne Chambers

The feline durability and dare-devil indestructibility of many of our modern-day, usually male, politicians serve to mesmerise and entertain us. Almost every year, further chapters in their political death-defying antics unfold. Where, we wonder, did they learn such skills in the art of survival? What Houdini-like coach schooled them to bob and weave, to duck and dive, to ensure their political lives? What manual of instruction, illustrated with case studies of notable historic survivors of the past, did they study to balance with such agility on the precarious ledge?

Until recently it is certain that one of the most remarkable survivors of past times was not on their list of case studies. This versatile exponent in the art of survival, overcame not merely the political pitfalls that confront all politicians but, in addition, had to contend with invidious and physically threatening obstacles of nature and society. The exploits of today's exponents in the art of political survival are liable to be well chronicled, debated and preserved for posterity. Yet this ingenious survivor, who outmanoeuvred and outlasted protagonist and ally alike throughout her life, in death fell foul to the conspiracy of neglect and bias that was perpetrated against her, as generally it was perpetrated against the contribution and role of women in our history.

But in the case of Granuaile (Grace O'Malley) more than mere male chauvinism ensured her dismissal from the pages of history. Granuaile committed an additional transgression by not fitting the mould determined and demanded by later generations of Irish historians. Until recently, Irish heroes and heroines were required to be suitably adorned in the green cloak of patriotism, their personal lives untainted, their religious beliefs fervently Roman Catholic, with an occasional allowance made for rebel Protestants. Granuaile, as one of her detractors wrote of her, was the 'woman who overstepped the part of womanhood'.[1] She superseded her husband in his sacred role as chieftain; assumed command of her father's fleet of galleys and hard-bitten crews; traded and pirated successfully for the space of fifty years from Scotland to Spain; led rebellions against the English Governor of Connaught when he tried to curb her power; allied with his Queen and her deputy in Ireland, when it was to her political advantage; attacked her own son when he sided with her enemy; trained another son so well in the art of survival that he fought with the English at the Battle of Kinsale. Granuaile, who allowed neither political nor social convention to deter her ambition, took a lover, divorced a husband, gave birth to her child on board her ship at sea, plundered Irish as well as Spanish and English, hardly fitted the rosy-hued picture of Gaelic womanhood painted by latter-day generations of male and often clerical historians. It is ironic that the *Annals of the Four Masters*, that seminal source of Irish history written in a time and in a place where the memory of Granuaile must still have been verdant, does not mention her name (except in ultimate ignominy when the editor, writing two centuries later, includes her name in a reference footnote to her husband and to her castle). Such bias erased from the pages of official history one of the most remarkable survivors of the past. Indeed without the English State Papers of the period and the folk memory of the people, all trace of Granuaile might well have been buried with her.

Yet the policy of survival which Granuaile pursued with such determination and success merely mirrored her contemporary political background. Granuaile was a product of her time (c. 1530-1603). For the greater part of the sixteenth century, Ireland was devoid of any unifying ideological stimulus, political or religious. Ireland had become detached from mainstream European development. It did not share a common history with the Continent and had been by-passed by the sweeping changes that had altered the social, political and religious fabric of Europe. Gaelic Ireland had in many respects remained virtually unchanged from its Celtic origins. It had not produced a centralised stable government or monarchy but had continued to nurture its fragmented tribal kingdoms. In sixteenth century Ireland, tribal warfare, cattle-raiding and blood-money were as much part of daily life as they had been in the time of Queen Maeve and Cuchulainn.

Having no central authority to mould the allegiance of the fiercely independent leaders of Gaelic Ireland, as had been done in England under the Tudors in the previous century, survival, not nationalism, was the spur of every Gaelic leader as it was for Granuaile. Their sole concern was to hold fast to their power and position: to protect themselves from either the encroachment of a neighbour or a competitor within the clan as much as from an English administrator, if they were strong enough. If they were not, then to ally with Irish, English or Spanish, whosoever was most likely to ensure their survival. Confederation against a common enemy, when it did emerge towards the very end of the century, under O'Neill and O'Donnell, proved too little too late. Until recently our history books preferred to ignore the earlier decades and to concentrate on the tentative nationalistic tendencies of the Ulster chieftains for the last nine years of the century. They shied away from exploring the more unpalatable but understandable survival motivations of the vast majority of their contemporaries, the myriad of minor chieftains who occupied the middle-ground between the fixed battle-lines of two fundamentally incompatible protagonists, the disintegrating old Gaelic order and the new English system.

As a female leader by sea as well as by land, physical rather than political survival was undoubtedly Granuaile's first challenge. Although born into a clan whose seafaring tradition was long established, it was no mean accomplishment on her part to master and excel in the skills necessary for survival on the wild Atlantic. Her ability to captain her ships to Scotland, England, and further afield to Spain and Portugal, rank Granuaile among the best seafarers of her time. The threat from English and Spanish warships out to capture her, or from competitors in the piracy trade seeking to relieve her of her life, as well as her cargo, augmented the physical hazards which confronted her. Her capacity to endure great personal hardship and danger was remarkable. Sixteenth-century seafaring was not for the faint-hearted. Conditions on board were primitive, privacy non-existent. To endure the barrage of wind and sea, the roughness of hawser, canvas and swaying boards, sodden clothing, little shelter and indigestible rations, to give birth on board a bucking galley as she did, on the high seas, seem to us in our cushioned lifestyle, unimaginable. To compete in such a hazardous occupation in such an inhospitable environment and to live to remember it in old age, was in itself a remarkable feat of survival.

If Granuaile's political stance is examined in isolation from the era to which she belonged then, she emerges as at best an enigma and at worst a traitor. Born into an ancient Gaelic family who had ruled their territory by right of ancient Brehon law and custom, her chieftain father, Dudara O'Malley, unlike his contemporaries, had not submitted to the English. Yet his daughter sought and gained the pardon of the English Queen whose policy was to destroy the very civilisation into which Granuaile had been born. At the height of her power Granuaile 'offered her services' to the Queen's deputy in Ireland, Sir Henry Sidney, 'unto me wheresoever I would command her'.[2] She promised the Queen at their historic meeting in 1593, as he recorded, to 'continue a dutiful subject' and to 'fight with our quarrel with all the world'.[3] Later, in a written petition to the Queen's secretary Lord Burghley, she vows that she and 'her sons and the rest will not only put their lives at all times in danger to the advancement of her highness' service but also pray for your honourable lordship's success long to live in happiness'.[4] Even allowing for the embellishments of the language of the day, hardly the words or actions of what we have been conditioned to accept as patriotic.

To these protestations of loyalty to the English must be added the seemingly contradictory observations of individual English administrators and military men on the ground during the period in Ireland, men who bore the brunt of the decidedly disloyal actions of their Queen's 'dutiful' subject, for a full picture of this exponent in the art of survival. 'A great spoiler and chief commander and director of thieves and murderers at sea',[5] the crusty President of Munster, Sir William Drury wrote after he had lodged her behind bars in Dublin Castle 1578. 'A notable traitoress and nurse to all rebellions in Connaught for forty years';[6] one with 'a naughty disposition towards the state',[7] her arch enemy the English Governor of Connaught, Sir Richard Bingham, complained to Court.

Bingham wrote with first-hand experience of Granuaile's duplicity. On three separate occasions she was actively involved in rebellion against his severe rule. She threatened and attacked officials and sheriffs whom he sent to collect Crown rents from her and her husband, the MacWilliam Bourke, and when Bingham eventually captured her and 'caused a new pair of gallows to be made for her

last funeral',[8] she again slipped through his fingers, leaving Bingham in possession of her substantial cattle herds rather than her
head. Despite the damning evidence he forwarded to the English
Court of her 'anti-loyal actions', Bingham failed to prevent her
presenting her case in person to the Queen. He was simply out of
his depth, outwitted by one who was more adept at playing the
game of survival. While opposing the English administration in
Ireland, whenever it impinged directly on her power and position, at the same time Granuaile ensured that she had friends in
high places in critical times. Dogged, duty blind, Bingham stood
little chance against her powerful sympathisers, the Earl of Or-
mond, Lord Burghley and Queen Elizabeth. How he must have
shaken his head in disbelief at the naïvety of the Queen who, after
meeting with the bane of his rule in Connaught, ordered him to
show 'pity for this aged woman'.[9] Despite her age, she had cun-
ningly elicited from the Queen her approval to continue her trade,
which she had euphemistically described as 'maintenance by land
and sea'.[10] Too well Bingham knew such 'maintenance' was no
more than the piracy and plundering at which the lady excelled
and on which he had expended so much to defeat.

Although to later generations of historians these political manipu-
lations might lack the requisite patriotic or nationalistic motivation, the fact that Granuaile's status as accepted leader among her
native peers was not diminished but rather augmented by her association with individual English administrators was proof of the
success and appropriateness of her tactics. The native chieftains of
Mayo, contrary to native Brehon law which excluded women from
the chieftaincy, accepted Granuaile as chieftain and submitted
hostages to save her from Bingham's gallows. Without any apparent opposition from the male hierarchy of the clan structure,
Granuaile petitioned and negotiated with the English Crown on
behalf of the extended clan family of the O'Malleys and on behalf
of her Bourke and O'Flaherty relations. In 1579, when her second
husband, Richard Bourke, the warlike and headstrong tánaiste of
the MacWilliams of Mayo, became embroiled in the rebellion of
the Earl of Desmond, Granuaile remained aloof. There was nothing to be gained from her husband's rash involvement in a rebellion that had little to do with Mayo. She owed little allegiance to
the Earl of Desmond whose lands she had previously plundered

and who was the cause of her imprisonment in Dublin Castle in 1577. Richard was subsequently defeated by Governor Malby who harassed him clear across Connaught to an island in Clew Bay.

It was Granuaile who negotiated her husband's reinstatement with Malby and with good reason. As tánaiste to the MacWilliam, Richard had been elected by Brehon law to succeed to the title. However the previous MacWilliam had agreed to rule by English law, adopting the English custom of primogeniture which meant that his eldest son, and not his elected tánaiste, would succeed to his title and estates. By playing the loyal card on this occasion, Granuaile was instrumental in 1580, on the death of the MacWilliam, and despite opposition from his son, in having the title conferred on her husband, uniquely by right of Brehon as well as English law. The letters patent from Queen Elizabeth (originals preserved in Westport House) creating Granuaile's husband the new MacWilliam must be one of the most revealing documents of the age, legitimising by royal patent a title which in fact was outlawed by English law.

To become an accepted leader in the sixteenth century, Granuaile had to battle and survive the social obstacles placed in her path in the decidedly male-dominated society which surrounded her. Brehon law explicitly excluded women from the office of chieftaincy. Succession was not by primogeniture but by the selection of the fittest male from among the members of the ruling sept. Young men aspiring to power were required by custom to prove their ability by cattle-raiding and plundering. The role of women was domestically orientated. That Granuaile defied both Gaelic law and convention to become an accepted leader of men is a tribute to her physical daring and psychological ability. There is no parallel in the sixteenth century for Granuaile as an active warrior chieftain. While a few formidable women, notably, Eleanor Countess of Desmond, Maire Rua O'Brien and Ineen Dubh O'Donnell, made their mark politically, they did so as wives of their chieftain husbands, not as Granuaile, a chieftain in her own right. Thumbing her nose at the legal and social obstacles in her path, Granuaile emerged as *de facto* chieftain of her husbands' clans, O'Flahertys and Bourkes and as matriarch of the O'Malleys. Her impact as a powerful player on the political scene is encapsulated by the inclusion of her name on the Boazio map of Ireland

published in 1599, the only woman so named. While her contemporaries might well have been astounded that a woman should
usurp male power and prerogative, the Gaelic bards, keepers of
clan genealogies, legends and folk history, could testify that Granuaile merely followed in the tradition of the women warrior rulers of Ireland's Celtic past, like Queen Maeve of Connaught, who
dominated society before the advent of Christianity and, with it,
the introduction of Salic law.

In order to survive politically or otherwise, a chieftain had to be
physically strong. To command respect and loyalty, he had to be
able to protect his followers, to risk the same dangers and in the
sixteenth century particularly, to contend with the momentous
political upheavals that were threatening his very existence as the
English administration with its sheriffs, lawyers and military men
sought to undermine his power and position. As a woman striving for power in a male preserve the problems were compounded.
To command the respect and retain control over her wild clans-
men and crews, to enforce her will, to keep her two hundred male
followers in thrall for over fifty years required some special characteristics.

That she was successful at her trade of 'maintenance by land and
sea' undoubtedly helped maintain her control. And her success
was substantial. Although not entitled by law, she took possession of Rockfleet (*Carraig an Chabhlaigh*) and Clare Island for
lengthy periods of her life, while her name is associated with Kil-
dawnet, Doona, Bosco's Fort on Inishboffin, Hen's Castle in
Lough Corrib, Bunowen and Ballinahinch and Renvyle castles in
Connemara. Her recorded plundering expeditions were frequent,
farflung and profitable. In 1577 she plundered the rich lands of
the Earl of Desmond in Munster. In 1589 it was the turn of the
Aran Islands and Ballinahinch in Connemara, while in 1591 she
led a reprisal attack on some Scottish mercenaries who had raided
her territory. The Dan of Limerick advised the English Council in
Dublin of another of her plundering raids in 1596, when at the advanced age of sixty-six, she sailed to Scotland in another reprisal
attack, this time on the MacNeill of Barra. As late as 1601 one of
her galleys was intercepted by an English warship allegedly 'to
do some spoils upon the countries and the islands of MacSweeney
Fanad and MacSweeney Ne Doe about Lough Swilly and Sheep-
haven'[11] in Donegal. By the end of her life she had amassed a herd

of cattle and horses numbering by her own admission 'one thousand head'.[12]

Her piracy career also brought rich rewards. The merchant ships plying their way along the west coast from England, Spain and France laden with cargoes of wine, Toledo steep, salt, damask, silk and alum, made rich pickings. In vain the merchant princes of Galway reported her activities to the English crown, accusing her and her crews of 'taking sundry ships and barks bound for this poor town which they have not only rifled to the utter overthrow of the owners and merchants but also have most wickedly murdered divers of young men to the great terror of such as would willingly traffic'.[13] For years the English had neither suitable ships to apprehend her versatile galleys nor the geographical knowledge of the remote and indented coastline over which she held sway, to capture her. Eventually when in 1574, a force out of Galway, commanded by a Captain Martin, entrapped her in Rockfleet, she succeeded in repulsing the attack and sent the besieging force scurrying for safety back to Galway. By the end of her life her combined trade by land and sea paid handsome dividends for herself and her followers.

As well as being successful, Granuaile had to be as daring and bold as the men she commanded and 'to take arms and by force maintain herself and her people by land and sea the space of forty years past'.[14] Militarily she was at least as expert as her male contemporaries. It was she who won back Hen's Castle in Lough Corrib when her first husband had lost it, dislodging the Joyces with admirable military skill. Withstanding a three-week siege of Rockfleet Castle and turning defence into attack required both daring and ability, as did her victory at sea over Algerian pirates who attacked her ship. Being, as Bingham accused her, 'nurse to all rebellions in Connaught for forty years'[15] denoted a proficiency in warfare. To command crews and navigate her flotilla of galleys on voyages of trade and piracy required unique talents and much bravery.

But not withstanding her success and physical daring, she undoubtedly possessed some additional spark, some charisma that forged such an enduring bond between herself and her men to make them willing to be led by a woman contrary to social mores and male pride. Her followers comprised members of different clans, each bearing tribal grudges which she had to subdue to mould them into a fighting force whose loyalty was to her. That she could offer the English Lord Deputy, Sir Henry Sidney, an army 'of two hundred fighting men'[16] willing to fight wherever she ordained, is testimony to her absolute control. Sidney could not fail to be doubly impressed when his own army numbered hardly more. She is reputed to have been proud of her men and to have said 'go mbfhearr léi lán loinge de Cloinn Conroí agus Cloinn Mic an Alaidh ná lán loinge d'ór'.[17] (That she would rather have a shipful of Conroys and MacNallys than a shipful of gold).

The career and lifestyle pursued by Granuaile hardly augured well for her commemoration by clerical analysts and historians. It is difficult to gild her actions with any semblance of a Christian, let alone Catholic ethos. Both legendary and factual sources suggest that in terms of religious leaning she was a product more of Ireland's distant Celtic pagan past than of her more recent Christian conversion. The blatant acts of piracy and plunder pursued by Granuaile, hardly found favour within the church and Granuaile was no Robin Hood. Her personal life was no better in accord with church teaching. Her unfeminine pursuits sat uneasily on the parchment page beside the more commonplace entries in praise of women known for their charitable good works and for being devoted wives and mothers. That Granuaile ruled both her husbands and her sons is too well recorded to be ignored. 'She brought with her her husband for she was, as well by sea as by land, well more than Mrs Mate with him,'[18] Sidney felt compelled to write of her in 1577. 'His mother Granny (Gráinne) being out of charity with her son ... manned out her navy of galleys and landed in Ballinahinch where he dwelleth, burned his town and spoiled his people of their cattle and goods and murdered 3 or 4 of his men ...',[19] Bingham recorded in 1593 after her attack on her second son, Murrough O'Flaherty, after she discovered he had sided with Bingham against her. The arrangement she choose for her second marriage to Richard-in-Iron Bourke, flew in the face of Catholic regulations regarding matrimony. Disregarding church and clergy, Granuaile opted for the Brehon secular form of matrimony which allowed for trial marriages and divorce. Tradition states that she married Richard for a period of one year and after the year invoked the divorce clause of their marriage contract and dismissed him from her bed and from his own castle. Even allowing for the decline in standards and the disarray of the church in Ireland during the course of the sixteenth century, the public and private life of Granuaile could not easily be accommodated or made to conform to the Catholic ethos.

If Granuaile's political, social and religious leanings debarred her from the pages of official history, her fictionalised life more than compensated. While analysts and historians neglected her, Irish poets on the other hand immortalised her memory throughout the decades by depicting her as a symbolic figure of fiery patriotism. While Granuaile might indeed be amazed at her elevation to such a pedestal, it is partly through this strange literary anomaly that her memory at least survived the passage of time. Similarly many fanciful novels were written about her which romanticised her memory further until her life appeared too fantastic to be credible. While literature in the past is to be commended for preserving her memory from complete oblivion, it must also be faulted for tending to preserve an image of her that bore little resemblance to her actual life. The English State Papers alone have preserved for posterity some of the historical evidence about her character and her career and her contribution to the traumatic age in which she lived. These tantalising cameos confirm her turbulent life and allow us a glimpse at one of the greatest survivors of them all.

Sources

Granuaile, The Life and Times of Grace O'Malley, c.1530-1603 (Wolfhound Press, Dublin)

Chieftain to Knight, Tibbott Bourke, 1567-1629, First Viscount Mayo (Wolfhound Press, Dublin)

Notes

1. S.P.I. 63/19, no. 56
2. Calendar Carew MSS. vol 1, 353
3. Calendar Salisbury MSS. vol IV, 368
4. S.P.I. 63/179, no 77
5. S.P.I. 63/19, no 56

6. S.P.I. 63/158, no 37

7. Calendar State Papers, vol CLI, 333

8. Ibid, vol CLXX, 132

9. Calendar Salisbury MSS, vol 11, 353

10. S.P.I. 63/170, no 204

11. Calendar State Papers, vol 1 CCVIII, 436

12. Ibid, vol. CLXX, 132

13. Ibid, vol. CCVII, 5

14. S.P.I. 63/170, no 204

15. S.P.I. 63/158, no 37

16. Calendar Carew MSS, vol 11, 353

17. Ordnance Survey, Mayo, vol 1, 1

18. Calendar Carew MSS, vol 11, 353

19. S.P.I. 3013, nos 62-66

CHAPTER 5

John Patrick Lyons:
'Liberation Theologian'

Kevin Hegarty

In common with other branches of theology, ecclesiastical history has witnessed new developments in recent decades. The main concentration of church history used to lie in biographical accounts of significant church leaders or in the study of church-state relations. Little attention was paid to the lives of 'ordinary' Christians because with them, it was believed, it was impossible to find out what really happened. This situation merely mirrored the trend in general history. Brecht challenged the historians' traditional bias in favour of the powerful, the wealthy, and the articulate, when he questioned rhetorically, 'Were there only places for the inhabitants of much-sung Byzantium?'

Under the impetus of new developments in historiographical studies, with their emphases on social and economic concerns, and in the light of the modern understanding of the church as the people of God, religious historians have been broadening their concerns and taking up the challenge implicit in Brecht's words. Jean Delumeau, in his *Catholicism between Luther and Voltaire: A New View of the Counter-Reformation* (London, 1977), presents an illuminating view of the average Christian during this period. The internal dynamics of the English Catholic community between 1570 and 1850 are outlined in John Bossy's fascinating and pioneering study.

Church historians in Ireland have lagged behind somewhat in responding to new trends, partly at least because of the problem of sources; due to our fractured history, the diocesan and parochial records on which such history is most fruitfully based are not extant as early or with the same continuity as in other European countries. Nevertheless some recent studies, most notably by Patrick Corish, have skilfully and imaginatively used whatever sources remain to show the gradual percolation of Tridentine Catholicism into the Irish religious experience.

These studies have been useful in challenging Emmet Larkin's hypothesis, in his controversial article, *The Devotional Revolution in Ireland 1850-1875*, that it was the cataclysm of the great famine which led the Irish people to seek their identity in Catholicism. According to Larkin, it was during the reign of Cardinal Cullen that 'the great mass of Irish people became practising Catholics which they have uniquely remained, both at home and abroad, down to the present day.' By showing that Larkin did not avert in sufficient depth to what had been achieved in this sphere before Cullen returned to Ireland in 1850, they have implicitly disproved Larkin's view. Before, however, any definitive synthesis of the story of the Irish Catholic community, between the humble Mass houses of the early eighteenth century and the Gothic splendour of the Victorian Cathedrals can emerge, detailed local studies of the development of religious life and practice will have to be undertaken. It is clear that there were differences in the rapidity and extent to which Counter-Reformation Catholicism took root in the maritime and subsistence economies of pre-famine Ireland. This article, through looking at the work of John Patrick Lyons, who served as a priest in the diocese of Killala between 1821 and 1845, offers a portrait of a Catholic community in the subsistence economy.

Though he was a native of the Archdiocese of Tuam, John Patrick Lyons spent all his priestly ministry in the Diocese of Killala. His early life is sparsely documented. He was born in the last years of the eighteenth century in Bekan, a parish which nestles between Claremorris and Knock, the son of a substantial farmer. The family employed a number of servants, and a brother and sister married into landed families. He entered the humanity class in Maynooth for the diocese of Killala in 1818. His choice of Killala, rather than his home diocese, was dictated by his family's friendship with Bishop Waldron of Killala who had earlier served as parish priest of Bekan. The poor priest-people ratio in Killala – the third worst in Ireland in 1834 – ensured that his course in Maynooth was short. Three years after he entered there, he was ordained by Archbishop Murray.

He was a man of literary and cultural interests. He was an excellent writer of English prose. His vast and valuable library, of over nine hundred items, indicates his profound interest in theology, literature and history. The library opens a window into his mind. Among the collection was a number of rare Irish manuscripts. He was particularly interested in the Irish language and antiquities. He encouraged Philip Barron to set up an Irish training school in 1835. It is unfortunate that his handwritten history of Erris has not survived, for John O Dovovan found the 'celebrated Dr Lyons' very knowledgeable about the antiquarian remains of Erris and Tyrawley during the Ordnance Survey mapping of Mayo. On a visit to Rome in 1842, he discovered in St Isidore's College, twenty-five volumes of Irish manuscripts. His accurate tracings of the chief heads of subjects in the entire collection are in the Royal Irish Academy.

After ordination, Bishop Waldron appointed Lyons as adminis-trator of Kilmoremoy (this mensal parish included Ballina, the largest and wealthiest town in the diocese). His progressive atti-tudes and commitment to the decrees of Trent were obvious in the four years he spent there; he streamlined parochial administra-tion; he started the practice of keeping parish registers of births, marriages and deaths, a relatively unusual practice in Connacht before 1850; he organised funds from the Kildare Place Society for the establishment of six schools; he acted as an intermediary be-tween repentant Ribbonmen and the authorities.

On John MacHale's appointment as coadjutor Bishop of Killala in 1825, Lyons was transferred to Kilmore-Erris. The transfer was in-evitable as Lyons and MacHale had always been at odds. He re-mained there for the rest of his life.

Erris in 1825: A general background

It is necessary to outline in some detail the social, economic and religious background of pre-famine Erris, for the problems in these areas constituted the agenda for Lyons' work in his new par-ish.

The barony of Erris is located in the northwest of the diocese of Killala, and before the great famine was easily its poorest and most inaccessible region. Given its desolate landscape, its remote-ness from the main centres of commerce, its high population dens-ity, and its primitive agricultural methods, it is not surprising that Erris was one of the most impoverished parts of pre-famine Ire-land. The witnesses from Kilmore-Erris, drawn from all its social classes, who gave evidence to the Poor Law Inquiry in the 1830s, convey a melancholic unanimity about the nature and extent of this poverty. Well over half of Lyons' parishioners lived in a constant state of tension between mere survival and destitution. Of the 1648 families in the parish, 371 were freeholders in a burlesque sense – having no land themselves, they sought access to a small plot from their neighbours in payment for duty work; about half the remainder were holders of land of no greater value than £1.0.0. to £1.10.0 per acre. The condition of Hugh O'Malley was typical of the majority in his parish.

> Rents three quarter of an acre; seldom gets work; has a wife and five children; his little holding does not have provisions enough for his family for five months; would most cheerfully work for 4d a day and his diet; his wife earns three halfpence a day by spinning, but she has not constant employment even at that price; his crop has failed this year; he has eaten all his potatoes already and he must now depend on providence; his family never begged except for three months in 1822 and for one month in 1833; but he apprehends they must beg this year; could not support himself last summer but for the Rev Dr Lyons who gave him some barley; he uses barrage, cabbage and wild rape as articles of food in summer; his children as well as himself are usually in rags, and such is the state of persons of his class throughout the parish.

The housing statistics of the 1841 census are a further index of the poverty of the Kilmore-Erris community. Over three quarters of the houses were in the lowest categories. Emigration, as an option, was confined to the sons of wealthy tenants who could afford it. The only way for most of the community to fend off starvation in times of distress was to beg from their neighbours or in the neighbouring barony of Tyrawley.

The central social and economic problem in Kilmore-Erris was the pressure of an increasing population on scarce and inadequately developed resources. The land-holding system in Erris was unmodernised. Though some of the landlords were beginning to modernise their estates, the main system of land-holding bore strong similarities to the Gaelic system. The general practice in each village was for three or four men to rent the land on behalf of all the inhabitants. The leader of this group was known as the King or *Ceann Fine*, a position that 'he attained through imperceptible degrees of mutual assent as the old king dies off.' This group regulated the collection of rent, the distribution of land and the organisation of labour in the village. They apportioned out, every third year, the amount of pasture and tillage each family could hold. They decided the number of cattle which each family could graze, and appointed a herdsman on behalf of the landholders.

This system militated against viable farming. No farmer was enthusiastic about improving land he might be deprived of after three years. Lyons found, in 1825, that agricultural methods there were one hundred years behind the rest of the country – harrowing by the horse's tail was a common practice until he got them to stop it.

This mode of land-holding also caused envy and rancour among neighbours. By providing relatively easy access to landholdings, albeit minuscule ones, it encouraged and facilitated early marriages. W.H. Maxwell wrote wryly of this practice in Erris:

> When they marry – for Malthus and his restrictions upon population are no more recognised in Erris than the Pope is by a modern methodist – they will obtain a patch of mountain from their patrons, erect a cabin, construct a still and, setting political dogmas at defiance, then and there produce a most excellent whisky, and add to the seven millions considerably.

In his evidence to the Poor Law Inquiry, Lyons talked of the profligate economic abandon with which his poorest parishioners entered marriage. 'Those who are more comfortable and somewhat educated wait longer, but persons unacquainted with comfort do not feel the want of what they can never know. They marry if they have enough potatoes to last a year, or indeed half a year.'

The economic poverty of Kilmore-Erris was reflected in its dilapidated and disorganised ecclesiastical and educational infra-structure. In 1825 there was no proper chapel or vestments in the parish. Mass houses were still the centre of worship and many people had to worship in the open air. In the neighbouring parish of Kilcommon-Erris, the community was unable to afford the money to roof a new chapel. In 1826 there were ten schools in the parish, four sponsored by the London Hibernian Society and six hedge-

schools, usually held in a common cabin. In one case the teacher
had no permanent schoolhouse but taught a week in succession in
the cabins of the pupils. An illiteracy rate of over 90% in the parish
testifies both to the small number of pupils who could afford the
paltry fees demanded by the teachers, and to the poor quality of
the education provided. The schools had a precarious existence.
Fortunes fluctuated due to economic factors. By 1835, the ten
schools of 1826 had been reduced to six, only one of which had
survived since 1826.

It is difficult to assess the quality of religious life in Kilmore-Erris
because of the absence of parochial records for the pre-famine
period. An impressionistic portrait is all that is possible. The 1835
report on Public Instruction indicates that out of a population of
9,400, just less than thirty per cent attended Sunday Mass. Though
twenty per cent would have been excluded from the obligation of
attendance by reason of age, we are still a long way from full attendance. The poor road system in this vast parish would have
meant that many people living in the outlying areas would have
found it difficult to attend, especially in inclement weather. The
custom, which continued in the remoter parts of the west almost
up to the present day, of parents attending Mass on alternate Sundays while one of them remained at home to look after the younger children, would also have reduced numbers.

The greatest factor in reducing attendance, however, was the poverty of the people. In his evidence to the Devon Commission,
Lyons pointed out that 540 families of his community could
'scarcely make their appearance in a congregation on Sunday.' He
told the Poor Law Inquiry, 'When I hold a station, persons commonly request of me to let them go early, as they must lend their
clothes to their neighbours, that they may come in turn.'

The stations were an important part of the religious life of the parish. W.H. Maxwell reported in his 'Wild Sports of the West' that
the priest in Ballycroy had to take a prolonged leave of absence
from hunting and fishing parties while the stations were in
progress. Held in each village on two occasions every year, they
provided the main opportunity for confession. Thomas Dixon, a
curate in Kilmore-Erris, reported to the Lords Committee on the
State of Ireland, in 1825, that the vast majority of the community
attended confession only on those two occasions.

Baptism records do not survive for Kilmore-Erris, but from the few records that survive elsewhere in the diocese, it is reasonable to assume that it took place very soon after birth. The available evidence suggests that confirmation was held irregularly.

In the area of sexual morality, the community imposed its own strict discipline. All the pre-famine observers of Erris – notably Otway, Knight and Maxwell – refer to the strong sense of sexual discipline there. In evidence to the Poor Law Inquiry, it was stated that illegitimacy was rare and, where it happened, the mother and child were outcasts from society. Abductions, however, seem to have caused particular problems. W.H. Maxwell said that a prosperous woman bent on celibacy should avoid Ballycroy!

It is not surprising that in an impoverished, illiterate community, superstition – a way of dealing with the seeming arbitrary reality of life – was a strong force. There were considerable early Christian remains in Kilmore-Erris, and around these a number of superstitions and convivial practices, in which the sacred and profane were incongruously mixed, had accreted. The pattern day of St Deirbhle, on 15 August each year, was the most prominent of these experiences.

The work of John Patrick Lyons in Kilmore-Erris

In an address to his parishioners on his second Sunday in Kilmore-Erris, in September of 1825, Lyons stated that his aim was to reform the religious life of the parish and to bring it into conformity with the structure in Ballina, which he saw as the model for the diocese. As a priest for whom the Tridentine decrees were the lodestar of his priestly life, this was an obvious objective. His concomitant involvement in the social, agricultural and educational reform of the parish should not been seen as the work of a man whose energies were unsatisfied by the demands of his ecclesiastical work. In *Catholicism between Luther and Voltaire*, Jean Delumeau, writing about France in the eighteenth century, claims that Counter-Reformation Catholicism could not find strong roots in the unpropitious soil of an impoverished and illiterate peasantry. Though Lyons did not explicitly articulate the assumptions behind his work in this way, he would have accepted Delumeau's views. All his activities were directed towards the religious, social and moral regeneration of his community.

Through a privately conducted census, which he regularly up-
dated, he was aware of the social and economic condition of all
his parishioners. A people from whom the tyranny of constant
hunger had been lifted, who were educated and adequately
housed, who had developed respect for public order, would more
easily assimilate and internalise the doctrines and practices of the
Counter-Reformation. His work in all these areas were individual
parts of a total approach to the modernisation of his community.

Lyons established Binghamstown as the ecclesiastical centre of
his parish. Under his aegis an extra curate was appointed to the
parish, which improved its poor priest-people ratio; its new ratio
of 1 priest per 2,980 people was much better than the diocesan
average. Throughout most of his ministry in Kilmore, he had a
say in who were appointed his curates, thus ensuring he worked
with people whose views resonated with his own.

His first task was the building of a church in the parish. At a meeting at Carnehill, in October 1825, his proposal that a church be
built was accepted by his parishioners, who declared themselves
willing to contribute what they could to the project. Lyons also received aid from influential friends in the building of this chapel
and by the early 1830s it was in use. He had built, out of his own
funds, a substantial house at Binghamstown, symbolic, in its own
way, of the major role he was to assume in the parish. He streamlined the system of parish collections, which, before his arrival,
had been arbitrary and open to abuse. The annual stipend was
fixed at three shillings, which was the highest sum to be expected
from any family, while the poorer families were expected to pay
nothing or a pittance. For this stipend the parish priest and curates were expected to celebrate Mass on all Sundays and Holy-
days, to preach, catechise, church women and to relieve the poor.

Lyons sought to curb the more blatant superstitious practices in
his community. He withdrew ecclesiastical sanction from the pattern day of St Deirbhle in 1827 because of the indecorous behaviour which he witnessed there. He claimed that his attempts to
stop obscene and heavy drinking at wakes were successful,
though in this he was probably too optimistic. Part of his approach was to give ecclesiastical dignity and discipline to the celebration of funerals. He liked to attend every funeral himself, be-
lieving, as he once wrote, that it was 'an appropriate occasion for

giving discourse to the people on a serious topic.' Where – as often happened in a parish where social distress was frequent – there were several funerals on the same day to different and very distant graveyards, it was impossible to attend them all. On such days he made a point of attending the funeral of the poorest person, and, for the others, he blessed some clay which was taken to the graveyard.

He believed that proper catechesis was an essential weapon in the attack on superstition. Attached to his new chapel at Binghamstown was a Sunday school where catechetical instruction was given and a devotional library established. Part of the problem of catechetical instruction in an Irish-speaking community was the lack of texts in the language. He found Jonathan Furlong's *Compact Compendium* of prayers and doctrine, *Compánach an Chríosdaigh*, especially valuable and, in a preface to the volume, welcomed it enthusiastically. On a visit to Rome in the 1840s, he found a substantial cache of the catechisms of O'Hussey and O'Molloy, which he brought to his parish.

His interest in catechetics was closely connected with his determination to provide a system of general education for his community. He believed that the school could be a major agency of catechetical instruction. A letter he wrote to the *Mayo Constitution* in 1838, in defence of the National School system, shows that his interest in education went way beyond the confessional. He saw education as helping to produce the disciplined and mature citizen for whom religious and civil obligations would be intertwined: 'A slight consideration of this mode of instruction will evince that it is eminently suited to secure other objects of great importance besides the mere acquisition of knowledge. It teaches habits of order and punctuality, and the boy who recollects the discipline and regularity of the school will know in after life how to arrange his household systematically and to make the most of his time and resources. The early training of such schools serves to correct and ameliorate the temper of youth and gives them a habit of self-control, of submission to proper authority and of respect for their superiors, and consequently it enables them, when they grow to maturity, to restrain their passions and feelings within proper limits, and to discharge the duties of good citizens and subjects. It also teaches them that members of society should co-operate for

their mutual benefit and that no one is so humble as to be incapable of rendering some service to the public or so exalted as not to
need the goodwill and offices of his neighbour. Youth is the proper
season for sowing the seeds of piety and industry and of learning
those relations between man and man which constitute the foundations of religious, moral and social duties.'

The total responsibility for education in Kilmore-Erris devolved
upon himself, for the resident gentry were uninterested in its provision. The presence, in the parish, of schools under the aegis of
avowedly proselytising societies rendered even more acute the
need to take a positive initiative. At a parish meeting soon after
his arrival, he had a resolution passed calling on parents of newly
baptised children to pay, as part of the baptismal stipend, money
that would be used in the provision of schools. The poverty of his
community dictated, obviously, that not enough money could be
raised in this way. He turned to the Kildare Place Society for help,
but his initiative proved unfruitful when the landlords refused to
give permanent sites for schools. Undismayed by this failure,
Lyons established a school at Binghamstown, out of his own
funds, and whatever he could collect of the baptismal fee, under
the tutelage of a trained teacher. Here over one hundred and fifty
children were given a basic education, which was free to all except those who had attained a knowledge of arithmetic.

Lyons realised that this was only a partial solution to the education problem. Lack of financial resources meant that he was unable to provide schools in other populous centres of his parish. He
found it difficult enough to keep the Binghamstown school open,
and it even closed for a while during the social distress of 1831.
Therefore he welcomed the establishment of the national system
of education in 1831, for it provided him with the opportunity to
set up a phalanx of schools throughout the parish. His early support and use of the system inevitably led him into conflict with
Archbishop John MacHale of Tuam, possibly its most intrepid op-
ponent. In a series of letters to the *Mayo Constitution* newspaper in
1837, he attacked MacHale's vehement condemnation of the system, asserting that, given the poverty of the west of Ireland, the
system provided an opportunity that should not be missed, and
that the dangers to faith, that the Archbishop discerned in the
new schools, could be averted by the vigilant involvement of the

priest. Between 1832 and 1841, he had seven national schools established in the parish.

The social and economic structure of pre-famine Erris teetered precariously on the abyss between poverty and famine. In particular, there were severe food shortages in 1831 and 1835. Lyons was involved, inevitably, in the relief of his community. Between 1827 and 1831, he made several visits to England to collect money for this purpose. The failure of the seaweed crop, in 1829, used to fertilise the seed potatoes, presaged two years of acute distress. Lyons was a leading member of the Mayo Central Relief Committee set up in 1831 to co-ordinate relief measures in the county. He used his allocation of funds to employ the distressed on the construction of roads in the parish, which served the two-fold purpose of improving its infra-structure and providing wages used to buy supplies. He arranged for the distribution of potato supplies from England to his distressed parishioners. Lyons was aware, however, that these measures merely met an immediate need. They assuaged temporarily, but did not solve, the central social economic problem. This perception led him to become involved in agricultural reform.

In his evidence to the Devon Commission, Lyons condemned the system of land-holding in the parish as a 'ruinous practice'. Major Bingham, the leading landowner in the parish, was uninterested in reform. The efforts of some of the smaller landlords to modernise their estates were vitiated by their tendency to charge higher rents before the new holdings could yield economic returns. He found that his verbal exhortations to his parishioners to improve their holdings fell upon unresponsive ears. In his book, *Sketches in Erris and Tyrawley*, Caesar Otway, a contemporary observer, records that one of his parishioners asked Lyons, 'Your reverence, that wants us to stick to the old way in religion, why urge us to give up the old way of managing our land?' This seemingly inexorable logic could only be answered by practical action. As Lyons said in his evidence to the Commission, 'I pointed out to the people the disadvantages of their mode of tillage without success, until I showed them by example on my own land how to farm their ridges, to make drains and duly prepare the soil.'

He rented, in the village of Shanahee, a large farm containing forty-five arable acres and 484 acres of mountain and bog. He hoped in-

itially that the Irish Cistercians, then searching for a base in Ireland as they were in danger of being expelled from France, would
set up a monastery and model farm there. His hopes were dashed,
however, by the decision of Dom Vincent to reject the site following a short visit there in 1831. Even the Cistercian capacity for aus-
terity was exhausted by the barren landscape of Shanahee. In his
diary, Dom Vincent wrote, 'I could not expose my brethren to the
dreadful consequences of settling down in such a place.'

Disappointed and somewhat nettled by the failure of Dom Vincent to share his enthusiasm – he said to him, 'How can you make
so many difficulties, while I for my part, can discover no difficulty
whatever?' – Lyons resolved to develop the farm himself. He retained about two thirds of the mountain land for reclamation. By
1844 fifty acres had been re-claimed, on which he hoped to settle
tenants. He had a surveyor divide the remainder of the land in
such a way as to give every tenant a separate holding for twenty-
one years. Those tenants were provided with new houses. By em-
ploying them in the work of mountain-reclamation, he enabled
them to earn enough money to pay their rents. In order to instruct
them in the methods of modern cultivation, he got a young man,
whom he had trained at an agricultural school in Dublin, to set up
a model farm.

Lyons' foray into the agricultural modernisation proved financially demanding. Although he did receive help from English friends,
by the early 1840s he was in difficulties. He could, however, claim
some success. In his evidence to the Devon Commission, which
considered the state of Irish agriculture on the eve of the famine,
he stated that the fifteen families whom he had settled on the farm
had become, 'the most comfortable people in the parish, from
having been the most miserable. They dress better and have more
cattle!'

Lyons also took an active part in the preservation of public order
in Erris. It was another aspect of his programme of modernisation
for his community. He tried to stop his parishioners plundering
ships which were wrecked off the coast of his parish. He believed
that such actions only served to strengthen in English minds that
the Irish were a primitive race and they deterred manufacturers
from investing in Ireland. He organised a campaign in 1831 to rid
Erris of Ribbonism which had broken out during the social dis-

tress of 1830-1. Faction fighting also incurred his displeasure. He welcomed Fr Matthew's temperance movement as a way of curbing the heavy drinking at fairs and patterns, which he saw as the cause of the fighting. For him, the temperance movement had religious and social benefits. Temperance parades were held regularly in Belmullet and Binghamstown. The high point of the movement in Erris was Fr Matthew's visit there in September 1842. At a huge meeting in Binghamstown, Lyons led the majority of his parishioners in taking the pledge.

It is the fate of all reformers to meet with opposition. In his work of social, moral and religious regeneration, Lyons was challenging the innate conservatism of a peasant society and its traditional vested interests. His activities led him into conflict with the leading local landlord, Major Bingham, who ruled Kilmore-Erris in a quasi-feudal fashion and had no interest in modernisation. He differed significantly with the most powerful pre-famine clergyman in western Ireland, Archbishop John MacHale of Tuam, particularly on national education. He once wrote of the controversy his actions generated, '(They) brought a host of foes on me. It was like putting my hand into a nest of hornets and bringing them with all their rage and venom upon my ears and eager to sting me, if they could get a spot to fix on.' The last decade of his life was a turbulent one as he was a central figure in the clerical conflict in the Diocese of Killala that followed on Francis O'Finan's appointment as bishop in 1835.

John Patrick Lyons died in March 1845 on the eve of the famine which was to obliterate many of his social and economic achievements. They had not sufficient time to take root. Today his name is almost unknown in the diocese and where remembered it is merely as an awkward man. The Welsh priest and poet, R.S. Thomas, has written in 'The Country Clergy':

They left no books
memorial to their lonely thoughts
in grey parishes.
Rather they wrote on men's hearts and on
the minds of young children,
sublime words too soon forgotten.
God in time or out of time will
rectify this.

Historical research, too, can do its part in restoring reputations. It is time to rescue the reputation of John Patrick Lyons from the twin hells of oblivion and misrepresentation, where it has languished for so long. His work in Kilmore-Erris provides a fascinating insight into the agenda faced by a priest in a western seaboard parish in pre-famine Ireland. He illustrates the overwhelming social and economic problems that the clergy faced as they sought to implement the vision of Tridentine Catholicism. His attempts to modernise his parish have a prophetic air. He exemplified an Irish theology of liberation in action. In an Ireland where, according to recent reputable surveys, poverty is still endemic, his life and work have a contemporary relevance.

CHAPTER 6

Mother Arsenius and the Eye of Providence

Eugene Duffy

Introduction

Agnes Morrogh-Bernard, better known in Co Mayo as Mother Arsenius, joined the Irish Sisters of Charity in Dublin in 1863. There she worked in various houses of the congregation before coming to Mayo in 1877, first to Ballaghaderreen and then to Foxford in 1891. She had imbibed deeply the spirit of her foundress who was totally dedicated to the service of the poor and who trusted in divine providence to sustain this work. While in Ballaghaderreen Arsenius did much to alleviate poverty in the area and raise the spirits of the local community by providing various opportunities for employment, education and spiritual renewal. Here she found ready allies in the local bishop and one of his curates, Fr Denis O'Hara, the great Land League priest. Denis witnessed the zeal with which Arsenius tackled the problems of the area and, so, when he was sent to Kiltimagh as PP, he asked her to establish a foundation in his new parish. Permission was given by her Superior General and the bishop but when it came to the final negotiations his own brother, Roger O'Hara, intervened and said Denis was doing a fine job without the help of any nuns. Thus that plan was abandoned.

The plans for Foxford

Although the plan for Kiltimagh did not materialise in 1889 the effort was not without its fruit. Mrs Deane, cousin of John Dillon and outstanding benefactor of the sisters in Ballaghaderreen, heard of the failed plan and then persuaded Arsenius to avail of the permission for another foundation to open a house in Foxford. At first, the Superior General, Scholastica Margison, said that it would not be possible due to lack of finances. Mrs Deane met her and said that the Order appeared to have sufficient money to provide 'splendid tessellated pavements in your halls in St Vincent's, yet you cannot afford to send sisters to that God forsaken district of Foxford'.[1] However, Mrs Deane herself volunteered to pay the interest on any loan which the sisters might take out in order to establish the convent. The Superior General, haunted by the needs of Foxford, eventually appointed Arsenius to negotiate the matter with the bishop. Arsenius asked him to help her secure 'a house in the town suitable for a lady in reduced circumstances with a large family'. The help of the local sergeant, a Protestant, was enlisted and he recommended a house which had belonged to the local parson. A friend of the bishop bought the house in his own name for which the sisters paid £475. The house itself was in a very dilapidated condition but this was not to deter Arsenius or her volunteers. The first two sisters left Ballaghaderreen on 6 April, 1891 and took up residence in the partly renovated house. The conditions were so bad that they spent the first nights sleeping on the floor in an upstairs room, which they named 'Providence'.

While in Ballaghaderreen, Arsenius had entertained the idea of establishing a woollen industry to give employment to the people of the area. Small looms and two operators had been procured. Although the move to Foxford had taken place before that plan could be brought to fruition, the idea of a woollen industry still remained an ambition. The extent of the destitution in the Foxford area, the availability of wool locally, the presence of a river and old mill, fuelled her energies for such a project. The next stage was to seek more professional advice. Eventually she was recommended to contact Mr Smith of the Caledon Mills in Co Tyrone. She wrote to him and asked him to come to Foxford to discuss her proposal. His reply commenced, 'Madam, are you aware that you have written to a Protestant and a Freemason?' He came to see her on 6 June, 1891, for discussions and at first scoffed at her ambitious plan, reminding her that accomplished businessmen had failed in this kind of work. In her own account of the exchange, Arsenius says, 'I, knowing it was God's work and under the Eye of Providence, persisted, "I am deeply grateful for your kind advice and for being so honest but I may as well tell you that we will go on without you. Providence will provide".'[2] At this, Mr Smith took off his hat and said, 'I place myself and my experience at your disposal ...' By August work was in progress, buildings were being prepared, second-hand machinery bought, and two operators had been sent to Caledon for proper training on the looms. Arsenius herself went along for a few weeks to familiarise herself with the industry. (While visiting Caledon she lodged with the St Louis Sisters in Monaghan, thus making a connection which was later to help her friend, Fr Denis O'Hara, to convince the community to establish a convent in Kiltimagh.) The work continued through the following year under the supervision of Mr Sherry, a young manager, who was sent to Foxford by Charles Smith of Caledon.

The wheels start turning

Money was urgently needed and the Mother General was among the first to come to the rescue with a loan of £1,000. It was welcome but far from enough for the scale of the project. Another source of assistance was beginning to open up for Arsenius. The Congested Districts Board was just established with a view to the alleviation of rural poverty. She set out for Dublin and made the acquaintance of Mr Charles Kennedy, a member of the Board, Horace Plunkett, the great advocate of rural development, and Fr Tom Finlay, SJ, an expert on agricultural co-operation on the continent. All of them shared something of her vision and gladly supported her plans.[3] On this same visit, although hardly any wool had yet been produced in Foxford, she canvassed orders in Dublin from Clerys and other stores.

The mill was officially opened on 25 April, 1892, just one year after the arrival of the sisters in Foxford. It had twenty employees. By May substantial orders for blankets were beginning to arrive. Towards the end of the year the fruit of her meeting in Dublin was evident as the Congested Districts Board came up with a loan of £7,000 for Foxford. As the community had no security to offer for the loan, the Mother General consented to give a mortgage on their Milltown property.

However, fresh obstacles were to be put in their way. The landlord, Lord Clanmorris, would not co-operate in making a small piece of land available for a school and another local notable, Mr Standish O'Grady, objected to the erection of a small weir on the Moy as attempts were being made to create a millrace on the river.[4] The latter objection was a very serious threat to the survival of the

mill. Without a proper millrace the water supply could not be regulated and so the mill would have had to close. Arsenius was in
dread of the outcome but the people of the town and others further afield protested so loudly that to have interfered with the
weir would have caused violent action to be taken. Not only was
the original arrangement left in place but a more significant alter-
ation was carried out so that a proper millrace was put in place.
This final work was executed amidst many minor misadventures,
such as a loss of the plans and the unavailability of an engineer to
supervise its building. A novena was offered that there might be a
speedy resolution and, on the day it was completed, a man arrived
in Foxford, a cousin of one of the CDB officials dealing with the
mill, plans in hand and very soon the work was under way. His
arrival was seen as the answer to prayer. As the work began the
sisters prayed for three favours: First, that the weather might be
fine; second, that no accident might happen; third, that the money
might be forthcoming to pay for it. All three were granted – just.
In the course of the blasting of the rock in the river-bed, large ex-
plosive charges were used. One day a fragment of rock, weighing
twelve pounds, hurled through the roof of the Infant School, during class, and missed one of the sisters who seconds earlier had
been sitting where the rock landed.

Arsenius was a keen business woman and realised the benefit and
necessity of good advertising. To this end she organised an Industrial Exhibition at Foxford in September 1895, hoping that it
would bring advantage to the factory and its products throughout
the country. It lasted for three days and its opening was attended
by people of different creeds, class and politics. The Conservative
Lord Chancellor and the Parnellite Lord Mayor of Dublin attended, as did the Conservative Horace Plunkett, MP, the local nationalist John Dillon. All shared the one platform. The vision and
achievements of Arsenius seemed to draw a united front of admir-
ation and support from people whose politics or religion were not
the same. There were over 2,000 entries for the various competi-
tions and the exhibitors came from as far away as Dublin and
Valentia. As well as the woollens, hosiery and fabrics made in the
factory, there was a comprehensive display of agricultural produce, all of which was to act as an incentive and reward for the
local producers to raise their own standards in farm production. It

was widely acclaimed in the local and national press as an out-standing success.[5] The outcome of the Exhibition was indeed greater publicity for the work being done in Foxford and more immediately the establishment of a Foxford Industrial Fund by Lady Arran which very quickly netted £1,000 as a contribution to alleviating the heavy interest which was still being paid on the accumulated loans.

Other developments

Apart from the work being done in the woollen mills, Arsenius was also encouraging the development of agriculture in the area, and the general improvement of living standards. In fact, she had been put in charge of most of the work being carried out by the Congested Districts Board within a five mile radius of Foxford. She encouraged the introduction of new breeds of poultry, the cultivation of new vegetables, new varieties of grasses, the proper spraying of potatoes, better housekeeping and the removal of manure heaps from the immediate environs of the house. The task was not always an easy one as old ways were often preferred by the cottiers. However, they were encouraged by prizes and awards offered for various improvements carried out on their holdings. When the second Exhibition was held in 1896, it was confined to people from the Foxford area and the number of entries was in excess of 1,600. The displays and the prizes served again as an important encouragement to local initiative and the spirit of competition was a significant fillip for ongoing developments. There were four Exhibitions in all at Foxford, the last being as well supported as the first with an equally impressive gathering of public figures. The Show of 1898 was to be the last, not because enthusiasm was lacking but because it was felt that its purpose had been achieved in raising the standards of farming, housekeeping and craftwork in the area. People at last had a sense of pride in their work, their spirits had been lifted. It was now up to them to follow the headlines they had been given.

As the conditions of the local farmers began to improve, the attention of the sisters was directed more to the mill and its development. By 1907 it had 130 employees. However, the beginning of that year, on 23 January, a serious fire in the mill threatened the livelihood of all of these. Fortunately, the fire broke out in the only

stone building on the site and so it was more easily contained. As
the fire raged and the people of the town were in panic trying to
extinguish it, Arsenius calmed them by saying that it was 'Providence's match-box'. In a very short time the damage was repaired
and by 1915 the number employed had increased to 150.

War and rumours of war

The outbreak of war in Europe in 1914, far from threatening Foxford, was another chapter in its success. At that time stores of
blankets were beginning to accumulate but no ready markets
were being found. Within a month of the war breaking out, orders
for thousands of blankets were being placed by the War Office.
The stocks were cleared and the employees worked long hours to
fill the major orders coming to the factory. In 1916, Arsenius beat
the restrictions on the purchase of wool and had large quantities
in stock before they came into force. Similarly with coal supplies,
as restrictions were introduced on its purchase, the Foxford manager had bought in large quantities in advance, so that the tur-
bines continued to turn and no jobs were lost in the course of the
war. In fact the workers were, at this time, in receipt of bonuses
and congregational loans were being paid off by the convent. Inevitably the sisters interpreted all of this as 'a kind and loving
providence putting forth his strong protecting arm'.

From that time on the mill went from strength to strength and at
its peak it employed over 200 workers. As well as providing work
it sustained a vibrant social life in the area, supporting sporting
activities, music and the arts. By the time Arsenius retired from
management of the factory and superiorship of the community in
1925, a new staff was adequately equipped to continue where she
was leaving off. The survival and growth of the industry for many
years afterwards are adequate testimony to that fact.

Spiritual renewal

If the sisters made their mark on the material prosperity of the
Foxford area, they also effected a spiritual renewal not only in
Foxford but in the Diocese of Achonry as a whole. As mentioned
earlier, it was through the influence of Arsenius that the sisters of
St Louis established their Convent in Kiltimagh. When the Sisters

of Mercy were having difficulties finding a suitable superior for their convent at Swinford, in the early 1890s, it was Arsenius who helped to resolve the crisis and introduced Mother Evangelist McCarthy to the community. It was on the basis of this community's strength that two new foundations of Mercy Sisters were established at Collooney and Ballymote, two towns which had been the object of Arsenius's concern years earlier. She was also responsible for the introduction of the Franciscan Brothers to Foxford in 1925.

When the sisters went to Foxford, morale among the people and their priests was low. The parish church was badly maintained. There was no weekday Mass; there was no sign of the devotional renewal taking place elsewhere in the country; and for the first two years of the Sisters' time in the town there was no homily given on Sunday. It was only after two years persuasion by Mother Arsenius that the Parish Priest eventually gave a homily on Good Friday.

Gradually, they effected a wonderful renewal of faith and devotion in the area. One of their first tasks, as earlier in Ballaghaderreen, was to begin catechism lessons for the children in their makeshift schools. For the adults they established sodalities and the Children of Mary, taking charge of these in the neighbouring parishes as well. They were responsible for starting the First Friday devotions and Corpus Christi processions in the parish. The first ever retreat for workers in Ireland was conducted in Foxford, during the Easter of 1913, by Fr Willie Doyle SJ. The Pioneer Total Abstinence Association was introduced by the sisters in 1914. A year later, Arsenius observed the Quarant 'Ore in Foxford, which was the first time this particular devotion took place in the Diocese of Achonry. What began in Foxford soon became a model for other parishes to imitate.

One of Arsenius' final projects as Superior in Foxford was the building of a proper convent chapel. Although she always wanted a worthy chapel for the convent, she was even more anxious that the needs of her poor be taken care of before such a building be undertaken. It was only when she was sufficiently secure financially that she undertook its building. It was designed by R.M. Butler, the foundation stone laid in March 1923 and it was consecrated in September 1926. Its rose window has the Eye of

Providence as its centrepiece, which was the trademark of the Foxford Mills from their inception, chosen by Arsenius to be at once a religious symbol and yet sufficiently subtle not to offend any who did not share her own faith or her remarkable trust in divine providence.

Arsenius retired shortly after the opening of the new chapel, already showing the burden of her years. Her final illness came in December 1931 but she survived until the following April. She died almost forty-one years to the day after her arrival in Foxford. She was predeceased ten days earlier by another founding member of the community, Sr Theckla, who was in her ninety-eighth year. Thus in a matter of ten days the foundation stones of the Foxford community were laid to rest.

Trials and tribulations of life

When Arsenius first came to Ballaghaderreen she got a warm welcome and wholehearted support from the bishop, Dr McCormack, priests and parishioners. Her relations with Dr Lyster, who succeeded McCormack, and the clergy in Foxford were not always as smooth. Often minor incidents, which she records, point to a certain tension in her relationship with them, which she found impossible to understand. Perhaps her determination and success, where they had failed for so long, generated a certain jealousy. The sisters were regularly deprived of a daily Mass; their efforts in the upkeep of the parish church were regularly rebuffed; they were not allowed to take due care of their own plot in the local cemetery and on several occasions both the Parish Priest and the bishop snubbed notable visitors, or important celebrations at the convent and its factory. At the same time, demands were made on them to meet the needs and whims of the clergy. On one occasion, a newly appointed curate demanded that the convent provide accommodation for him. He was given one of the houses which was used as a residence for the teachers. As if this were not sufficient, he then demanded that they provide a stable for his horse, which they also did. Much of these difficulties were patiently endured by the sisters and they never showed any signs, to their parishioners or workers, of the pain they felt at being so badly treated.

However, Arsenius was not one to be rebuffed when important

matters were at stake and any opposition from the clergy was dealt with firmly. There is one incident, from her career in Foxford, which illustrates her commitment to the poor and her fearlessness in dealing with ecclesiastical authority. The incident occurred around the time of the 1892 General Election and, so, shortly after the Parnell split. The factory had on its staff people on both sides of the political divide, but this was not an issue for the sisters. That summer, while the parish clergy were on their annual retreat, the sisters and their staff carried out what had become an annual cleaning of the church. On their return from retreat the priests called to the convent. Arsenius recalls in her memoirs, many years later, the sequence of events:

> Naturally we might have expected their visit to thank us for the work we had done and they did thank us and were very pleased ... but then my astonishment was great when the PP informed me that he had spoken to the bishop and come back with authority to ask me to dismiss from our employment our carpenter, Mary Henehan, our work teacher in the school and four girls, all notorious Parnellites. These had joined in a demonstration in the street and behaved rudely to the PP, booing and hooting as they passed. They were in the wrong, I could not excuse them on that point, but neither could I dismiss them. I saw at once the drift of the thing, our mill was to be made a party machine ... and I felt bound to make a firm stand and I refused emphatically to agree to their demand. 'We Sisters of Charity have no politics. When I entered religion my people were all Conservatives. Now I do not care what they are ... I came here to help the poor, non-sectarian, non-political. So long as they require my help, they shall have it, and I will submit to no interference. We are not Sisters of Mercy under local authority. I am under that of my Superior General and recognise no other. If we are not allowed to do the work we came for, then we go – we have been sought for other places and are sure of a welcome elsewhere. I am ready to close down the mill, to leave on short notice and leave you the care of your own poor, the responsibility is with you'. The priests went away dissatisfied. The week passed somehow ... On Saturday the CC called to tell me that our school was to be placed under

'Interdict'!!! if the delinquents did not make a full apology. I repeated what I had said a week ago and added that I considered my community was being badly treated. Our schools and grounds were private property and I would allow no action to be taken there that savoured of politics. I conceded the point that these employees of ours had been rude to their priest, and that a public apology was due and that I undertook should be made. That evening I sent for these parties and I explained my views ... I told them I would go with them next day and before the congregation after last Mass I would speak for them. It was a vital moment, the life or death of our work in Foxford depended on it. I insisted that the two priests should come to the church door, and there I made my first and last public speech, and read the apology I had written out for them. The culprits were forgiven with the exception of Mary Henehan. The parish priest said that the bishop reserved her case ... A month later [the bishop] came over and spent hours here, and the subject was again threshed out. 'God arose and scattered his enemies' and our little barque once again weathered a violent storm, which had threatened to submerge our work, and leave the banks of the Moy as destitute as they had formerly been. [6]

The relationship between the bishop and Arsenius seems to have remained strained for the rest of his life. On one occasion he visited the convent to inspect the mill's accounts. She regarded this as somewhat *ultra vires*. The next time the accounts were audited she sent a sister over to his residence with an abstract of the accounts, sufficiently complex to prevent enlightenment and with strict orders to the bearer that she have them home with her that evening. When Dr Lyster died, in 1911, he endowed each convent in the diocese, including two other foundations of the Irish Sisters of Charity, but omitted Foxford.

Trust in providence

As the story of Mother Arsenius unfolds it becomes obvious that all her undertakings were the result of prayerful reflection and intercession and the outcome was always integrated positively into the whole scheme in which she was involved. Her work often

seemed to defy the normal laws of economics and sound investment.[7] Yet, her utter trust in divine providence gave her the courage to forge ahead in spite of obstacles or opposition. Whatever
she needed, whether premises, finance, materials, expertise, personnel or markets, always seemed to come her way and her plans
materialised to the advantage of those whom she felt called to
serve. It cannot be said that she was ever possessive of her projects because in each situation in which she worked she was always ready to move on and respond to other needs elsewhere.
While in Ballaghaderreen she was ready to volunteer for Kiltimagh. When this plan fell through she was ready to go to Foxford
and no sooner was it established than she was ready to go to Belfast to found a new community there.

What then of providence?

Among women religious, this outstanding trust in providence
would not seem to be unusual. A simple indicator illustrates the
point. There are at least thirty-four congregations of religious
women with the word *providence* in their title as against two
groups of male religious.[8] Despite the prominence given to providence in the life of the church, the theme has received relatively
little theological attention, especially from Catholic authors. However, recently, a number of women religious in the United States
have been attending to this omission with the result that the Catholic Theological Society of America devoted its annual convention
to this topic in 1989. With the help of this and other recent literature some attempt will be made to present an overview of a theology of providence and to assess the work of Mother Arsenius in
its light.

At its simplest, providence is a doctrine which asserts that the
same God who created the universe continues to govern its
affairs, constantly renewing and sustaining it with a loving presence. It points to a definite movement in creation towards the realisation of its potentialities. Providence is also the ground for our
own participation in history and the ongoing work of creation.
But here, of course, lies another aspect of providence, its ambiguity, the obvious presence of so much that is evil and destructive in
the world, so great in fact as to make any facile claim to the goodness of reality or being almost untenable. The same events can

often be interpreted, on the one hand as evidence of the goodness of God, and on the other as punishment or just evil. The Exodus event could be interpreted by the people of Israel as an instance of God's providential care of them and by the Egyptians as evil and destructive of their people. Belief in providence often has to be held in the face of facts which appear to contradict it. It can be said that providence is an aspect of our faith and of our hope which can be shown to be a reasonable stance towards life in the world.

John Macquarrie in his book, *Principles of Christian Theology*, writes:

> Belief in providence, like belief in creation itself, is founded existentially. It is through happenings that increase and strengthen our being – that do so not because of our own efforts primarily, but sometimes even in spite of our own efforts – that we come to believe in providence; and we do so because in these happenings we have become aware of the presence of Being, acting on us and in us, and giving itself to us. Historically, it has been through classic happenings of this kind, such as Israel's exodus from Egypt and the cross of Christ, that communities of faith have come to believe in God's providential dealing. In the case of most individuals, they have probably learned the doctrine first in the community of faith and then confirmed it in their own experience. This existential or personal basis of the belief in providence prevents us from regarding it as mere mechanical process.[9]

Macquarrie goes on to show how the biblical view of providence is developed through the course of Israel's history. One can see in the Old Testament story of Joseph, who was maltreated and sold by his brothers, a case of God's providential care, not just for Joseph but for the community as a whole. In such an instance the personal interpretation had to be checked against the community experience lest it become a merely subjective, individualistic assertion of divine favour. In the scriptures there is a movement from any individualistic interpretation of God's favour to a community recognition of the God of the Covenant who is constantly renewing and guiding people to their destiny amidst the events of history. This community awareness is eventually pushed beyond the realm of human history to include all of creation which is viewed as good and part of God's providential rule. Even in the face of much that might seem to contradict that belief, there is the underlying confidence, expressed by Paul, that 'in everything God works for good' (Rom 8:28). Belief in providence is not a matter of blind fatalism or an unambiguous acceptance that 'what will be, will be'. Rather, it attempts to make sense of events, to interpret them as they unfold in the context of one's faith experience and that of the whole community of faith. Thus some events can be seen to move with God's desire for the fuller being of creation and of all God's people. Other events reveal God's judgement and the awareness that they may not be in the direction of greater being. To know which is the case is the task of Christian discernment. Consequently, some events may invite our co-operation while others may require the prophetic word to be spoken or a prophetic stand to be taken.[10]

Divine providence and human engagement

These considerations take us on to look at two other aspects of providence. The first is that of the underlying hope which characterises trust in divine providence. Underlying any ability to accept the role of providence in life is the virtue of hope, a virtue not always as appreciated by Christians as it might be. Hope, according to Karl Rahner, is even more fundamental than faith and love. He defines hope as:

> that *act* in which the uncontrollable is made present as that which sanctifies, blesses and constitutes salvation without losing its character as radically beyond our powers to control ... Hope alone is the *locus* of God as he who cannot be controlled or manipulated ... [11]

Hope is directed to the future and is the basis for a Christian attitude to the world which is in fact always revolutionary, ever anxious to renew it according to its acceptance of God's promise of salvation. This attitude towards renewal is never one which accepts any human project as definitive, but as provisional and dispensable. Hope confronts the Christian with the choice of holding on to the past or the present as a possession or letting go on pilgrimage into an unforeseeable future which is understood to be embraced by God's promise of salvation.

The second corollary from our consideration of divine providence is that, far from making us passive, conservative or fatalistic, it calls us to responsible engagement in the world. It recognises that

God involves the agency of human beings in shaping the future through the exercise of their freedom and responsibility. In fact, this is such an important aspect of Catholic thought that it tends to stress this secondary causality more than it does divine providence. In this way it has safeguarded human autonomy on the one hand, and avoided the idea of random divine intervention on the other. The Catholic tradition did not deal with this issue explicitly but did so implicitly in its moral theology, in terms of the relationship between the natural and the eternal law. The position is summarised thus by Charles Curran:

> Life in this world is ruled by natural law which is the participation of the eternal law in the rational creature. Through human reason reflecting on human nature, human beings can determine what they are to do and what God wants them to do. The understanding of natural law coheres with the understanding of providence as based on mediation and the fact that God works through secondary causes. Providence thus in theory does not alter or change human responsibility to discover and act in accord with natural law. The general tendency within the tradition denies that God could grant dispensations from or exceptions to the natural law because in so doing God would contradict God's self. Thus a belief in providence does not affect the requirements of human morality in this world, for providence in the Thomistic tradition works through the natural law.[12]

So, in fact, the traditional teaching on the natural law enables us to understand how we implicitly co-operate with the action of divine providence in the world. Thus the natural law itself, as a participation in the eternal law, requires the human person to act in the world as a responsible co-operator with the divine plan of salvation.

Providence and prayer

Finally, it must be said that one's view of providence also conditions one's view of prayer. If one sees providence in terms of an interventionist God, then petitionary prayer will expect God to intervene in dramatic or abrupt ways to answer the prayer of individuals. However, this view of providence, as we saw above, cannot be sustained in a reasonable fashion, despite the fact that it has much popular appeal. An equally unsatisfactory alternative is to say that God has created the universe and let it off according to its own impersonal laws. In such a scheme of things, petitionary prayer would have no effect on God because God does not change but the petitioner may be changed, becoming more open to the presence of the divine life in others and in the world itself. Both options have points in their favour yet neither of them is adequate to the notion of providence being outlined earlier. So a third option is needed, and this is one proposed by Jack A. Keller, basing himself on the thought of Langdon Gilkey. He suggests that God is one source of power in a world with a plurality of agents of power. In petitionary prayer, we, as agents of limited power, join with the divine power. Thus we seek to open ourselves to the divine power and to co-operate with it. Still, that divine power can appear to be thwarted by human freedom or other non-divine actualities.

> In each moment God offers the best real possibilities for the achievement of value that can be built on the past. But God does not force the best on any creature. The divine power functions only as a persuasive lure, which can be ignored or rejected ... God cannot unilaterally direct the course of events, large and small, as one of the actors. To the degree that there is receptivity (conscious or unconscious) to the divine will, God's power – and our prayers that are consistent with God's will – are efficacious. [13]

Even though God's power may seem thwarted to some extent, this is not a reason for us to stop praying because God's love is inexhaustible, it endures for ever. From this perspective, providence means that God cares about creation and humanity, individually and collectively, and works constantly for our well-being, which takes us back to the Pauline confidence that 'in everything God works for good'. In this understanding of providence, prayer is part of our effort to align ourselves with the creative power of God's love, it is to be open to the kingdom which is coming into existence and expressing a readiness to participate in it. It acknowledges the sovereignty of God and the need of others, so that whatever is sought in petition is asked for in a spirit of openness and receptivity to the reign of God itself.[14] Thus while some may claim that petitionary prayer is not to be the primary form of

Christian prayer, it is nonetheless appropriate as an expression of our willingness to be co-workers in furthering the reign of God. In the end we can still rest secure in the old adage: Work as if everything depended on you and pray as if everything depended on God. This conclusion still appears valid in the light of current thinking on divine providence.

Conclusion

The attitudes and activities of Arsenius can be seen to stand the test of a current theology of providence. She had a sense of the goodness of creation and drew out its gifts so that a fuller life could be offered to her people in a genuinely holistic way as she attended to the needs of body, mind and spirit. She was never defeated nor overwhelmed by the obstacles which came her way, whether the forces of nature or human obstinacy, poverty or war. There was nothing fatalistic in her attitude, rather with a deep sense of hope and confidence in the sustaining love of God, she forged ahead in the realisation of her plans to enrich the lives of the poor. Aware of the ambiguities of all human endeavours, she could discern what was positive and consistent with the ongoing work of creation and co-operate with it. Alternatively, when she encountered contradictions of goodness or truth she was able to take the prophetic stand and voice her objections, showing how it thwarted the divine plan for the fulness of life. Despite her indisputable gifts in establishing and managing the mill and other enterprises, she still had a healthy sense of her own dispensability and never clung jealously to any of them. Readiness to move and take on new works was a constant feature of her life, pointing to that deeper reliance on God than on her own talents. A deep sense of hope seemed to underpin her attitude to life and what it presented. All of her undertakings were enriched by prolonged periods of reflective prayer. Although she had recourse to novenas and other popular practices of the time, she could never be accused of attempting to manipulate God. Rather, her whole life was characterised by a remarkable openness to God as she trusted in God's love for the world and its people, knowing that in everything God works for good. She was without doubt a co-worker in advancing the reign of God in both prayer and action.

When we look back at the life and work of Agnes Morrogh-Bernard we see in them a reflection of many of our contemporary social and theological concerns. She was committed to the poor; she was a feminist before her time, capable of meeting the men of church or state on equal terms, but also able to bring a uniquely feminine perspective to her projects; she was non-sectarian and ecumenical in her religious disposition and non-partisan in her politics; she was sensitive to the ecology of the area and used its natural resources for energy and industry, never putting more efficient machinery before the need to provide an extra job. She was a woman of vision and of action; a woman of prayer and practicality. Her unshakable trust in divine providence was no escape from the deployment of all her own human resources to effect the plans which she had for the alleviation of poverty and the enhancement of the lives of those whom she was called to serve. Although she may not have used the terminology, her motivation was the building up of the reign of God in a world afflicted by poverty and injustice. She brought hope to a destitute people not only for material improvement but also for a deeper communion with God in prayer and worship. Her life is an invitation to all concerned with survival and salvation in Mayo to look afresh at the possibilities latent in our present situation. Her achievements survive her and are still evident in every corner of Foxford. The mill, the schools, the interpretative centre, much of the housing in the village, the thriving brass band and, latterly, Hope House, all stand as a caution to any who may be tempted to give up the struggle for survival in Mayo. And in that struggle for survival, under the Eye of Providence, is found our salvation.

Notes

1. *The Memoirs of Mother Arsenius* (Dublin: Archives of the Irish Sisters of Charity)

2. Ibid.

3. *cf* Lyons, F.S.L., *Ireland Since the Famine*, Collins Fontana, 1973, 202-216

4. This particular controversy was discussed for months in the national and local papers of 1893, the cuttings from which were kept by the sisters in what was known in Foxford as *The Big Book*.

5. Gildea, D, *Mother Arsenius of Foxford*, Burns, Oates and Washbourne, London 1936, 132

6. *The Memoirs of Mother Arsenius.* According to her letters to the bishop, the root cause of the problem seems to have been that the curate in the parish had tried to persuade one of the sisters in the primary school to use the children to pressure their parents, who were Parnellites, to change their political views. When this failed he wanted them dismissed. The problem with Mary Henehan seems to be rooted in a much earlier difference between her family, her father in particular, and the Parish Priest.

7. Her efforts were not without critics at the time. See P. Murray, 'Novels, Nuns and the Revival of Irish Industries: The Rector of Westport and the Foxford Woollen Mill 1905-1907', in *Cathair na Mart: Journal of the Westport Historical Society,* 1988, 86-99

8. Hofmann, K., 'Vorsehung' art. in *Lexikon für Theologie und Kirche,* Verlag Herder, Freiburg, 1965 Vol X, 890-892

9. First Edition, SCM Press Ltd, London, 1966, 220

10. *cf* Langdon Gilkey, *Reaping the Whirlwind: A Christian Interpretation of History*, Seabury Press, New York, 1776, esp. 263

11. *Theological Investigations: Writings of 1965-7,* Vol X , trs David Bourke, Darton, Longman & Todd, London 1973, 254-255

12. 'Providence and Responsibility: the divine and the human in History from the Perspective of Moral Theology', in *The Catholic Theological Society of America Proceedings* 44 /1988, 49. See also in the same issue A. Carr, '"Not a Sparrow Falls": Providence and Responsiblity in History', 19-38

13. 'On Providence and Prayer', in *The Christian Century,* Vol 104, No 32, (Nov 4, 1987) , 968

14. *cf*. Collins, R, F., '"Lord Teach us to Pray" (Luke 11:1) A Reflection on the Prayer of Petition', in *Louvain Studies,* Vol X, No 4 (Fall 1985) 354-371 esp. 367; also Dorr, D., 'Prayer and Providence' in his *Spirituality and Justice* , Gill and Macmillan, Dublin , 1984, 236-255

PART III

If education could save ...

CHAPTER 7

The Schooling Revolution in Mayo

Christina Murphy

Education has always been very important in Mayo; with little industry and few jobs, education has traditionally been seen as the passport to employment. Even before free education, parents were prepared to make large sacrifices to meet the fees for secondary education.

Interestingly, education has been taken just as seriously for girls as for boys and the participation rates in secondary education have often been higher for girls than for boys and more girls have stayed on in school, for example, to do the Leaving Certificate than have boys. In the case of boys, there was the family farm to provide a livelihood or they could do the Group Certificate in the vocational school – universally known as 'the tech' – and opt for a trade. But, for girls, with little or no local job opportunities, a good education was vital. Indeed, participation rates for girls have even been higher in third level education in some years than for boys. So, there was very little notion of 'Oh, sure she's only a girl' when it came to schooling.

In this context of a native high regard for education and a big economic incentive to educate one's children to as high a level as possible, the coming of free education had a huge impact on Mayo. In the period of twenty years from the 1960s to the 1980s a virtual revolution took place in education, which changed forever the educational, career and job expectations of young people in Mayo – and many other rural Irish counties – to the extent that in the most recent survey of participation in higher education, while Dublin had only a 19% participation rate, Mayo had a 30% rate.

As someone who went to school in Mayo in the 1940s and 1950s, i.e. pre free education, I have had first hand experience of the impact of the changes. Going back and examining education in Mayo now is like looking at a different landscape; it is as if it were a different century since I went to school there, rather than a few decades. As the eldest of six children, I have seen the changes in my own family. I am a child of the fifties educational system, my youngest sister, seventeen years younger than me, is a child of the seventies system and it is as if a great chasm separated us educationally.

I went to a two-teacher national school with outdoor dry toilets, an open fire to heat the classroom, no running water, no project work or arts and crafts, and a curriculum mainly designed to drill us for the Primary Certificate exam at the end; few of us went to secondary school; if we did we paid fees, had no careers guidance, no expectation of going on to higher education, and followed a curriculum where everything was learned off by heart.

My sister had flush toilets, central heating and no exam at all in the same national school; her secondary education was free, there was a school bus to transport her, career guidance teachers to counsel her and grants to go on to university. Today the two-teacher national school of my childhood has eight teachers and a brand new school; the secondary school which had what seemed like dozens of nuns and just two lay teachers new has just a handful of nuns and dozens of lay teachers.

National school

I started at Breaffy National School in 1946 in response to an appeal from the altar for every possible child to be sent to school in order to preserve the third teacher in the school. With high emigration and low birth rates, enrolments were falling rapidly in Mayo in the 1940s and holding on to a teacher was a vital priority for schools. My sister started school the following year at an unbelievable age of three and a half, in response to a similar plea.

No high-minded discussion in those days as to whether to start school at four or wait till five – it was holding on to the teacher that mattered. But our efforts were in vain; by 1950 enrolments had fallen so low that the third teacher had to go and from then on to 1969 Breaffy was a two-teacher school.

We walked to school – as everybody did – in our case about a mile and a half, but for many children up to five miles. Nobody was ever accompanied to school; it just never occurred to anyone that there might be any danger. In any case there was hardly any traf-

fic on the roads, so there was no cause for worry. For some reason
I can never fathom, nobody ever cycled to national school either.
Perhaps the bikes were needed at home during the daytime, but
everybody walked.

There were three teachers and three classrooms and the eight
classes were divided among them. There were open fires in all
three rooms and each family bought a cart of turf to the school in
turn or we paid, I think it was one shilling, towards buying fuel. It
was co-educational, but it might as well not have been. There
were two playgrounds with a wall – a very high wall – between
them and we never, ever played with the boys or mixed with
them in the playground. In the classroom, boys sat on one side,
girls on the other. (Even the church was divided, men on one side,
women on the other on Sundays.)

At the end of each playground there were two dry toilets, messy
and smelly most of the time, it has to be said. Every now and
again a travelling man came and for a few shillings cleaned it all
out and buried it in a hole away down at the far end of the field.
There was no running water, but there was a big corrugated iron
barrel with a tap on it in the girls' playground which collected
rainwater.

Nobody found any of this odd as we had no running water, electricity or flush toilets at home either. Electric light arrived at the
school around 1950 with the arrival of electricity in the parish of
Breaffy through the rural electrification scheme.

The curriculum was very basic; no arts and crafts, no nature
study, though we did have singing. We did a little history and
geography, but not a lot as the all-important Primary Certificate
was examined only in English, Irish and Maths and passing it was
vital. There was a dusty map of the world on the senior classroom
wall and we assumed that someone, at some stage, must have
studied world geography in our little classroom – perhaps when
the school still had seventh class and kept pupils up to age fourteen. In the bottom of a musty cupboard there was a collection of
scientific instruments, relics, no doubt, of when science was
taught in primary schools prior to its being abolished to make
way for compulsory Irish in 1922.

The girls went down from the master's class to do sewing with a woman teacher and we also totted across the road with her on Fridays to clean and polish the church altar and arrange the flowers. We felt enormously privileged to be allowed to do this.

The school year was longer and we didn't get holidays until well into July. When the weather got hot, we loved to go to school barefoot, the soft, warm tar oozing up through our toes; we would be beseeching our parents as the weather got warmer to allow us shed our shoes.

Corporal punishment, as in most schools at the time, was the norm, though I never remember the women teachers hitting us. The master had a thick stick and we got slapped for being late, for missing our lessons and – mainly the boys – for misbehaving. The stick was raised up and you had to hold your hand out and wait for the slap. The sound of it swishing through the air heralded its arrival on your hand. The effort to continue to hold your hand out, knowing the pain that was about to descend on it was almost unbearable. Everyone got slapped, even what would be known as slow learners or even mildly mentally handicapped in today's terms. I can still remember the blank, incomprehending look on the round, innocent face of one such child who obediently held out his hand day after day; he never knew his lessons, because he never could.

And so we learned our spellings and our maths and all the rest of it and duly passed the Primary Certificate. Few went on to post primary education; many simply stayed at home, others emigrated. One or two went to secondary school in Castlebar, a few to the 'tech' and that was it.

Secondary school

I was utterly and absolutely terrified of secondary school. I had no idea where to go in the vast sprawling complex that was the 'convent', where to leave my bicycle, what to do. The majority of the class were girls from the town, who had attended the convent primary school, so for them it was just a stroll across the yard to another building; they were totally familiar with everything. For the minority of us from country schools, it was foreign territory and nobody bothered to explain anything to us. There was no question of applying in advance for a place, putting your name on a waiting list or having an orientation day; you simply turned up, made your way to the first year classroom somehow or other and that was it.

I was the only girl from Breaffy school and so I knew nobody. Country girls got teased mercilessly in the beginning by some of the 'townies' and you were made to feel a right hick. It was a strange world where thirteen-year-old girls dressed in black dresses, long black stockings – there were no tights in those days, so long stockings meant you had to wear suspender belts; nylons were not allowed, so they had to be thick stockings and we wore a hard white plastic collar at the neck – a bit like a priest's collar, but reversed.

I myself gradually became a sort of hybrid; as someone from the country and who went to a country national school, I was by origin a 'culchie,' but I made friends mainly with town girls and lived near enough to the town to be hopping backwards and forwards after school on my bicycle, so I more or less fell between two stools. I made extraordinarily good friends among girls from the town and must honestly say that I encountered not a trace of snobbery among them personally.

Most of the daughters of professional people in the town sent their girls to posh boarding schools like Mount Anville or Sion Hill in Dublin. And in the case of the odd one who did end up in the local convent, the nuns seemed so pathetically grateful that they quite literally fawned over the unfortunate girls. Many of the nuns were irredeemable snobs. I don't think they realised this themselves, but it was inevitable. After all, even within their own convent, they had two different classes of nun, the professional sister and the lay sister and we were left in no doubt that the poor nuns who washed the clothes and scrubbed the dishes were of a different class from the ones who taught in the school.

Within the classroom there were subtle layers of class distinction; top of the pile came to the odd child of an important local professional or business family who happened to go to the local school; next came the boarders – well you had to be reasonably well off to board; next came the local girls from the town and bottom of the pile the 'culchies' who cycled in from anything up to ten miles to school. I think they thought of country people as a bit uncivilised really – though often very bright, amazingly.

It wasn't their fault, they were merely reflecting the attitudes of society as a whole at the time. Country people were very much looked down upon in the towns; the social divisions seemed to be more town/country than middle class/working class – perhaps because there was so little working class.

Amazingly, when you think of the distances that some of those girls cycled to get there, the school made no effort at all to provide any facilities for them; despite having a boarding school – and thus cooking lunch for boarders – there was no hot soup or anything offered to day pupils at lunchtime, no facilities provided to dry their clothes when they had cycled to school through torrential rain; you simply hung your coat – on top of dozens of others – in a tiny cloakroom.

The boarders lived up at the end of the lawn in Lord Lucan's old house; day pupils got to see this – well the study part of it – once a year during the annual retreat which was held there. On fine Sundays the boarders went for a walk; we'd see them sometimes, in full uniform, marching in Indian file past our house, a pair of nuns ahead setting a brisk pace.

Confined by syllabus

In the beginning secondary school was exciting with all the new subjects, but gradually it got boring. There was a huge amount of learning by rote and the nuns clearly saw their job as drilling us to pass the Inter and Leaving and get us into the Civil Service or semi-state bodies as clerical assistants – or into teacher training if we were very bright. The word 'university' was hardly ever mentioned; you had to be pretty well off to go to university. There was one girl in the class who said right from the beginning that she was going to 'uni' and we all knew she would; it had nothing to do with intelligence, we knew she was well enough off to afford it.

If someone had said the word 'career guidance' to us, we wouldn't have known what they were talking about. Nobody ever mentioned to us what we wanted to do or what career we might choose; basically, there was no choice. If you passed those exams, you got into the Civil Service or teaching and that was about all there was. Once when Sr Perpetua, a very nice English teacher, said that I wrote very well and maybe I should think about writing, somebody said you'd need a BA to go into journalism and that was the end of that.

We never did anything that was not on the exam syllabus; there was what we called a 'library' at the end of one of the classrooms – it was actually a large bookcase – and it was locked. We had no access to it and I never once remember it being opened except by teachers taking out books they needed. But we did have a library.

There was a science laboratory downstairs, with sinks, gas burners and all the accoutrements – but we never used it either. We never had one single class in it. I suppose they had taught science seriously at some stage in the past, but by the 1950s, we did no science subject; instead we did a subject called Physiology and Hygiene which, it was explained to us with not a trace of irony, was a subject specially provided for girls and that girls did not manage things like science very well.

In first year, the subject choice was between Latin and Domestic Science as it was then called. I took Domestic Science because if you wanted to become a national teacher you had to do a sewing test, so it was recommended to those who might get the Leaving Certificate results for teaching. Nobody explained that you couldn't get into university without Latin, but then nobody expected us to be going to university. After a disagreement with the Domestic Science teacher – my recollection is that she hit me with a saucepan, but I could be wrong – I transferred to Latin in second year – luckily, otherwise I would not have been able to go to university years later.

Looking back on it, the curriculum was amazing; we never once in five years of English read a single novel or a full book. We had this extraordinary prose anthology, from which we read pieces, totally out of context and we never discussed the author or the full book or his other writings. These were the set pieces of prose; questions on the exam paper would be set on them and only on them, so we learned them. Poems were the same; you studied the set poems, but never ever discussed the poets or any of their other work. We did read *Macbeth* in full because it was on the syllabus, but I honestly think that if someone had said to us that this was a play that you could actually act out on stage we would have been astonished; to us it was a book you read and studied for the exams, nothing more.

In history, I don't remember having a textbook at all for the Leaving Certificate. The teacher dictated notes to us which we assiduously wrote down in our copies and learned off by heart. She picked topics which she felt would come up in the exam with the result that I ended up with the most disjointed view of history. We 'did' Napoleon, for example in total isolation from anything that went before or came after him in French history. We did the 1916 revolution in Irish history, but nobody told us anything about what came after it.

The convent was actually in the grounds of what had been Lord Lucan's house and the boarding school itself had been the house; this was never once mentioned to us and I only discovered it much later. The same nuns who ran the school ran the County Home, as it was then called, where thousands of famine victims died and on whose records much of Cecil Woodham-Smith's book on the famine was based. Yet we learned about the famine without one mention of the County Home. It was as if the famine had happened in another country. It was something that you learned off and parroted back in the exam, not something that had happened in your own town to your own ancestors. We never discussed the battle between the French and the crown forces in Castlebar in 1798 or the routing of the British in the famous 'Races of Castlebar', despite the fact that several streets – and indeed a pub – in the town were named after the events. It wasn't on the syllabus, so you didn't do it. Learning was something sterile, something which seemed to happen in total isolation from real life.

The convent ambience

It wasn't the nuns' fault; they were doing nothing, no different from dozens of other schools around the country; and they were doing what the parents expected of them: to drill pupils to pass exams which would get them jobs. They were following the curriculum laid down by the Department. They got little or no money and no educational support from the Department of Education; some of them were not even trained teachers or certainly not trained in the subject they were teaching. In-service training was virtually unheard of. They were running a school on annual fees per pupil of £10 and ploughing their own salaries back into the school. They were well-intentioned and were doing what they – and most of society around them – saw as the best for us; and some of them didn't know an awful lot more than we did.

And it's not as if we didn't have some good times, too; some of the
nuns were quite good fun and we would chat and joke with them.
A number of lay teachers came and went during the five years I
was there, but there were never more than two lay teachers in the
school at one time. There was, of course, no staffroom or cloakroom for them. (I presume they went up to the convent if they
wanted to go to the loo, but like most of us they probably waited
till lunchtime. The pupils' toilets were away down at the end of
the yard and it would take you a full five minutes to get there, so
the townies waited till they got home and we used them mainly at
lunchtime.)

The convent itself was a sacred place and totally out of bounds to
us. At the end of the Intermediate Certificate classroom, a door
opened into the convent and through it the nuns came and went
to school; one of our favourite activities was to speculate on what
went on behind the door.

If you were doing music, you actually got into the convent once a
year when the music examiner came. She did the examining in the
convent parlour. You sat outside and waited in the hallway which
reeked of furniture polish in the way which only convents did.
(Did they have a special convent polish, I've often wondered?)

Leaving school and choosing a career

There was a big drop-out rate after the Intermediate Certificate.
Many of those girls went to do what was then quaintly called a
'commercial course'. The real posh ones went off to places like
Loreto College in Dublin to do it, the next most prestigious was
the Louis Convent in Kiltimagh, while the rest made do with the
local tech – which, if the truth be told, was probably better than
any of them – but it didn't have the same 'connections' with top
notch employers.

I did my Leaving Certificate in 1959 and came out with a fair
sprinkling of honours; we didn't have As and Bs in those days,
just honours or pass. There was no great hullabaloo about the results, most of us had no idea what the other girls in the class had
got; there was no class get-together, no discussions of where are
you going or what are you doing; we just went our own ways and
nobody in the school asked us either. We had done the civil ser-

vice, ESB and other entrance exams and, in time, they hoped we'd get the 'call'. The great thing was to get the 'call'. But the real 'call' was to teacher training – national teaching, that is. Strangely, that was regarded as a far higher honour than going to university and the school really boasted about the number of 'calls' its pupils got, whereas you never heard a squeak about who went to university – but then any old gobdaw with a pass Leaving Certificate could go to university if she could afford it, whereas you had to be really brainy to get the 'call'.

I got honours in English; on paper, I was an honours English student with high marks in English literature; in reality I was totally ignorant about English literature. I had never even heard of James Joyce; I don't mean I hadn't read him – you'd hardly expect that in a convent school in the 1950s – I mean I never even knew the man existed or wrote anything – but I was an honours English student.

I didn't know that such a thing as the *Irish Times* existed either. We got the *Irish Independent* at home and I read it every day, but in five years in school nobody ever mentioned or I never heard the *Irish Times* referred to. I never saw it in the newsagents either. I persume a few people in the town got it and had it on order, but I never saw it displayed. Later, I was positively amazed to discover that Ireland had a *Times* as well.

I would have given my right arm to have been able to go to university, but there was no way we could afford it. We briefly explored the possibility of going to UCG and staying with an aunt and working part time to cover my expenses, but the aunt didn't think it was possible to work and study at the same time, so that was that. I went abroad, wandered around Europe doing different things, and came back to UCD in 1964.

The changes

So what has changed? Everything. Socially, as well as educationally. From being looked down upon as a backward place in the 1950s, the country has now become *the* in place to live socially. The countryside around Castlebar is festooned with spanking new bungalows, built in many cases by people who work in town but prefer to live in the country. We would have been astounded in the fifties if someone who could have lived in town opted for the country. Even the Principal of our local national school gave up his teacher's house near the school to move into a new house in the town.

So, Breaffy school has grown and grown. It now has nearly 200 pupils and eight teachers and a brand new school with big windows, lots of light, a toilet suite and arts and crafts area in each classroom, too. There is lots of colourful children's artwork and projects displayed around the walls and the children do projects on local history and nature trails around the area.

The 'New Curriculum' of course, is child-centred and has resulted in the Primary Certificate exam being abolished. There is much project work, PE is part of the curriculum and it is unlikely that any child would leave the school without knowing a lot about her or his local area. When the new school was built, the old one was converted into a community centre and its first activity was a local history exhibition which included a classroom laid out as it had been in the nineteenth century. It was a world away from the beautiful, bright new school, but oh, so like my 1950s classroom.

No longer are slow learners beaten or left at the back of the class; the school shares a remedial teacher with a number of others and in Castlebar there is a special school for pupils with learning difficulties.

Not only is the local school-going population increasing but, in a reversal of the trend of the 1950s, some urban parents now prefer to drive their children from the town to Breaffy school; small country national schools are now flavour of the year. They are seen as having smaller classes, being 'safer', better and providing a more congenial environment than the sprawling, urban schools; the country has become posh. There is a board of management with parents as well as teachers on it, parents visit the school to discuss their childrens' performance and the Principal discusses which second level school might be best suited to their needs.

Nobody except those living extremely close walk to school anymore and there is a large traffic jam outside Breaffy as parents arrive in their cars at 3 o'clock to pick up their offspring.

At secondary level, all has changed, too. There are no fees anymore. The schools hold 'open days' for parents and students to visit the schools in advance and enquire about what they have on offer and work out if they are suitable to their children's needs.

There are parents' meetings and management boards and it is quite common for parents to visit the school and enquire about their childrens' progress. A fleet of yellow buses ferries in children from the surrounding area, free if they have a medical card, for a fee if not. There is plenty of project work and local history forms a sizable part of the history programme. Under the new Junior Certificate programme there are no set texts at all, so pupils are encouraged to read a wide selection of literature. It is extremely unlikely that anyone has failed to hear of James Joyce. There is a career guidance counsellor and every student has an appointment with her and discusses what career she might choose. And it is worth bearing in mind that it is the same order of nuns – and in some cases the same nuns – who have introduced these reforms.

But perhaps it is the availability of higher education grants which has changed the scene most. Free secondary education and the school buses have been given much credit for the educational and social revolution in rural Ireland; not nearly as much attention has been paid to the effects of free higher education. Every girl in the Convent of Mercy secondary school in Castlebar now knows that she can go to university if she wants to and gets the points. Large numbers do and others go to the Regional Technical Colleges or the Post Leaving Cert (PLC) courses. The biggest revolution, to my mind, is that all of the girls I meet nowadays quite automatically assume that it is simply a question of deciding which career or course they are going to opt for. If they are very bright they can aspire to becoming doctors more easily than the professional family's daughters who may not get the high points – and that is a real revolution. I don't think anyone looks down their noses at country girls anymore – they are more likely to assume that farmers are all filthy rich through EU subsidies! They don't look down their noses at the 'tech' anymore, either, which has metamorphosed into the spanking new VEC-run Davitt College, which gives both the convent and the brothers' school fair competition for pupils – and it is actually built on part of what were the former convent grounds.

Now Castlebar is getting its own sub-Regional Technical College, so it will end up with a third level institution as well; young people will not always have to consider leaving the area in order to go to college.

Sometimes, it seems to me that when we – rightly – criticise what is still wrong with Irish Education and lobby for reform and improvement, that the impression is created that we have an appalling system or that nothing has changed since the dark ages. The INTO talks of Ireland having 'the largest primary school classes in the developing world', for example, without taking into account the fact that we have been steadily reducing our class sizes.

The reality is that, while much remains to be improved in the Irish as in many other education systems, the amount of change which has taken place over the past twenty-five years is staggering. In the year I sat the Leaving Certificate, 5,000 students sat the exam; last year it was 63,000 which represented almost 80% of the age cohort; 30,000 go on to university or RTC each year and another 20,000 to various other forms of further education and training including PLCs. Methods of teaching and the approach in the classroom have changed dramatically as have the syllabuses pupils follow; parents are no longer strangers in schools.

The pity is that with all of the advances in education, the increased access and provision, the enormously increased participation levels and the huge numbers advancing to higher education, we have not been able to make similar advances in the employment market and provide jobs for them at home. Because the reality for many from Mayo as elsewhere is that much of this education is leading to emigration – exactly as it did in the fifties. The best one can say is that at least now they are emigrating with qualifications.

CHAPTER 8

Separate Churches: Separate Schools

Eoin de Bhaldraithe

Should Catholics have separate schools? This is the obvious theological question to ask about education in Ireland today. When the national schools began, they were to be for Catholics and Protestants together, but eventually education became denominational. The dramatic episodes of this development were acted out on stages set mainly in the west. To tell this story again will help us to understand and review our present policies.

The National Schools

The non-denominational beginnings

In 1814, with general Catholic agreement, the Kildare Place Society received grants from the government to assist schools. As an effort to be neutral between the denominations, the scriptures were to be read 'without note or comment'. Some money, however, was given to proselytising groups and this led Daniel O'Connell to oppose the Society.[1] Eventually two thirds of the money was going to Protestant Ulster. [2]

So in 1831 the government decided the money would be administered through a National Education Board. Those schools would have 'combined moral and literary and separate religious instruction'. The two archbishops of Dublin, Daniel Murray and Richard Whately, sat on the board and it was realised that they were pillars of the system.[3] Murray had told a government inquiry that there could be no possible objection to a Protestant teaching secular literature to Catholic and Protestant children together.[4] He also suggested that a gospel harmony and a book of scriptural extracts could be used for teaching in common.

Both the government and the board wished that 'the clergy and laity of the different religious denominations should co-operate with one another in conducting national schools'. A 'General Lesson' was composed by Whately and approved by Murray. It was to be taught and displayed in every school and could be abbreviated as follows:

> Christians should endeavour to live peacefully with all, even those of different religious persuasions. Our Saviour, Christ, commanded his disciples to love one another and even their enemies.

> Many hold erroneous doctrines, but we ought not to hate or persecute them. Jesus Christ did not intend his religion to be forced on men by violent means. Quarrelling with our neighbours and abusing them is not the way to convince them that we are in the right and they in the wrong. We ought to show ourselves followers of Christ by behaving gently and kindly to everyone.[5]

James of Kildare and Leighlin

This harmonious spirit comes as quite a surprise to us nowadays, so it is helpful to look at some of the attitudes of the time. James Doyle, Bishop of Kildare and Leighlin, is best known for his letter on the union of the Roman Catholic and Anglican churches. The king and government should bring together bishops who were conciliatory and if agreement were reached, an act of parliament would settle the matter.

'It is pride and points of honour,' he said, 'which keep us divided on many subjects and not a love of Christian humility, charity and truth.'[6] The following shows how he regarded Protestants.

> We consider that whoever is baptised is incorporated with Christ, and has no 'damnation in him' and that if he retain the grace of that first adoption pure and unsullied until death, he enters heaven – no matter to what sect or denomination of Christians while on earth he may have belonged.[7]

Apart from the obvious references to St Paul, his contemporaries would have recognised an allusion to the Council of Tent. He is saying that all the baptised are in the body of (incorporated with) Christ and so belong to the one church of Christ. For us it is a remarkable anticipation of the second Vatican Council decree on ecumenism.

The evangelicals of the second reformation were already at work. Doyle said they were sincere but doubted if their sincerity was founded on truth. However, 'if a Catholic choose to become a Protestant, he might do so, by all means,' for Christ only 'knows if they fell away freely and culpably from their first faith.'[8]

While Doyle did not get much support, he was not alone in his views. Archbishop Murray said that 'at present' we seldom use the word 'heretics', but refer to Protestants as 'our dissenting or separated brethren'. The young John McHale took issue with Doyle, but the then Archbishop of Tuam, Oliver Kelly, was favourable to his scheme for reunion.[9]

It is in this context then we must place Doyle's evidence before a parliamentary committee.

> I do not see how any man wishing well to the public peace, and who looks to Ireland as his country, can think that peace can be permanently established, or the prosperity of the country ever well secured, if children are separated at the commencement of life on account of their religious opinions.

This is how he sees it from a political point of view. Separate schooling would endanger the public peace which, he believes, is not yet permanent. The prosperity of the country also depends on keeping children together. He goes on to deal with the effect separation would have on the children themselves.

> I do not know any measures which would prepare the way for a better feeling in Ireland than uniting children at an early age, and bringing them up in the same school, leading them to commune with one another and to form those little intimacies and friendships which subsist through life. Children thus united know and love each other as children brought up together always will and to separate them is, I think, to destroy some of the finest feelings in the hearts of men.[10]

Evidently Murray and Kelly were in agreement with those sentiments. Doyle was pleased with Whately's 'General Lesson' and commended it to his clergy in a circular as the schools began in 1831.[11]

When Paul Cullen succeeded Murray as Archbishop, he found the attitudes of the predecessor an embarrassment and refused to take his place on the board. The main reason for the great change of attitude was the experience of proselytism in the west of Ireland in the 1840s.

Reformation and Counter Reformation

Souperism

We are indebted to Desmond Bowen for an account of the second reformation in Ireland and all the accusations that went with it. The fly leaves of his book on 'souperism' carry his map of the dioceses of Killala and Achonry. It should make compelling reading for westerners but, of course, its significance is universal.

After describing the rather harmonious relations between priest and parson in the early 1800s, he goes on to outline the mission of the evangelicals. George Gubbins established the Dingle colony of newly converted Protestants in 1831. The conversions, which included a Catholic priest, were loudly announced in the British press and attracted many subscriptions.

Another famous colony was founded by Edward Nangle on Achill Island. Alexander Dallas came from England to work mainly in Cong and Clifden. He believed that famine was the means God was using to open the hearts of the people to the true religion.

Bowen says that the 'ultra-Protestant' activity was resented by most Anglican clergyman 'who had deep roots in the Connaught countryside'. The tithe war took place mainly in Leinster and Munster. The parsons were glad that Connaught had escaped the turmoil but this new dispute stirred up religious emotions which were not easy to control.[12]

The evangelicals considered Connaught the best hunting ground. After planting the colony 'they invaded the entire diocese (of Tuam) North and West'. In many parts of the diocese there were no Protestants at all, but more important there were no national schools.[13] Most of the preaching was done in Irish and it was mainly Irish speakers who converted and were called 'jumpers' from the Irish *d'iompaigh*, (he) turned, pronounced 'jumpy'.

Bowen gives a moving account of how in the Spring of 1847 most of the parsons in the west ran soup kitchens with food supplied by the government or more usually by the Quakers. They kept many thousands of people alive during that terrible year. He successfully defends them from any guilt of souperism. The only people to whom it might apply were some of the evangelicals.

By 1850 the danger of famine had receded but by then the religious dispute had heated up and Bowen refers to the next ten years as 'religious war in Connaught', mainly Mayo and Galway.[14]

Counter Reformation

At the instigation of O'Connell, the Vincentians went to Dingle on a 'mission'. Most bishops were reluctant to agree at first, but the mission soon became a feature of Catholic culture. James Murphy regards the movement as the 'Irish counter-reformation'.[15] The emphasis was on catechism and doctrine rather than morality. While the evangelicals ridiculed statues, medals and scapulars as superstitious, the missioners emphasised them as tokens of faith.

Murphy insists that they were really setting up a different culture and their spiritual teaching had social and political implications. All the emphasis was now placed on those matters that distinguished Catholics from Protestants. It was a swift departure from Doyle's insistence that on most beliefs, 'there is no essential difference between Catholics and Protestants'.

In Dingle they concentrated on reaffirming the Catholic faith. Later in Oughterard, Co Galway, they went further and preached ostracism of the jumpers. They wanted a public engagement from the people

> not to speak to them, not to lend or borrow from them; not to allow them into their homes nor upon their land upon any pretence whatsoever; and to show on all occasions their horror of their crime.

Again we have only to remember the words of Doyle to see what a radical change of policy this was. Not only did the missioners insist on people withdrawing their children from the evangelising schools but from now on 'schools which merely brought Catholics into contact with Protestants were the object of mission attack.'[16] The Redemptorists soon joined in the mission work and their policy of burning the bible in public is celebrated in a well known cartoon from 1852.[17]

The practical result of the whole conflict was a hardening of attitudes, a loss of a certain liberal spirit in both Catholic and Protestant clergy. Cullen now claimed that any situation in which Catholics came under the influence of members of the establishment was, of necessity, a proselytising situation.[18] How different to his predecessor who had no objection to Protestant teachers!

The ostracisation which was so strictly enforced in Oughterard became an ideal for the whole country. The first sectarian riots took place in Belfast shortly afterwards, from 1857 to 1864. Their purpose and effect was to impose strict area segregation. The one may not have been the direct cause of the other, but both conspired to create effective boundaries.

The formation of church policy
The bishops and the schools

The setting up of the national system was regarded as something of a victory for the Catholics, so the Presbyterians and many Church of Ireland clergy refused to join the system for a time.[19] Murray put considerable pressure on Edmund Ignatius Rice to take part in the project. Six of the Christian Brothers schools joined, but Rice withdrew them six years later in 1837.

Archbishop MacHale was in favour of the schools at first, saying that 'a feature of promise' was that the Protestants disliked them.[20] In 1837, however, he underwent a sudden change which his biographers are at a loss to explain. It is clear, however, that he was influenced partly by the Rice decision and partly by the fact that the Presbyterians were forcing change in the rules and would join the system in 1840.

He withdrew the few schools of his diocese which had come under the national board. Only after his death in 1881 would government money be available for schools again in Tuam diocese. He wrote to the press complaining that Murray had too much power. Murray replied defending the system. So was MacHale 'instrumental in depriving a large section of a generation of an education'.[21] But for the tenacity of Murray that would have been true of the whole country. According to David Akenson, he had 'the patience and disposition of a saint'.[22]

It is often said that separate schooling follows from a divided society, that in Belfast segregated housing necessitates denominational education. Yet that was not how it happened historically. The Belfast segregation, if not a consequence, was at least a sequence to the battle over the schools. Would it have been so absolute if the counsels of Murray and Doyle prevailed? The latter was certainly prophetic when he warned of the danger to the public peace.

Cullen and McHale may have differed on many things but they were agreed that Murray was too conciliatory to the Protestants.

They looked to a Catholic country like Italy as a model. For the mission orders, the ideal was rather the France that expelled the Huguenots. The ostracisation led to a partition of minds and eventually to a Catholic state and to another one where the alienated minority became a dominant majority.

Church policy in Ireland today

John Fulton, on the basis of papers by two cardinals, a bishop and a priest (William Conway, Cahal Daly, William Philbin and Denis Faul), outlines current teaching in Ireland: the only way to educate Roman Catholic children is in a school controlled by Catholic clergy and permeated by Catholic ethos. Fulton believes that this line is at times so strongly stated that education almost becomes indoctrination. He is surprised that even preparation for the sacraments takes place in the classroom.[23]

Philbin said, 'The law of the church is quite definite, quite universal in this matter. It is that there is an obligation to go to Catholic school ... It is the same in Northern Ireland as any other part of the world.'[24] We are also told the story of how two Dublin priests were able to stop the building of an integrated school by telling the people they were obliged to send children to Catholic schools.[25]

Fulton says that the bishops must defend the schools with 'universal' type arguments if they are to retain control. Also they must vigorously deny any connection between schools and the 'Troubles'. There would have to be a major pastoral strategy to prepare children for the sacraments if anything happened to the school system. The bishops would not admit that sin might be involved in the structure itself. An ethnic sense of identity has grown up among Catholics. The schools are both cause and effect of this.[26]

Church teaching

Vatican II

The recent council began its document on Christian education by saying that all people have a right to education suitable to their destiny, ability and culture.[27] This is said to be in line with the United Nations Declaration on Human Rights.

Christian education, on the other hand, is for all who are baptised. This is what we usually call catechesis and the council describes it in terms taken from the New Testament. Christians should be trained to live their lives as sanctified in the truth and be able to give witness to the hope that is in them.

Parents have the first obligation to educate their children. The church is also under obligation to provide education and this is principally catechesis which develops the life of faith.

Only now does the document proceed to speak of schools. Again catechesis is the priority, so there is special mention of the great number of children being taught in non-Catholic schools. They need special teaching in Christian doctrine and parents have a grave obligation to see that this is provided.

When it comes to Catholic schools, we are told that the church has a right to establish them. Catholic parents have a duty to send their children to Catholic schools when possible.

There is a progression, then, from 'the gravest obligation' to educate one's children, to a 'grave obligation' to provide them with Christian teaching, to the 'duty' to send children to a Catholic school when possible. This duty is not termed grave, so genuine reasons would override it. Further, the reference here is to choice between a Catholic and non-Catholic school. It would not apply to a choice between a Catholic and an interdenominational school which is partly Catholic.

Such is the doctrine of Vatican II, much less categoric than we might expect. The document is of course composed by a very wide international body, and not all bishops give the same emphasis to Catholic schools as do those of the English-speaking world, who are naturally influenced by their origins in nineteenth-century Ireland. Indeed the document seems to be satisfied that if catechesis is done properly, then all kinds of schools are acceptable.

So what does this mean for the Catholic school? Colm Burke raised the question in a short note some years after the council. Once the Catholic church insisted that the ideal was that the church should be 'established', that is that the state grant it monopoly rights. But, he says, this is no longer 'an ideal at all' and 'the same may be happening to the ideal of a Catholic school.'

First he quotes the decree on religious liberty which says that in spreading the faith there should be no hint of coercion. Parents ought to have a free choice of schools or education. While this means that there should be Catholic schools available to Catholics, it also means, Burke insists, that they should be free not to send children to such schools.

He then quotes the document on education. The ideal school brings students of diverse backgrounds together and fosters understanding among them; indeed the school becomes a centre for the entire community. Burke says that if a school is not denominational, this does not mean that it is non-religious.

He believes that if the ideal were accepted, then the fear that many mixed marriages might result would be eased. The Catholic system causes 'trouble in the South and suspicion in the North', and so he asks us to consider if non-denominational schools would be a way of improving community relations.[28] Since writing that, however, the integrated or interdenominational school has made its appearance and changed the situation somewhat.

Developments since Vatican II

We may describe the current situation quite simply by presenting the findings of a conference on the Catholic school held in 1991. Perhaps the biggest surprise is that none of the five speakers make 'any attempt to distinguish Catholic and Christian education'.[29]

Dermot Lane emphasises the change in Vatican II: openness to the world; respectful recognition of other churches; concern for religious liberty. Since then the church has accepted a distinction between 'parish based catechesis' and 'religious education in schools'. This was first suggested by the German bishops and is now official Catholic policy.[30] This is further ratified in the document from the synod on the laity which says that parishes should be communities where the faithful can communicate the Word of God and express it in service and love to one another.[31]

At the conference, John McDonagh asked, 'How fair is it that year after year we expect teachers to prepare for the sacraments children who experience little or no religious faith-commitment in their homes?'[32]

Herman Lombaerts speaks of the stories of the founding of

schools in a way that history is given 'power and authority' over the present situation.[33] In former times the schools were essential for maintaining the monopoly of the Catholic church. This is probably why Lane says that we need a new story.

Would the conference be in favour of abandoning the Catholic school? Nobody has said so even though several arguments seem to point in that direction.

Adult Faith

The renewal of the liturgy was the most visible effect of Vatican II and the *Rite of Christian Initiation of Adults* was by far the most radical innovation. Its effects will be felt for a long time ahead.

The adult rite has become a model for many other liturgical actions. The new ritual for infant baptism says, 'When parents are not yet ready to undertake their duty of bringing up children as Christians, it is for the parish priest to determine the time for baptism of infants.'[34] This means in practice deferring baptism rather than refusing it. Children should only be baptised in a faith community. Such is the clear policy of the church today.

Pastors who must defer baptism, normally inscribe the infants as catechumens. This gives them partial church membership. After catechesis they may make a realistic decision for or against baptism. Meanwhile they may take part in the liturgy of the word and, if they die, re ceive Christian burial.[35]

It is sad to contemplate, but this means that many people will grow up as non-Christians in our society. Yet if faith is to be free, what other option can there be? This situation is already far advanced on mainland Europe. We are told that in all major cities of North-West Europe 'more than half of all infants are no longer baptised'.[36]

The School For The Community

Education is a human right according to the United Nations charter and now according to the second Vatican Council. Today we are engaged in an experiment of supplying free second level education to all. Church language on choice of schools is now outmoded as it comes from the time when only the wealthy were educated. Today it is choice within schools that is important. 'One school for one community, answerable to that community', seems to be the official ideal and has a solid basis in Vatican II.[37]

In our nearby town of Castledermot, the technical and convent schools merged some years ago. There remained a Catholic primary school and a much smaller Protestant one. The situation is similar in many towns in Ireland. Surely the two primary schools ought to have merged as well. Many Protestants would agree, if there were a system of management which gave equal status to the clergy of both denominations.

The parish should take over preparation for the sacraments. Preparing children in classroom for the sacraments is not just unfair, as McDonagh says, but also disloyal to church policy which does not want baptism or eucharist outside the context of faith.

At present, Protestants in a Catholic school feel rather isolated when the rest of the class prepares for first communion or confirmation. If preparation for the sacraments were done in the parish, this would not only foster religious liberty, but would also greatly facilitate integrated schools.[38]

There are over twenty such schools in Northern Ireland at present. Since they receive full funding, the movement is set to grow. Yet it is still less than two per cent of all schools. The Opsahl commission said that integrated education 'would represent a small brick in the wall of peace-building.'[39]

Education for ecumenism

Even when catechesis is done in a parish context, there will still be need for religious education in the school. A Catholic school will need a serious ecumenical dimension and an integrated school will need to have both separate and combined education.

The Opsahl Commission heard the Belfast students ask for more religion to be taught, not less. They asked for mixed religious education classes where they could hear other young people talk about their religion.[40]

The commission commended the programme of Education for Mutual Understanding (EMU) introduced in Northern Ireland. The more recent report on sectarianism endorses this initiative more strongly: 'It can and does get under the skin of sectarian myth and prejudice'. That report also welcomes 'the promotion of programmes of contact between schools' and mentions in particular the 'the depth of misunderstanding and lack of contact between North and South is very large'. [41]

The success of EMU is dependent on the teachers who implement it. They need special training, together if possible. This is the view of the Cultural Traditions Group who recommend that 'integrating the teacher training colleges should be tried again.' [42]

One great achievement in Northern Ireland is a common syllabus for religious education agreed by all the churches but flexible enough to include the specific teaching of each church. This reflects the agreed statements between the churches themselves. However, one is concerned to see a continued emphasis on certain Catholic specifics, including even medals and scapulars, a sign that the boundaries are still be ing maintained. [43]

In 1976 an interchurch commission recommended an extensive programme of ecumenical education for schools. The basic need was to bring Protestant and Catholic young people together at school level. They recommended an exchange of teachers between schools especially on the sensitive subjects such as secular and church history, Irish language and culture. In particular people from other traditions should come to schools to explain their religious views and so avoid common stereotypes. There should be joint projects and fieldwork on these matters. The teaching of religion must be fully ecumenical.

While not agreed on integrated education, they do express agreement on 'shared sixth form colleges'. Catholic and Protestant schools tend to play different games, but they should really take on each other's games.[44] Opsahl insists that the churches need to give those matters urgent attention. In practice this would mean, for example, that every second level school in Mayo ought to be twinned with a protestant school in the north.

Church leaders then are agreed that all second level schools urgently need a thorough-going ecumenical dimension to education. Earlier we asked if the Catholic school should survive. Now we may ask an easier question: Is there much difference between the genuinely ecumenical Catholic school and an integrated school? Could not the difference be catered for in one community school with choice of courses inside it?

Surely the practical way forward is as suggested by All Children Together. They ask for 'the goodwill of the churches voluntarily giving up some of their places on the school boards to parents and representatives of other churches to allow integrated schools to develop'.[45]

Conclusion

An old story

Even better than a new story is an old story newly understood. St Patrick tells us how in his youth he was dead in sin and unbelief. According to Daniel Conneely 'we must interpret him here as meaning exactly what he says'.[46] While he was a slave, perhaps in Mayo, God literally made him a believer. This is clearer if we realise that Patrick was not baptised at this time.

He prayed several times in the day and night, for 'the Spirit was fervent' in him. This means that the Spirit had come upon him now for the first time. Like the Gentiles who came to Cornelius, he received the Spirit before baptism. Then when he returned to Britain or Gaul he was baptised and ordained.

His contemporary Augustine was reared by a saintly mother yet, as was the custom at the time, she did not baptise him. The confessions of both, then, describe a sinful unbelieving youth and adult conversion. As well as Augustine and Patrick, their near contemporaries, Jerome, Basil and Ambrose were baptised and ordained in quick succession.

This is the system Patrick brought with him to Ireland. The Irish Penitentials, of some centuries later, ask that children be made catechumens on the eighth day, just as happened to Augustine.[47] They were then baptised at a mature age. Many surviving holy wells, which were clearly suited for baptising adults, prove that the custom continued for a long time.[48] This is how the faith St Patrick brought us was expressed in sacrament.

This story points to a future where our religion and our patriotism will be separated. The school, like the fatherland, would belong to all including those who seem to us to have a wrong faith or even no faith. But we will invite all to accept the gift of faith freely and join the communion of saints where they will be taught by God's own wisdom.

Notes

1. Coolahan, J., *Irish Education: Its History and Structure*, Dublin: 1981, 11-12

2. Stated in parliament by E. G. Stanley, Chief Secretary of Ireland. Durcan, T.J., *History of Irish Education from 1800*, Bala, Wales 1972, 14

3. Akenson, D.H., *The Irish Education Experiment: The National System of Education in the Nineteenth Century*, London 1970, 131; Durcan, *History*, 18

4. Durcan, *History*, 18, Akenson, *Experiment*, 95

5. Durcan, 15-16; Akenson, 159

6. Letter on the Union of the Churches, Joly Pamphlets 221 (1824), National Library, Dublin.

7. This was in reply to William Magee, Archbishop of Dublin, who said that Doyle's use of the word 'catholic' excluded all others from the church of Christ. The quotation is from W.J. Fitzpatrick, *Life, Times and Correspondence of Dr Doyle I* (Dublin 1880) 216, who tries to limit it to 'the well known doctrine of invincible ignorance'.

8. Quoted from McNamee, B., 'J.K.L.'s Letter on the Union of the Churches'. *Irish Theological Quarterly*, 36 (1969) 46-69 (62-63)

9. Bowen, *Souperism: Myth or Reality? A study of Catholics and Protestants during the Great Famine* (Cork 1970), 77-78

10. Committee on the State of the Poor in Ireland; Durcan, *History*, 221, 282; Fitzpatrick, *Doyle*, I, 10

11. Durcan, 24

12. Bowen, *Souperism*, 91-92. Majerus, P., The Second Reformation in West County Galway, M.A. thesis, University College, Dublin, 1991.

13. Ibid. 127

14. Ibid. 135-150

15. Murphy, J., 'The Role of Vincentian parish missions in the "Irish counter-reformation" of the mid nineteenth century', *Irish Historical Studies*, 24 (1984), 152-171

16. Ibid. 170

17. MacWhite, E., 'Vladimir Pecherin 1807-1885', *Studies* 61 (1972) 23-40; see 24-25 on 'The Bible-burning trial'; cartoon in Norman, E., *The Catholic Church in Ireland in the Age of Rebellion: 1859-1873*, Longmans, London, 1965, 213

18. Murphy, 'Irish counter-reformation', 168

19. Coolahan, *Education*, 14-16

20. Akenson, *Experiment*, 206

21. O'Hara, B., 'Archbishop John MacHale', *Mayo: Aspects of its Heritage*, Galway 1982, 276

22. Akenson, *Experiment*, 131

23. Fulton, J., *The Tragedy of Belief. Division, Politics, and Religion in Ireland*, Claredon, Oxford, 1991, 189-192. Fulton teaches at the Roman Catholic teacher training school in Strawberry Hill, London.

24. Ibid. 180.

25. Ibid. 181-83

26. Ibid. 195-97

27. 'Declaration on Christian Education', Flannery, A., (ed.), *Vatican Council II*, Dublin 1975, 725-37

28. Burke, C., 'The Catholic School', *The Furrow* 23 (1972) 180-181.

29. *The Catholic School in Contemporary Society*, CMRS, Dublin, 1991), 124. I owe my introduction to this conference to Sr Mary Fagan.

30. Ibid. 83-84, 90-91, 111

31. *Christifideles Laici* 26 (1988): kindly pointed out to me by D. Lane.

32. CMRS, *The Catholic School*. 74

33. Ibid. 105-6

34. *Rite of Baptism of Children* 5.

35. Upton, J., 'A Future for Infant Baptism', *A Church for the next Generation: Sacraments in Transition*, (Collegeville 1990) 63-78

36. Kerkhofs, Jan, 'Confidence in the Spirit of Jesus; European Religious Respond', *Religious Life Review*, 32 (1993) 294-302 (297)

37. This view is attributed to 'a former Minister for Education' by Walsh, M., 'The Future of Catholic Secondary Schools', *Doctrine and Life* 42 (1992) 171-80. She also speaks of the 'anticipated evolution of a single school serving the needs of the community'.

38. This view was put to me by the Reverend Robert Dunlop, Baptist Pastor of Brannockstown.

39. Pollak, A., (ed.), *A Citizens' Inquiry: the Opsahl Report on Northern Ireland*, Lilliput, Dublin, 1993, 107-8. In its reference to Vatican

II, the report seems to exaggerate the duty of attending Catholic schools.

40. Opsahl 121.

41. *The Report of the Working Party on Sectarianism* (Belfast 1993) 74, 110.

42. Crozier, M., (ed.), Cultural Traditions in Northern Ireland: Proceedings of Conference, March 1989, Queen's Belfast, 1989, 78, 85

43. Faul, D., 'Integrated Education', *The Sunday Press*, 28 November 1993.

44. *Violence in Ireland: A Report to the Churches* (Dublin: 1976) 86-87. Co-chairmen of the Joint Group were Bishop Cahal Daly and Revd Eric Gallagher.

45. Letter to the *Irish Times* on behalf of the directors of All Children Together, 19 November, 1993.

46. Conneely, D., *St Patrick's Letters: A Study of their Theological Dimension*, An Sagart 1993, Maynooth, 111

47. 'On the eighth day they are catechumens (*Octavo die caticumini sunt*). Thereafter they are baptised on the solemnities of the Lord, that is Easter, Pentecost and Epuphany'. Second synod of St. Patrick, 19. Bieler, L., *The Irish Pentitentials* (Dublin 1963) 191-92. The parallel practice of the Eastern church shows that this meant baptism at a mature age.

48. See our account of the Easter baptisms in an early Celtic church, 'Kildare and Tulrahan', *Béacán/Bekan: Portrait of an East Mayo Parish* (Ballinrobe 1986) 116-18

CHAPTER 9

Education, Salvation, Human Liberation

Mary Fagan

Introduction

When John the Baptist was in prison he sent his disciples to Jesus to ask him,

> 'Are you the one who is to come, or are we to wait for another?' Jesus answered them, 'Go and tell John what you hear and see: the blind receive their sight, the lame walk, the lepers are cleansed, the deaf hear, the dead are raised, and the poor have good news brought to them. And blessed is anyone who takes no offence at me.' (Matthew 11:3-6)

This is nothing short of a proclamation of a mission of freedom, liberation and new hope for the most oppressed in society, and the gospels are an account of how Jesus, by his work, his life style and his death and resurrection, worked to fulfil this mission. His attitude and his decisions were always from the perspective of the outcasts as is seen in the parables, the miracle stories and the accounts of the people with whom he shared meals. The stories of his preference for the downtrodden are all the more revolutionary when we know that, at the time of Jesus, to be deprived in any way was understood as a curse brought about by one's own or one's family's failure to be faithful to the law of God as prescribed by Moses. Jesus' life's work then can be seen as an effort to change the prevailing value system and adopt totally new criteria on which to base one's attitudes and actions. This new perspective would include everyone; there would be no distinction on the basis of race, gender, class or economic status. God's love is freely given to all peoples. The gospels tell the story of the efforts Jesus made to educate in the truth about God's relationship with all people and in the loving response that was fitting for this God. This objective necessitated the freeing of the people from false notions about God that were, at the time of Jesus, condemning large sections of society to slavery and misery.

The starting point then, for any discussion on education, salvation and human liberation is the gospel story. It is the yardstick against which we measure our attitudes and actions and indeed our whole life style, to decide whether or not we are both educating and being educated according to the principles laid down by Jesus. The context of this educative process is the Christian community which is described for us in the Acts of the Apostles.

> All who believed were together and had all things in common; they would sell their possessions and goods and distribute the proceeds to all, as any had need. Day by day, as they spent much time together in the temple, they broke bread at home and ate their food with glad and generous hearts, praising God and having the goodwill of all the people. (Acts 2:44-47)

While we do not sell our belongings and live communally – the first Christians didn't either because we know that they met in each other's houses to celebrate the eucharist – there are certain norms of behaviour and attitudes to life that would be seen as characteristic of Christian living. This demands constant vigilance and dialogue, on the one hand with the prevailing norms and standards of the secular society, and on the other hand, with the structures and practices of the Christian community itself. This two-pronged approach calls for an examination of the values and aspirations of the secular society to identify what in them militate against our efforts to remain faithful to a gospel calling. It also calls for a constant re-evaluation of the institutions of the Christian community, or the church, to ensure that they are helping and not hindering us in our quest for true freedom as proclaimed in the gospels.

Religious education will be much more rewarding and Jesus-centred when we educators revise the settings in which we educate, when we integrate our liturgical celebrations into the process and when our language is inclusive and liberating. For me, a woman, a member of a religious community and a catechist, my search centres around my work in school, my need for authentic Christian community in which to worship and my understanding of myself as a woman in the church. Consequently, I plan to address these three issues, namely the role of the religious education in the school, the need for a better understanding of the eucharist and an appreciation of the role of women in the church. How can I uncover false notions about God that lie unexamined in these three areas and are inhibiting growth toward freedom and liberation as understood by Jesus in the gospels?

The settings for religious education: School, parish, community

Religious education is on the curriculum of all community and second-level Catholic schools in Ireland. Catechists or religion teachers are paid salaries by the state and, in addition, chaplains are employed in community schools. This is an expression of the value that both the state and the church place on religious education in our schools. However, difficulties surrounding the teaching of religion abound, calling for a total re-evaluation of the current practice.

This need to examine the situation arises because of the increasing pressures on the school to respond to the demands of society. Schools are rated primarily on their ability to produce results that will enable young people to qualify for courses that seem to be in very short supply, thus the emphasis on the points system in the Leaving Certificate examination. The values that these pressures encourage are ambition, individualism and acquisitivism. Excellence is confused with competitiveness and schools inadvertently find themselves carried along in this value system. The overall message for young people is 'look after yourself ', 'forget about your neighbour ' and 'make friends with those who can help you'. The reality is that within this framework, while religious education is desirable, it is no longer essential. It is perceived by parents as good, but really on the periphery of the real purpose of schooling. This attitude is borne out at parent-teacher meetings when parents are more anxious to meet the teachers of examination subjects and either ignore the catechist or meet her/him out of a sense of politeness. There is also a sense that parents are not quite sure what the catechist is trying to do, so it is easier for them to leave well enough alone.

If this is a true description of the reality of the school, then one must conclude that it is unsuitable as a medium for religious education. How can one seriously promote values of co-operation, care, sensitivity to the needs of others and the sharing of knowledge and expertise? How can one engage students in issues such as world poverty, the arms race, the environment or more enlightened attitudes to race and gender? I feel that the reality prompts us to reflect on a statement made by Herman Lombaerts:

> Shifts in the global pattern of society and culture call the established and evident continuity of a given tradition to a halt. Any institution which refuses to integrate the fundamental changes is condemned to die or to survive as a closed, anachronistic system. [1]

Well might you ask why do I continue working as a catechist in a secondary school. Am I behaving like the ostrich just sticking my head in the sand? No, I don't think so. While I'm acutely aware of the limitations of the school as a context for leading young people to maturity of faith, I'm also aware of the possibilities and opportunities in it for journeying with young people in their search for freedom as understood in the gospels. The school is one of the most important areas of socialisation for young people between the ages of five and eighteen years so, in short, we cannot but be there. Yet I can only justify my mission in school by holding to my conviction that religious education or catechesis is a life-long process and does not end with the Leaving Certificate examination. This conviction, when an integral part of one's approach to catechesis in the school, ensures that religious education is not judged by the same criteria as academic subjects. I also approach my work with the conviction that catechesis or religious education is occasional and ongoing, not concentrated and terminal. My methodology differs from that adopted for other subjects because it focuses on sowing seeds and raising consciousness rather than following a syllabus. Not all moments of deep insight and moments of newly discovered truths about the value of life and the goal of Christian living occur in the classroom. Such events can be the annual school retreat, a class liturgy, the dramatisation of a gospel story or the involvement in a project on, for example, poverty, ecology or justice.

As a catechist, I have memories of many such high points which make my work rewarding and affirm me in my own journey as a member of the Christian community. On one occasion I was teaching the Exodus story to a class of second-year students. We had read the text, drawn maps, illustrated the ten plagues and sung 'Go Tell It On The Mountains'. Finally we had a class discussion on the significance of the Exodus event for us Christians today. The class was in a reflective mood when one student asked, 'How is it that God told the Isrealites very clearly what they had to do? Why doesn't God act as directly with us?' We then discussed situations in their own lives when God could be as close to us as God was to the Hebrews. I concluded by suggesting that the student keep asking her question. This was a moment in the space afforded in the religion class for a reflection on an image of God as our constant friend, companion, father or mother.

Real life issues are an important factor in the religion class and help make the necessary connection between the classroom and the world of reality. A class of transition year students did a project on world poverty; they amassed so much information that one could write a thesis on the subject. My problem was, how could I encourage the students to respond to these facts in a humane rather than an intellectual manner? How could I get these facts to impinge on the lives of a class of broadly based middle class people in one of the richest countries of the world? So we decided that the class would be a microcosm of the world. We prepared a meal for our world when 65% would eat rice, 30% chips and sausages and 5% a four course meal. Each student contributed the same amount for the meal but twenty-one got a bowl of rice, seven had chips and sausages and three had a four course meal. We then concluded that people ate, not according to the dictates of justice, nor of their needs but according to their status which is the result of unjust social structures that perpetrate injustices, hunger and evil.

But all these experiences will remain isolated and doomed to die if they are not nourished in the wider Christian community. The responsibility of the local church to forge links with the school and involve young people in community ministry and activities cannot be overestimated. I always think it strange that the church confirms young people in their faith at the age of twelve years and fails to pursue this status with any form of involvement in ministry. Why can they not become ministers of the word or of the eucharist at parish liturgies? If we are really serious about avoiding the development, as described by Herman Lombaerts, we need to start making real connections between the school and the local church.

It is encouraging to note some developments in forging links between the school and the local church. Many parishes now have
programmes in which secondary school students become faith
friends to children preparing for eucharist and penance. A senior
student befriends four or five children during the months prior to
the reception of the sacraments, meets them on a weekly basis and
shares with them his/her own understanding of the sacraments.
Projects such as these enrich the lives of the older student even
more than they do the lives of the young children and give an
important dimension to the religious education of second level
students.

The celebration of the eucharist

The second Vatican Council introduced far-reaching changes in
the way we celebrate the eucharist. We are now so familiar with
these changes that we have almost forgotten what our Mass was
like in pre-Vatican II days: the priest standing at the altar with his
back to the people, the silent congregation and the whole ceremony conducted in Latin. After the Council programmes were introduced to help people understand the need for the changes, the
word *eucharist* was now used instead of the Mass as a more authentic form of expressing the reality of our celebration. The term
Mass was derived from the Latin phrase 'Ite missa est ' meaning
'therefore go you are sent' and, as such, is a misnomer whereas
the word eucharist means thanksgiving and has been used since
the time the early Christians met in each other's houses to celebrate the Lord's Supper and recall with gratitude the first eucharistic meal when Jesus commanded his disciples, 'Do this in memory of me '.

These changes in the celebration of the eucharist were brought
home to me in a very real way when, two years ago, I attended a
silver wedding celebration in a rural parish in the west of Ireland.
The festivities started with a get together, a party and a dance in
the local hotel. The following morning we gathered again in the
family home to celebrate the eucharist. This time the family room
was packed with family, neighbours and friends. The children,
now in their teens and twenties, had planned the whole liturgy
with their parish priest who was the celebrant. They had chosen
the readings, composed the prayers of the faithful and, with their

friends in the parish folk group, had provided the music. At the offertory they brought to the altar gifts that symbolised the things that make up the home. The wedding rings reminded us of the commitment and the trust that make up a marriage. The home-made bread and the basket of turf told their own story of the daily struggle of the parents to keep bread on the table and the house warm. The flowers, the candles and the school books, the guitar and the deck of cards symbolised the beauty, the brightness, the learning and the joy that are part of the family life. The children themselves, who, with their parents, brought the gifts to the table were the greatest gift of all. The fruit of the marriage, it was their love, their gifts and talents that had added meaning to the euchar-ist. It was truly a celebration of thanksgiving centred on and sus-tained by the memory of Christ.

What a contrast this silver jubilee ceremony was to the pre-Vatican II nuptial Mass twenty-five years before. The priest then took full responsibility for the liturgy as if he alone was the one qualified to do so. He stood apart from the congregation, his back turned to them as he offered the sacrifice of the Mass on their be-half. There were no prayers of the faithful, no offertory procession and no involvement of the laity. We were outsiders, spectators at what should have been a communal celebration.

While the contrast in this situation is very noticeable, it is not typi-cal. By and large the renewal envisaged by the Council has not ef-fected the radical change in our understanding of the eucharist or impacted on our lives to any great extent. The way we celebrate eucharist today does not exert any significant influence on the life of the Christian community. Maybe, apart from cosmetic changes, the thinking is still nearer the nuptial Mass of twenty-five years ago. When Jesus said, 'Do this in memory of me' he certainly meant more than merely change bread and wine into his body and blood. We know that St John omits the account of the institu-tion of the eucharist, given by the other evangelists. He thus high-lights the service dimension of the eucharist. And yet, our experi-ence of eucharist is still mainly confined to the act of consecration. David Power expresses the situation when he states:

> Reductionism obstructs communication, as when bread and wine come to represent only the physical body and blood of Christ, and cease to symbolise the community participating

in his life and mystery, as one in him, the new creation in Jesus Christ.[2]

Of course bread and wine become the Body and Blood of Christ but David Power is telling us here that there is much more to it than that. It also symbolises the Body of Christ which is the community.What Jesus had in mind was the transformation of the worshipping community into a group of people who would take seriously the vision of the gospel to work for justice and inclusiveness in our world. Changes are taking place. Many theologians writing on the eucharist feel that we are only beginning to understand the possibilities of the eucharist to effect change and consequently to lead us to salvation and human liberation. It is precisely because I can be part of eucharistic communities, that are constantly involved in this search and actively engaged in bringing about equity in our world, that I get upset when I don't experience a dynamic community but only mere tokenism.

A few years ago, I was fortunate to be part of a small community gathering for weekday eucharist. The celebrant always gave a short homily on the scripture readings and gathered our intentions into two or three intercessory prayers. Since he knew approximately the number attending this early morning celebration, he used large hosts which he broke and shared with us at communion and, of course, we always had the opportunity of receiving under both kinds. These were small points but they made the difference between a meaningful community celebration and a routine individualistic type performance.

This kind of practice, which can gradually lead to understanding, is not the norm in our parish liturgies. Do some priests still perceive themselves as celebrating eucharist for us rather than with us? Language too sometimes seems to be disconnected from the actions it stands for. How can the celebrant justify addressing the assembled community of men, women and children as 'brothers' or expect them to profess their faith in such words as 'for us men and for our salvation'? In the second Eucharistic Prayer the celebrant addresses God on our behalf and states, 'We thank you for counting us worthy to stand in your presence and serve you' when he is the only person standing. There are many references to our being nourished by the Body and Blood of Christ and we say in the eucharistic acclamation, 'When we eat this Bread and drink this Cup we proclaim your death, Lord Jesus, until you come in glory', when in fact the priest is often the only person who eats and drinks. The symbolism of the breaking of bread and the sharing of the cup is lost when, even at a small gathering, the celebrant breaks bread and then returns to the tabernacle to get the ciborium for the community. These may be seem small contradictions in themselves but when words are not aligned to actions authenticity is lacking. Sociologists call this type of experience 'cognitive dissonance'. To justify such behaviour by statements such as, 'Well, we know that the eucharist is a mystery and we don't understand it anyway', is to move closer to magic than to mystery. Such practice underlines the discontinuity between our lives and the demands of the eucharist and fails to strengthen us as a community to face the injustices in our world. In this sense we could be described as a dysfunctional community, as defined by John H. Westerhoff III:

> Dysfunctional communities encourage regressions into withdrawal or denial, fail to comfort affliction, and provide a fantasy world of escape. They also encourage activity in churches to be only a sign of devotion and provide no transition to interdependence. Functional religion is known by its fruits. If religion has no prophetic imagination, it becomes dysfunctional.[3]

The Christian Feminist Movement

One of the great hopes of saving the church from this threat of degeneration into a dysfunctional community lies, I believe, in the Christian feminist movement. The sense of connectedness and the challenge to continual growth and change in it contrasts sharply with the sense of powerlessness that I often experience in the traditional church structures. The attitude of certainty about practically everything, including the God question, dismisses the experience, the intuitiveness and even the expertise of women, leaving them voiceless and disempowered. The understanding of our faith as an objective reality that can, somehow, stand on its own, independent of our journey, thwarts growth and fails to engage us in life's struggles.

On the other hand, the Christian feminist movement engages both women and men in an exploration of who God is for us today. God's self revelation to us, the interpretation of the mission of Jesus and his stance on the side of the oppressed, is often learned not in an intellectual way but in an experiential way that can touch the very woof and warp of one's life. I recall one such incident when, during a Christian feminist conference, women from Dundalk mimed the following story written by Ann Shanahan.

Reflections on the gospel story of the haemorrhaging woman

There was a woman who overheard in the marketplace that Jesus was coming to town. No one told her this, no one would speak to her, she was an outcast. She was an untouchable of her time. She had been bleeding from her womb for twelve years. The very symbol of her femininity was a problem for her. She was bleeding and regarded as unclean, therefore she was marginalised. She had no friend at all in the world. She spent a lot of time thinking about this man Jesus who was a great healer, a performer of miracles and her heart leaped. She thought to herself: this could be my chance, maybe I could be healed. Then a voice inside her said: 'You old fool, he wouldn't heal you, he wouldn't allow himself to be made unclean by touching you. You are an unclean bleeding woman.' So she remained where she was imprisoned in her painful state, alone with her miserable condition.

The next day around noon, she was indoors when she heard the commotion outside. She dragged herself over to the window and as she peered out she could see a huge crowd gathered. She heard them shouting to each other, 'He's here, Jesus is here.' Watching them she became eager and excited and she longed to be near him. Suddenly her inner voice mocked her again, choking her excitement, paralysing her eagerness.

As she stood and peered through the sunlight, she spotted him in the distance and, with a courage unknown to herself, she was out of that house and into the crowd. She covered her head with her shawl and, keeping her head bent low, silently, stealthily, sure footed, she wove her way through the crowd, right up behind him when one of the disciples stopped her. 'Move back woman, get out of the way. Can't

you see the Master is busy?' She was familiar with this language of rejection, but she was determined to meet him. She
really believed that this Jesus would heal her. Without any
hesitation, she grasped the hem of his cloak. Jesus felt the
power go out from him as she touched that hem. He turned
and looked at her and he loved and accepted her. In his look
she felt a renewed sense of who she was. With him she
sensed equality and experienced a restored dignity.

For her, he was indeed a miracle worker, she was freed from
her rejection and oppression. She was filled with wonder
and awe in his presence and was empowered by his presence. He confirmed her with love and gentleness with his
words: 'Woman you are healed, because your faith has
made you so.'

Afterwards one woman told her story and how she felt a sense of
liberation during the drama. She had separated from her husband
twelve years before, after a marriage that left her emotionally and
physically scarred. She decided to make a new life for herself and
her two small children and so became a separated spouse. While
she was accepted in her community, she often felt as if a finger
were pointed at her; she was a failure, not an example for the
young women in the community, someone not to be fully trusted.
In a subtle way she also felt that the church regarded her with
some suspicion. But having journeyed with the woman during
the mime, she experienced a sense of freedom and acceptance. At
last she felt vindicated for the decision she had taken twelve years
before. She told us that it was as if Jesus put his arms around her
during the reflection. She was now free to accept her own story
and her own history. Is not this the kind of freedom and liberation
that the gospels promise us?

Conclusion

Any discussion on a religious topic focuses ultimately on the God
who leads us out of slavery. There is an urgent need for us to examine our ideas and images of God to see if they are authentic.
Christians, raised on a patriarchal salvation history in a male-
dominated church, often have a narrow range of images of God
and any effort to question these images is discouraged. Many people, and especially women, experience a crisis of faith when they

realise that the male God whom they accepted unquestioningly
for years no longer satisfies their search for justice and freedom.
The process of re-imaging God is a painful one but, once one em-
barks on the journey, there is no turning back. However, the consequences for the Christian community of re-imaging God are
mind-boggling. Our prayers, both liturgical and non liturgical,
our hymns, not to mention our school text books, would all have
to be re-written. It is an exciting prospect. I sometimes wonder if
we are on the verge of a shift in thinking as radical as the shift
necessitated when Gallileo discovered that the earth was not the
centre of the universe.

Notes

1. *The Catholic School in Contemporary Society*, CMRS, Dublin 1991,
'Society, Culture and the Catholic School: Partnership for what
Future?' 105

2. Power, David N., 'Households of Faith in the Coming Church',
Worship 57 (1983), 239

3. Westerhoff III, John H., 'Celebrating & Living the Eucharist: A
Cultural Analysis', in *Alternative Futures for Worship, Vol 3*, The
Liturgical Press, Collegeville, Minnesota 1987.

CHAPTER 10

Lay Theology:
The Search for a Living God

Nuala Bourke

Theology and Lay Theology
Defining theology poses many problems and occasionally it has
been a suspect activity even for professionals. Certainly any lay
woman expressing an interest in the subject was, and perhaps still
is, very likely to be misunderstood. She must surely have designs
on the priesthood! But in spite of its complexities, theology may
be described as a study of the relationships between God, ourselves and the world we live in. It is not the preserve of ordained
men, but is open to all. The term *lay theology* then, is not intended
to refer to some kind of inferior discipline set aside for the unor-
dained. Although how we might 'do' theology may differ according to our vocation, the study of theology remains the same for
everyone – male, female, cleric or lay person. Indeed for anyone of
faith it is a necessary journey towards understanding and sustaining belief.

Religious education but no theology
Faith has been and continues to be central in the lives of the vast
majority of people in Ireland, and perhaps especially in places like
Mayo. Ours is almost completely a rural county and it is largely
because of our people that studies like those of Fr Micheál Mac
Gréil can show such a high average of belief in God, of Mass attendance, and of reception of the sacraments. Superficially, there has
been little change since the days of my childhood. During World
War II while Hitler rampaged through Europe, the west of Ireland
slept. It was the very epitome of De Valera's vision of a people living happily in frugal comfort. Life had a certain security where
day followed day with little disturbance from the distant war, and
joy and sorrow alike were declared to be the will of God. There
were no doubts about his existence and we were happy in the

knowledge that he had saved us from all that evil because we were faithful. There was little emphasis then on God's compassion and love. If you were good you would go to heaven, and if you transgressed you would be punished. The Council of Trent had done a very good job and a well trained and highly respected clergy ministered very paternalistically to a laity which seemed happy to pay and to pray. Everyone knew where they stood.

Although we knew nothing of theology, we were taught religion. Primary school took care of the basics with the catechism. Its certainty was marvellous, even when it confidently declared the world to be about 4,000 years old! For those who had the privilege of a secondary education, Hart's *Christian Doctrine* and Sheehan's *Apologetics* supplied the rest. In theory, at least, there was nothing we could not answer. It seems strange now that in all those years most of us never remarked on the absence of the Old Testament from our studies, and equally strange that there was little or no discussion of the emphatic answers in our books. Cleverer men than we were had worked them out and who were we to question them? Indeed those who did so were considered anti-clerical and a bad influence. They were to be avoided.

The challenge of teachers abroad

Like many others, I emigrated from Mayo in the 60s. Armed with all this righteous certainty, I found myself teaching in an RC school in dockside Liverpool, where every Catholic teacher was required to teach religion. What a shock! In a class of forty children, two knew 'their prayers' and even those devout little souls had never heard of the Angelus or the mysteries of the Rosary. If I could console myself that these youngsters came from an underprivileged background, I could find no such good excuse when confronted with the unbelief of some of my own colleagues and other young professionals with whom I came into contact. They were openly scornful of my pious catholicity and humble acceptance of other peoples' answers. But perhaps the greatest distress of all was caused by my own uncertainty in the continuing validity of my beliefs, and my inadequacy in the face of this challenge to them. I had to admit that I was amazed and impressed and indeed troubled by their knowledge of and interest in the scriptures. They seemed so much better able than I to think things through for themselves, to make their own decisions and to take responsibility for them. This then was the uncomfortable beginning of my journey in search of the real God.

Vatican II

Because England was in general an unbelieving society, it afforded a freedom of discussion and open questioning with no loss of face, no accusations of giving scandal. Enquiry was encouraged and dissent was no disgrace. Around this time Vatican II broke upon us and the fresh air allowed by Pope John XXIII was more than welcome. Religious freedom, primacy of conscience, the universal call to holiness and other equally 'extraordinary' advances in thinking were debated openly. For the first time since perhaps the early church, we heard of the central role of the laity. We were the church. Sadly it was all too much for us. We were like children freed from parental control with no education for liberty. In England, and more so in Ireland, changed proved difficult and unsettling, and many were unable to adapt. Priests and people ran for cover, and a world of opportunity was lost.

Practice and belief

In spite of the fine words of *Gaudium et Spes*, very little progress has been made in this area of educating the laity. We have all failed to scrutinise the times and we have therefore been unable to interpret them in the light of the gospel. Even a glance at the situation in Ireland today bears this out. Over 90% of our population is considered to belong to the RC church and there is a very high level of religious practice, particularly in rural areas. However, this does not necessarily indicate a correspondingly high level of belief. At least some of those who attend Mass regularly may do so out of habit or to please others or to conform in some other way. In spite of outward appearances, many remain apathetic and Sunday Mass has little to do with the rest of their lives. There are also those who look for spiritual nourishment and who would probably be interested in a meaningful way of expressing their faith, but for them too, Sunday Mass is often an isolated and unsatisfactory experience. Week after week great opportunities are being lost to 'feed the hungry' and to begin to develop some theological awareness in those whom we continue to describe as the

church – the people of God. In general, there seems to be little or
no movement towards a thinking and more vibrant church.

Devotionalism and its dangers

Almost miraculously, people are still praying and in recent years
there seems to have been a revival or a return to a certain kind of
devotionalism. Many who sincerely missed the support of pious
practices have welcomed the reintroduction of the perpetual ex-
position of the Blessed Sacrament, and novenas – solemn or otherwise. Without questioning the need for or the power of prayer,
there is I feel a danger here that without a parallel development of
theological understanding, we will again be comforted rather
than challenged. We will be lulled into a false sense of security
with no response to the threat posed to our society by increasing
secularism. If we do not foster a questioning church, we will fail
to find solid ground between moving statues and open cynicism.
The devout may become easy prey to some forms of extreme
evangelism, while others pursue a lifestyle which leaves no room
for God. The people of Mayo are undoubtedly prayerful and their
support for shrines such as Knock, and for pilgrimages like the
Reek, bears eloquent testimony to their reverence for and dependence on God. They are certainly convinced that he should play a
vital role in their lives. Nevertheless, universal education is chip-
ping away at this kind of religious commitment and although my
generation will continue to go to church regularly, it is less likely
that our children will continue to do so. Unless more relevant
links can be made for them between religion and life experience,
they may be unable to withstand the pressures of either affluence
or unemployment in spite of mothers who are no less persistent in
prayer than St Monica of old. If this happens, in another thirty
years we will be looking out on this most beautiful county of ours
full of regret because we have lost the opportunity to 'renew our
hearts and minds' and have sought instead to restore inappropri-
ate supports for our spiritual life. It is still not too late. The remedy
is available and must involve us all. This will be our most important pilgrimage – our journey towards understanding the real relationship which exists between God, ourselves and the world.

The education system

I feel we must begin with the system of education. Over the last
thirty years, there has been a complete renewal of the religious

programmes in Primary School, and valiant attempts have been made to give young children a more wholesome vision of God. But at the same time, many parents have watched with dismay the decline of the status of RE in our secondary schools. Some very good programmes have been devised, but there seems to be no organised approach, and I think many teachers, even catechists, find religious class at secondary level very difficult. Students' lives are necessarily dominated by the points system and it is therefore very difficult to arouse their interest in a subject which to them seems superfluous and lacks academic credibility. To date, there has been some debate about the inclusion of religion as a points subject with sincerely held views being expressed by those for and those against. Fr Dermot Lane, who was director of Mater Dei, has written of his opposition to the inclusion of religion in the CAO, CAS. While I sympathise with his desire to keep faith out of the examination rat-race, I feel strongly that there is a pressing need to provide an academic base or background for Religious Studies. I also feel that being obliged to study a subject need not necessarily blight interest in it. Many a student who struggled with Shakespeare later learned to love the English language. Without the basics which were part of an exam prospectus, they might not have had the resources to proceed further. By providing the opportunity for serious biblical and theological study in our second level schools, we would ensure a nucleus in the wider community who would be properly prepared to engage in critical public debate on issues which necessarily arise in our day-to-day living – the referenda on divorce and abortion being two very obvious cases in point.

Theology at third level

Moving on to third level education, the scene is no less depressing. Only two of our universities teach theology – Maynooth College and Trinity College. Although we have been extremely well served by our Maynooth trained and based theologians, the situation has undoubtedly contributed to the perception of theology as a male clerical preserve. Trinity too must surely suffer from having to uphold the independent banner alone. These difficulties are regularly exploited by media which sometimes seem more interested in headlines than in getting at the truth. Labels such as liberal and conservative are often inappropriately applied to one or other establishment and the two colleges become relegated in the public mind to the Catholic and Protestant ethos respectively. At the moment no other university has a chair of theology. In Dublin, All Hallows and Milltown are endeavouring to redress the balance, but for the people of Mayo, and for the West of Ireland as a whole, there is no facility for theological study and at least three hours in a train separates us from pursuing such an interest. While we are aware that there are laws preventing the establishing of a faculty in the NUI colleges, it seems unreasonable to lay people that such statutes are allowed to remain in place. One wonders if more persistence on the part of our bishops and theologians would produce better results. In a country which is as nominally religious as Ireland, it is surely absurd that there are no graduate or post-graduate theological studies available to students attending our National University.

Access for lay people

With such limited access to theological education, it is small wonder that, until very recently, almost all our theologians were clerics. Lay people could not be blamed for feeling that theology was a no-go area, likely to be too academic or risky. There are thankfully signs of change and we now have a number of lay theologians, both men and women, but the situation remains far from satisfactory. Lay people in general feel ignored by theologians and excluded from the world of theology. Much of the important work done rarely filters down to the public at large, and there seems to be a very wide gap between those who study religion and the ordinary worshipper. This is not true of any other discipline. We read every day of recent advances in scientific thought and discovery, and we are regularly encouraged to explore the enchanted forests of art and literature. At the same time, new and attractive ideas of God fail to reach us and we remain locked into the traditional image of him as male and all powerful. Belief in God is still strong in Ireland, but it is surely threatened by such a lack of development. While some are content to worship a God who requires letters of thanksgiving to be published in newspapers, an increasing number find such an image inadequate, irrelevant and even distasteful. There is a serious challenge to us all then to re-image the divine and to make a real connection between belief in God and our experience of life. God the father was used even by Jesus Christ to portray the best and most universal qualities when the male was the only significant parent – a loving, protecting, providing father who would not reach his child a stone in place of bread. But in the modern world, with its emerging gender equality and a deepening crisis of authority, this particular image is rapidly becoming outdated, if not offensive. In many households to-day, Christian and otherwise, the male parent is significant only by his absence, and for some, both men and women, a feminine aspect to the divine is beyond question. One might also usefully ask what the 'Good Shepherd' has to say to the high-tech generation, or the Triune God to the socially disadvantaged? Indeed what kind of God can we believe in when our county is being decimated by emigration? And what kind of protest can appropriately be made by people of faith when meagre livelihoods are being wiped out by big business and the lure of gold seems to threaten even our sacred places? While we can quite properly look to our theologians and our clergy for scholarship and leadership, we lay people should be actively involved in exploring the relationship and relevance which God has to our everyday lives in the created world. We have much to contribute to a theology of emigration and unemployment which would protect our human dignity, and a theology of land and sea and lake, which would find a middle way between mere conservation and exploitation. Without critical reflection we can do neither. Without theological education we won't know how or where to begin.

A questioning, thinking church

Gone for ever are the days when we could propose the 'will of God' as an adequate explanation in times of individual or social distress. Gone also are the days when other people's answers were satisfactory. If we fail to educate the laity, there will be no cover to run to and faith may disappear forever from the lives of our otherwise well-informed young people. A questioning, thinking church is not a spiritual luxury or a pious aspiration, it is a necessity. We must find that solid ground which will safeguard us from the emotionalism of visions in the heavens, and spare us the derision which they invite. We must learn and be convinced that the divine is in everyone of us and we are all involved in the continuing work of creation and salvation.

We are the Church, we are the family of God, and there is much to be learned from this analogy. The secular family to-day is having to devise new models in order to survive the chill winds of change. Parents can no longer make rules and issue orders. They are now in the much more difficult business of explanation and negotiation. They see the need to educated their children for freedom by equipping them with knowledge and skills to make good choices in adult life. We lay people, the children of God's family, also need education for liberty so that we too can make our own decisions and take responsibility for what we believe and how we act. The God whom we find ourselves is the *real* God who will bring us to the wholeness of salvation. May we, as St Paul prayed, 'have the strength to grasp the breadth and the length and the depth of God'.

PART IV

Missionaries and Migrants

CHAPTER 11
Mayo and China:
John Blowick, Missionary Priest

Brendan Fahey

The vision and its presentation

The vision for an Irish Mission in China existed in 1916; some of the blueprint even was already in place. But to put the nuts and bolts of a society of Irish missionary priests into place, required unremitting labour, and on-going sacrifice. This was the task that Belcarra-born Mayoman, Fr John Blowick, took on. The remarkable thing is that the young twenty-eight-year-old, who up to then had focused his considerable mental and physical energy on academic achievement in Maynooth College where he taught theology, was now able to channel that same energy into developing this new missionary endeavour.

This became evident in the days immediately following the Irish bishops' approval of the mission plan which John Blowick had submitted to them at their Maynooth meeting on 10 October, 1916. Within days, he had produced a booklet about the mission, 10,000 copies in the first printing, followed soon after by 25,000 more. His own comment on this production indicates the intensity of his application to the task: 'It was ready by Friday night (13 October) and my head was ready for the surgeon.' It cost but a penny; in fact, he would refer to it himself later as 'a miserable production', but then adds another comment which he brought to all this work. 'No effort, no matter how mean and poor, will go without doing some good in this work; it is often the trifles which count most!'

The 25-page pamphlet gives a good insight into the programme to make the vision of an Irish Mission in China come true. Reading it today, you cannot fail to be aware of the spirit for mission that burned in the man himself. One central tenet in this thinking is that the whole of the Irish people must be drawn into this project. It is hardly an exaggeration to say that he aimed at involving every man, woman and child to some degree or another in the work of the mission. The first page of the booklet reproduces the written

permission given by the bishops to commence the work of founding a society of priests in order to establish a mission in China. He
then described his strategy:

> The six priests who had by this time committed themselves
> to this work will commence preaching immediately. They
> will visit *each* of the 1,100 parishes in Ireland. They will use
> pulpit, platform and press. Their immediate purpose is first,
> to arouse and stimulate the interest of every Irish Catholic in
> this great work for God; second, to collect money to estab-
> lish a missionary college, and third, to direct the minds of
> young Irish boys and girls to the great harvest of souls that
> lies waiting in China.

This direct appeal to the Irish people, individually and collectively,
is repeated again and again throughout the pamphlet: 'This our
National Mission, our destiny in the world. Help its realisation ...
Let us bring China to Jesus. Everyone of us, every Irish Catholic,
lay person, nun, brother and priest.' The rallying cry became:
'You the people of Ireland must first show that you desire to convert China and that you mean to do it. Your place is in the van-
guard.'

This message was carried across Ireland principally through the
use of church pulpits. John Blowick wrote to each of the Irish bishops for permission to speak at the Sunday Masses in each parish
in the diocese. With the exception of the Archbishop of Dublin, all
the other bishops consented. Because the six priests were far too
small a number to cope with the work that lay ahead, he enlisted
the help of priests from Maynooth, All Hallows and also from the
Redemptorists, the Passionists, the Dominicans; and sometimes
the parish priests themselves undertook the task so that the majority of the Irish people could be contacted and their help and
support enlisted in the shortest time possible. Sisters also offered
their help as John Blowick later acknowledged: 'The nuns of the
country have done much for the mission, and no one but God can
ever know the large part they have played in its success.'

Preaching the mission

All this involved very considerable labour and effort week in,
week out. John Blowick himself remembers how each weekend he
would leave Dublin (he had now, through the help of friends, an

address in Sandymount which he used as a mailing address and office) and journey to the bishop's house in whatever diocese the appeal was taking place. Saturday night was an opportunity to talk with the bishop, explain to him about the mission and give him information about the progress to date. Then on Sunday he would make the mission appeal, maybe at as many as five Masses in the cathedral itself or the adjoining parishes. On Monday he would journey back to Dublin and continue the office work through the week.

The voice in the pulpit was the best means of communicating with the rank and file of the Irish people. In the days before radio and television, not only was it an effective means of contacting the vast majority of the people; the spoken word, whether in church or on the political platform, from the time of Daniel O'Connell through Parnell and on to Pearse and his contemporaries, had proved to be a powerful force in the mouth of a gifted speaker. That is why John Blowick was willing to undergo any labour in order that the voice of the Chinese mission would proclaim itself from every parish pulpit in the country. He also made use of the national newsapers – those who favoured the birth of an Irish nation were the most co-operative – and the provincial papers. In addition, the *Far East*, the project's mission magazine which appeared in January 1918 and which would find its way into a great number of Irish homes, aimed at making the Irish people mission-minded and confirming their active participation in the on-going work of the mission. The first issue of the magazine reported that, in the previous year, one hundred and ten students had applied to enter the Chinese seminary, twenty of that number coming from Maynooth. The work from the pulpit was clearly achieving its aim.

Negotiations with Rome

Meanwhile the work-load of John Blowick continued to increase. About this time also he began a correspondence with Rome to negotiate for territory in China, to establish an Irish Vicariate. For this he enlisted the help of the Rector of the Irish College there, Monsignor O'Riordan. The rector was most co-operative, took a deep personal interest in the project, and offered invaluable counsel about procedures and negotiations with Rome. It also meant that the Irish outpost had an involvement in the project, offering its services to obtain from Rome the permission for the canonical sanction of an Irish Mission Society.

A memorandum from Blowick at that time notes: 'I got up each morning at 5am and went to bed at midnight.' Yet a central feature of his overall plan was still waiting implementation, namely, establishing a missionary college. Without it, there would be no continuity, no assurance of being able to supply personnel for an Irish Vicariate in China, nor could the growing momentum among the people be sustained. Despite the heavy burden he was already carrying, he now threw himself whole-heartedly into that work.

Dalgan Park

Fr Edward Galvin, on home leave from China and the other prime force behind the new mission venture, joined John Blowick in the quest for a suitable property and location for the college. Naturally they first looked at Dublin, but the archbishop there was unforthcoming, so they were forced to look elsewhere. The kind of house or property they had in mind belonged for the most part to the old landlords, people unlikely to be disposed to deal with priests regarding the sale of their properties. Blowick and Galvin met with four blank refusals; others were not so blunt but they still refused. Finally, near the end of their tether, they found an old Georgian building with a farm attached outside the village of Shrule on the Mayo/Galway border. Hardly ideal when you consider that the nearest railway station was in Tuam, twelve miles away. However, the Bishop of Galway made them welcome, so with a sigh of relief they ended their long quest and set down their bags in Dalgan Park in October 1917.

The work of preparing the place and making it ready to receive the first group of students began immediately and continued at a hectic pace over the next seven weeks. Blowick now applied himself with the same thoroughness he had shown in his academic studies to co-ordinating all the practical matters involved in setting up house. As he himself remarked, 'everything from the beds down to the last salt spoon' had to be provided. I myself remember him relating how he went to Dublin to one of the large retail establishments and purchased all the necessary cutlery, delph, and household items.

On 29 January, 1918 the first group of students arrived. Nineteen in all, at various stages on the path to priesthood, they had come from practically every ecclesiastical college in Ireland. John Blowick recalled that first night when the students and the priests who had been involved in preparing the house for their arrival, all gathered together in the ballroom which was 30' x 20'. 'It was very bare,' he wrote, 'and there were oil lamps on the walls. There were three altars made from packing cases. There were some chairs for sitting on, but many of them just knelt on the floor.'

He read the gospels to them, particularly John 17 (the prayer of Jesus for the disciples). Straight away he began to inculcate in them the spirit he hoped to see come alive and grow among them, a spirit that would shape their living as a Columban family. He emphasised ' a perfect and never-failing charity among all the priests and students' as the core of that spirit. He also wanted to eliminate that separation between staff and students which would have been the normal situation in the ecclesiastical colleges then. So, as well as furnishing the material fabric of a missionary college, he was also faced with an even greater task of providing a type of spiritual training which, while fostering personal development, would also enable a group to grow into community, into family. There is no doubt that in many of the practices he introduced into the training of the students he was influenced by, and indeed may actually have borrowed from, the regime that Pearse had established in Scoil Eanna. This contribution that John Blowick made to the training of Columban students would come to be known as the 'Dalgan spirit'.

Even in those years, when his energies were almost entirely absorbed in the practicalities of establishing the foundations of what was to become known as the Society of St Columban, he still found time to pursue his earlier career as a theologian. Around the mid-twenties he wrote a series of essays which were published under the title, *The Supernatural Life*. Early in the thirties a large work appeared, entitled *The Priestly Vocation*, and was adjudged to be the best work on the subject to have appeared in English. These writings were an attempt to express the basis of his own lived faith-commitment. Just as his own theological reflection on Christ's command to his church, 'Go and teach all nations', led him to make a decisive turning point in his own life, he strove to make theology a tool for others, a means of helping them to love more fully the mystery of Christ. In later life he seemed to have been deeply saddened with the way the teaching of theology appeared to him to be failing to achieve this, as is revealed in a remark he made in 1966: 'I have been all my life convinced that dogma as taught was little better than a farce, in as much as it has little or no impact on our lives and that for all practical purposes we would be as well off doing advanced algebra.'

The first ordination of Columban students took place the same year that students had entered Dalgan. In 1918, ordinations in Maynooth were brought forward from June to April. The reason was that the British Parliament was proposing to introduce a Conscription Act which would make Irishmen liable for conscription into the British Army. The bishops sought to forestall the possible effects of such an Act by bringing forward the time normally set for ordinations in a year that afterwards would be referred to as the year of the Lloyd George Ordinations.' Together with the band of men being ordained for their respective dioceses in Ireland, five 'Dalgan men' were ordained for the mission in China. On 18 April, 1918, The Maynooth Mission to China was born, to be baptised later as 'The Society of St Columban', in honour of its patron, one of the great names from the first Irish missionary movement in the sixth century. It was less than two years since John Blowick had petitioned the body of Irish bishops at the time of their annual meeting in Maynooth. The dream was coming true, but the negotiations being conducted in Rome to obtain territory for an Irish Vicariate in China had not yet brought any results.

Roman approval

Finally, approval from Rome came in 1918, and in June of 1919 the first General Chapter was held. John Blowick was elected Superior General. He began to move urgently on the business of obtaining an Irish Vicariate in China. Men were being ordained for the mission and some of the bishops were clamouring that they be sent out without further delay, but he and others held tenaciously to the view that the identity of the Irish Mission to China would be sadly obscured unless they had a territory of their own. Yet, it was now late 1919 and still no one had gone to China. Finally, at the end of that year, the negotiations with Rome were brought to a successful conclusion and a territory was allotted, around Hanyang City, situated near the junction of the Han and Yangtse rivers, about six hundred miles west of Shanghai. It was the kind of highly populated but neglected area for which they had hoped.

Road to China

John Blowick at once directed his energies to organise the sending out of the first group of missionaries to China. As Superior General of the Society he would travel with them, see China for the first time and try to assess the situation there. Their departure was seen and celebrated as a special event in the history of the Society and in the history of the Irish church. On 17 March, 1920 a formal departure ceremony took place in Dalgan Park, attended by some of the bishops and by Dr McCaffrey, then President of Maynooth, who had befriended John Blowick and Edward Galvin from the very beginning. At the ceremony in Dalgan, the sermon was preached by the Archbishop of Tuam, Dr Gilmartin. There were eleven, including John Blowick and Edward Galvin, in the first group (they would be joined en route by five more then working in the States, bringing the total to sixteen). Dr McCaffrey invited the whole band to a farewell banquet in Maynooth on 20 March, and the following day the President of All Hallows College invited John Blowick and his comrades to another farewell dinner.

Reflecting on these events in his diary, Blowick writes: 'Again we experienced the same kindly spirit as we did in Maynooth and are embarrassed by the words of the President ... We have a great deal to thank God for in giving us such generous and sincere friends.' This aspect of their leave-taking continued to attend them even when they crossed over to Liverpool to board the *Carmania* for the USA. Priests from Liverpool, Manchester, Birmingham and Leeds came to the wharf to bid the missionaries farewell. Also a large crowd of Liverpool Irish thronged the dockside and some of the final farewells were spoken in Gaelic. The same sort of response greeted them in the States and indeed their departure from the States was marked by a Pontifical Mass, celebrated by Archbishop Harty on 29 April in the cathedral of Omaha, Nebraska, the city where the Columban Society had established its headquarters in the States. This initial band of sixteen missionaries for

China continued their journey by boat from San Francisco, stopped at Japan en route, and finally arrived in Shanghai on 16 June, just three months after they had set out from Dalgan Park.

An Irish vision

The response generated by the launching of the Chinese Mission points back to the vision of John Blowick and Edward Galvin to involve not just the people of Ireland, but the diaspora Irish in England, Scotland, Australia, New Zealand, the United States and even Argentina, in the missionary works of the Irish church. Very early on, the *Far East* magazine was published in US and Australian editions. John Blowick was well aware that the missionary spirit he was hoping to rekindle in the Irish church and the Irish people was helped by the historical climate in which it began to catch fire. The era from Parnell to Pearse was a period that was vibrant with ideals and at a time when there was not yet an Irish State, the term 'The Irish Race' gained widespread acceptance and became a lens through which people could begin to see the shape of a new dawn for Ireland.

The Chinese mission had been launched in October 1916, a year that has such significance in modern Irish history, marked as it is by the Easter Rising. Did that event, and subsequent new horizons in Irish nationalist thinking, influence the new missionary movement? John Blowick, a man not given to exaggeration, gave his own answer:

> I am strongly of the opinion that the Rising of 1916 helped our work indirectly. I know for a fact that many of the young people of the country had been aroused into a state of heroism by the Rising of 1916 and by the manner in which the leaders met their death. I can affirm this from personal experience. And, accordingly, when we put out appeal before the young people of the country, it fell on soil which was better prepared to receive it than if there never had been an Easter Week.

During his China visit, where John Blowick came to view Hanyang as the ideal mission – completely Chinese, no churches, virgin mission territory – it became clear that his own contribution to the mission would not be there. No one carried the same weight

in Ireland or in Rome as he did. Edward Galvin was the China expert and he remained on in Hanyang, later to become its Perfect
Apostolic and eventually its first bishop.

Sisters and brothers

Back in Ireland, John Blowick continued his missionary labours
and he was instrumental in founding the Sisters of St Columban,
who began in 1922. Around the same time he admitted men into
the Society of Columban Brothers. At Rome's request he became
part of the Missionary Union of Clergy in Ireland and launched a
magazine entitled *Pagan Missions*, later called *Ensign*.

The year 1924 marked a turning point for John Blowick and the
Society of St Columban. A General Chapter was held in May
which elected Dr Michael O'Dwyer as Superior General. Major
financial problems were looming because money badly needed to
run the college in Ireland was being sent out to meet urgent demands in China. There was a danger that Rome might even close
down the Society if the situation worsened. The situation called
for someone who could take drastic steps to balance the budget, a
task for which temperamentally John Blowick was less suited. He
was appointed Vicar General, Superior for Ireland, but his direct
influence on daily affairs lessened. At this time also his health
began to show signs of strain, a result of the terrific work load he
had shouldered since setting his hand to the plough in 1916.

The new Dalgan

In the decades after 1924 he was engaged in plans that were forming to move the Columban seminary from its original home to a
more suitable location. The growing numbers also called for more
extensive accommodation. In fact, the first thing he did was to
take the architect to Europe to visit the different seminaries there
and to experience the latest and most advanced thinking on seminary building. Of course, the money needed to build a new seminary had to be collected. Again it is an indication of the esteem
and affection in which he was held by the Irish people, and the
missionary identity they accorded to him, that the new Dalgan
was built by the pennies of the people who could not afford it.
When Dalgan Park seminary, which rose up out of the plains of
Meath under the shadow of the Hill of Tara, opened its doors in

September 1941, it was free of debt. It is a building that bears the imprint of John Blowick's own thinking and personality: a blend of simplicity and grandeur, a durability overlaid with a sense of good taste. Something of that is echoed in a story I heard him tell himself about the building. At some stage he was on the continent still pursuing ideas on seminary building when word came to him that some were advocating terrazzo for the Dalgan corridors, some of which were fifty or sixty yards long. Terrazzo was a new material at the time and its likeness to marble gave it a certain attraction. As he told the story you heard him heave a sigh and then in the flat, gravelly Mayo accent which he never tried to disown, he commented: 'I had to hurry home quickly before they turned the whole place into a public lavatory!'

Final years

John Blowick not only moved with the times, he also moved the times in which he lived. He was a churchman and in that capacity he inspired the Irish church to rekindle the missionary spirit which so marked its beginnings in the post-Patrician period, but which in the course of Irish history in subsequent centuries had gradually been stifled. He had the ability to identify and tap a latent energy in the Irish people. In that little booklet he compiled at the very beginning of the movement, he stated: 'Thousands of Irish today are inspired as much as their forefathers were with a spirit of bravery, chivalry and sacrifice. They are looking for an outlet by which they may renovate the world by the frenzy of their soul and their religion. We have found such an outlet.'

He died in June, 1972. It was the immediate post-Vatican II years, when a new understanding of mission and a new assessment of missionary approach and methods was developing in the church. It would be his wish that the missionary society which he had helped to found would move with the changing times, indeed that it would as far as possible spearhead the movement towards change, just as he had done in his day. His passing was felt as a personal loss by all Columbans living in 1972. Columbans among themselves always spoke about him in a personal way. He was known to them simply as 'JB', sometimes referring to the man, more often, perhaps, to the spirit of the man.

CHAPTER 12

Survival and Faith in the Horn of Africa

Mairéad McDonagh

As a young girl growing up in Mayo, I remember vividly the many visits my uncle, Fr Frank, made to our house. He spoke of Africa and of a people with a closeness to and love of the land and nature, and in these words I found a bond with these far away strangers, for I too was a child of the land.

As a young secondary school student in Convent of Mercy, Claremorris, I wrote an essay for a religious class on Third World poverty. Much to my embarrassment, the sister read my essay aloud to the class.

I still remember the final paragraph of that essay. It was from Matthew's gospel, 25:35-40:

> I was hungry and you gave me to eat,
> I was thirsty and you gave me to drink,
> I was a stranger, and you welcomed me,
> I was naked, and you clothed me.
> I was sick, and you visited me.
> I was in prison, and you came to me.
> Truly I say to you, 'Whenever you did this to one of these,
> my brothers, you did it to me.

This reading of Matthew's gospel always challenged me, and I always feel a need to fulfil those words in some way.

Later, during my nurse training, I dreamt of working in Africa many times. In May 1987, the urge to go proved too strong to resist. I applied to the Third World Agency GOAL and met John O Shea. I was amazed at his energy and his vibrancy in helping the poorest of the poor. I was sent on a preparation course for one week, and I received the usual injections. During this time my family and relatives were hoping that I'd decide against the journey but I became more and more excited at finally visiting this 'mystical' land. Yet I also felt apprehensive and fearful of the unknown. I now know that God was with me all the way.

I was being sent to a place called Migdadu in the North Eastern Highlands of Hareigha Province of Ethiopia. The clinic and school in Migdadu was run by the Fransiscan Missionaries of Our Lady for a catchment area of 10,000 people. This area nestled among the higher mountains, was very poor and had little or no medical service.

My first glimpse of Africa (Ethiopia) was approaching the airport in Addis Ababa. The terrain was very brown and settlements of dozens of oblong huts were visible – I remember my heart racing with excitement. I saw the huts for the first time. I knew that I finally had the first part of my dream come true – 'to see Africa'.

The struggle to survive

With Visa and travel pass, I set off for Hareigha with another GOAL nurse. The first three hours from Addis Ababa to Nazareth town were good and we chatted along the way. The land was flat and monotonous and the road had many army tanks travelling North to Eritrea and Tigray where civil war was raging at that time.

The roads gradually deteriorated to a mountain dirt track and the mountains became closer and eventually the track was all that we had. Cliffs of hundreds of feet stood on one side, and the jeep (4 wheel drive) rocked back and forth up steep hills and down into valleys. The heat and the dust were rising and in the distance clouds quickly piled up. As we drove on, the rain came thundering down (it was the rainy season), and we got stuck in the mud. Long lean tribesmen came to help push the jeep out, and women and children came to giggle and wonder at the *faranje* (foreigners). We finally abandoned the jeep and belongings which contained medicines, hired two mules, and two village tribesmen to take us to the sisters in Migdadu. Darkness fell quickly and rain poured down. At this stage, feeling exhausted, lonely for the warmth and security of my home in Mayo, aching from riding the mule up and down steep hills, and a fear of the two accompanying local men, I questioned my previous longing to be in this mystical land which had become deepest and darkest Africa. I realised also that my friend's mule took off at a steady pace, and I was travelling at a slower pace, and eventually I was on my own with two African men guiding me along in the dark. Of course, my imagination played games, and I was fully convinced that these two men would take me to an unknown destination and that I would never be seen or heard of again. On that evening I reached the depths and I remember crying out to God! I felt so helpless and out of control. I reached for my rosary beads and started to recite the rosary and I cried at the same time. After travelling for about three hours (two hours on mule, one hour on foot) a flashlight shone and Sr Margaret called out my name. My friend apologised for straying away from me. (She was already three months here and familiar with the track.) I realised that I had reached my destination of work among the very poor. I wanted to abandon my dream and return to Mayo the next day.

Sr Margaret, an Ethiopian sister, became a wonderful friend in the many months to follow.

All people, no matter what creed, cult or codes they applied to living their lives, were seen at our clinic. Each individual was treated equally and fairly. The people realised this and travelled days by foot to reach us. We then commenced several outreach mobile clinics travelling two to three hours each morning to take health, vaccinations, and education programmes to the outlying areas.

Many of my Sunday afternoons were spent visiting people in the local villages, who were once very ill, now recovered, and had especially invited me to their homes. Their homes were called *tukuls* (huts) made of wattle.

Eight to twelve people can live in one *tukul* because they have no personal belongings, apart from their land (one hectare), its products and their livestock. Every object is communal – for storing and grinding grain or for cooking or serving food.

Their hospitality was overwhelming even in the midst of this extreme poverty. The woman of the house would greet you outside with a welcome handshake and a kiss and guide you inside to be welcomed by the remaining members of the household or *uhhagers*. They were always generous, considerate, friendly and gay.

A story of salvation

Salvation means helping each person to develop as a whole, and not just spiritually, but here in Ethiopia also to cope with disease and poverty.

I witnessed at first hand faith, courage and love by many of the poorest of the poor. Two of these people were Mohammed and Fatuma, a Muslim man and his wife.

She was carried for two days by a group of people from her village. She was in obstructed labour for two to three days, and was becoming weaker and weaker. I examined her, found that the baby was already dead, and the uterus had the signs of rupturing which would eventually lead to Fatuma's death. I only hoped and prayed that she would live until dawn, when I could set off to Nazareth town, the nearest hospital with an operating room facility. I knew that a complete hysterectomy was all that Fatuma needed to save her life. Due to the rough terrain, I had no choice but to wait until the first signs of dawn. I corrected shock by commencing intravenous infusion of dextrose/saline, high doses of antibiotics, pain relief and sedation. At 4am I put Fatuma on a mattress in the rear of the jeep, her husband behind supporting her, and my health worker and I set off on the long arduous journey. With every boulder the jeep rocked back and forth like a boat on the high seas and Fatuma cried out in pain. At 11am – seven hours later – I finally reached Nazareth hospital. To my horror and disbelief the surgeon was in Cuba on holidays. I had to continue on another three hour journey to Addis Ababa. I prayed silently all the way to Addis, stopping from time to time to check Fatuma. I reassured Mohammed as best I could. After driving through the city for the first time, I finally reached the hospital, and Fatuma was alive, but she was deteriorating rapidly. The doctor agreed with my diagnosis of Fatuma but refused to operate unless I obtained two pints of blood prior to surgery. I looked at him in disbelief. He said 'no blood, and she dies'. I ran to haematology, demanded her blood group, ran to my health worker and took him and Mohammed across the other side of the city to the blood bank. I was met with resistance, and refused the two pints of blood. At this stage I bargained for the blood. I offered to donate blood myself to replace what was taken from the blood bank. Due to civil war in the North, blood was in short supply. I donated the blood and my health worker had high blood pressure due to exhaustion and could not donate blood. We returned quickly to the hospital, and Fatuma had by now become very ill and weak. I approached the doctor with the blood and he said he would operate at 8pm. It was now only 6pm.

I cried with anger and again prayed silently for a miracle. Mohammed said that he was thankful for all I did for Fatuma, no matter what the outcome. I sat with Fatuma and held her hand. The men fell asleep. She squeezed my hands many times with the anguish of pain. We each had a different language but there did not seem to be any barrier between us. They finally came to take her for surgery, and she came out two hours later, alive.

I returned to Addis three weeks later to bring her home. They both kissed and hugged me tightly. I felt so happy and so loved by these special people.

The call to return

There were many people like Mohammed and Fatuma, and in similar situations. Many did not reach a happy ending in this life. Every experience becomes a memory to be carried through life and I feel that every act of human compassion and love will never die as long as there is a human memory to cherish it. I had just returned from Ethiopia when tragedy struck Khartoum, Sudan, by flooding. The slums and shanty towns were the worst hit areas. Again the powerful media photography touched me.

I packed my bags, repeated my vaccinations, and arrived in Khartoum, Sudan. Here I worked with the displaced people ten kilometres north of the city. It was a refugee camp situation – a feeding and medical unit. Hundreds of people, the poorest of the poor, attended daily, each person with their own anguish and story to tell. With the limited resources available in a desert slum, the rampant disease and starvation shocked and saddened me. Although we did the best we could for these people, it never seemed to be enough. Many children were dying daily from severe dehydration and tropical diseases. I remember vividly a mother putting her twelve-month infant into my arms. The infant looked at me with big glassy helpless eyes and took its last breath of life. I shed a tear, and many people gathered around me. The mother said 'Do not cry, it is the will of Allah.'

The people of the Horn of Africa whom I worked with had a quiet inner dignity. Their values seemed to be more in place than the values of the affluent. Their grinding poverty had deprived them of everything except an inner peace. They knew what was important in life. I felt that in the midst of the daily blood, sweat, and tears, it was so easy to become consumed by the endlessness and helplessness of it all. I forgot these feelings when children would gain weight, stand for the first time in months, learn to smile and play again. The pain and suffering for these was over. Optimism and hope would eventually overtake the negative feelings. The world would feel warmer again. After a few months working in Africa, one clearly sees that despite the poverty and disease, the harsh climates, the extreme struggles, there is a wealth of self-acceptance. The simple joys and wonders fill their lives. To witness this is to witness their innocence and also their freedom – the freedom of happiness. In witnessing the patience, kindness and laughter that fills the tiny mud huts, I also feel that I'm witnessing the survival of faith. These people definitely had a level of self-understanding, self-possession, which was also their salvation in their harsh planet earth.

Over a year ago, the media brought the plight of the innocent victims of civil war and famine once again to our living rooms. It was the plight of the Somalian people.

Testing of faith

While I was working in Somalia my faith was tested many times. All wars shed the blood of the innocent, all war becomes morally wrong. Intolerance and discrimination against people of different colour, beliefs, political groups or creeds are so ugly. Amnesty International say that torture is used in more than a hundred countries worldwide. I saw at first hand the effects of a brutal civil war on innocent people. It was so obvious to see, after two years of brutality, the lack of compassion and of love for each other. Their homes, crops, animals and the little possessions they owned were looted; they fled, and they became refugees.

I often felt disillusioned and frustrated when so much aid and effort was wasted and misused by corrupt authorities. But when a child is starving does one withhold food to punish a corrupt government? Children of all ages, wandering alone in villages, orphaned, starving, are not interested in politics, religion, or strategies. They only want to be fed, to be warm, secure, and most of all loved. There can be no fear worse than being abandoned, unwanted, nowhere to go, that inevitably leads to a degrading and humiliating death, dumped upon a human rubbish heap.

Many of the children who survive war and famine will always be afraid. I have fond memories of the many orphans whom I cared for. With time and patience, we may be able to heal some of their wounds. When the children were admitted to the orphanage they were frightened. Their faces were expressionless. With time, they gradually became like real happy playful children. It was clear to see that it was not our medicine or food or clothing that was of importance to them, but to be touched, rocked, hugged and kissed. This was an essential part of their daily diet. This was the way forward in their salvation and survival in their part of the world.

Of course, many did not survive. Adults and children in the Horn of Africa die from what in Mayo would be a quickly cured illness. A young girl can lie in agony for weeks, dying from simple bed-sores because they have become so severe that her entire skin structure has broken down. She screams at each dressing change, because there is no pain relief available. After a time you don't hear her; you can't or your heart would break from her terrible pain, and her hopeless fight to live.

And there are wounds from bullets and mines; horrific wounds that tear apart limbs and gut and heads. It is so easy for us to accept a shooting. We say it quickly, just as we say he died on the cross quickly, and it is as if it was over as quickly. We talk of his death so ritualistically, but it was a living torture. We talk of Africans being killed by bullets so blandly, but their dying is so often hours of unspeakable agony. To watch a child die in such horror, where you have no drug except prayer to ease their suffering, is as much the test of aid work as to reflect on the suffering of Christ is a test of our faith.

Survival of faith and people in this part of the Horn of Africa is difficult because of human weaknesses. I believe that by seeing what is good in all people, and by letting our kindness and care shine out, that we will overcome evil. Many people in Somalia whom I met, whom I worked with, thanked me for showing them my care, and for travelling from Ireland to help them in their time of great need. I have always hoped and prayed that in those lives I touched briefly, that something they may have seen, may have shown them something of faith. This may one day allow for the survival of faith among these people.

In the midst of such suffering, joy seems to dance more visibly among the poor than in the avenues of the rich. Perhaps this is also their way in surviving a very poor world. I cannot stop wars, I cannot feed everybody, but perhaps I can and did change myself, and brought some joy into my little corner of the world. Mother Theresa was asked if her work in the slums of Calcutta was not a futile and hopeless waste of effort, just a drop in the ocean. 'Perhaps,' she replied, 'but it is my drop, my humanity. Nothing is hopeless.'

Back in Mayo

But when I returned to Mayo from fieldwork in the Horn of Africa I felt saddened by the lack of genuine interest in the other culture and its people. People will listen for a few minutes, and make comments on how interesting the people look. Soon the conversation returns to local update. *Neighbours* and *Coronation Street* are spoken about with such passion and enthusiasm that one returns home wondering if Africa and Mayo are the worlds of illusion and imagination, while Ramsey Street represents reality.

The acceptance of Ramsey Street and pub life as the only reality goes hand in hand with the acceptance of Mayo's problems of unemployment, emigration, alcohol abuse, pursuit of the material interest. Recognition and acceptance of another culture might result in recognition that there are other ways of life, and if there are other ways then perhaps there is another and better way for Mayo. When Mayo people begin to take a genuine interest in the lives and challenges facing other Christians in far off lands, it will be an indication that Mayo is ready to take charge and to change its destiny so that the next generation can know a life of hope and promise and ensure survival of faith. I still have faith in the words of Martin Luther King:

> I have the audacity to believe that peoples everywhere can have three meals a day for their bodies, education and culture for their minds, and dignity, equality, and freedom for their spirits. I believe that what self-centred men have torn down other-centred men can build up. I still believe that one day mankind will bow before the altars of God and be crowned triumphant over war and bloodshed, and non-violent redemptive goodwill will proclaim the rule of the land. And the lion and the lamb shall lie down together, and

every man shall sit under his own vine and fig tree, and none shall be afraid.

I believe that we shall overcome.

CHAPTER 13

The Prayer, the Poetry and the Praxis: A missionary in Latin America

Suzanne Ryder

Ver, juzgar, actuar: to reflect on reality, to weigh it up and to do something about it, is the essential rhythm of 'doing' theology in Latin America. It seems to me akin to the melody of my given title. Like the *Ver, juzgar, actuar* principle, each step of Prayer, Poetry and Praxis flows into the next, no one part being separate from its neighbour. As the aftermath of action is the occasion for reflection, praxis too calls us to pray.

Prayer, in my Latin American experience, is active and alive. It has flesh and blood, sight and sound, even its own smell. Poetry is everyday. It is in the drama, the aside, the juxtapositioning of the apparent and the true. It is written on the blank face of poverty and heard in the deafening silence of the Andes. And then the Praxis: the doing, the trying to change or at least affect the experienced reality. This is what puts us *entre la espada y la pared*, between the wall and the sword. From here, where can we go – if not to our knees?

Many missionaries go to Latin America. On arrival they are stripped of language, culture and identity itself. The landscape is entirely new. This is the first pain. But later, if we are honest, a far deeper pain is to realise that we carry within us prisons of prejudice, reams of racism, and the most well disguised of all diseases, goodwill – that desire to fix up everything and everyone – recreating all in sight into our own myopic image.

My own hope is that the person arriving in Latin America from the Irish experience, and in particular coming from a place like Mayo, can grapple with such mindsets in a special and creative way. S/he knows many faces of poverty from personal experience as well as from the collective and historic experience of our people. So that when plans come to nought and dreams disappear, that person is in a unique position to *accompañar*, to really 'stand with' the oppressed. And it is only from such a stance of openhanded powerlessness, that any real and longterm future can be seen.

Prayer

Señor de los Milagros,	*Lord of the Miracles,*
a ti venimas en procesión	*to you we come in procession,*
tus fieles devotos,	*your devoted followers,*
a implorar tu bendición.	*to implore your blessing.*
Faro que guía, da a nuestras almas,	*Light that guides, give to our souls,*
la fe, esperanza, la caridad;	*faith, hope, charity;*
tu amor divino nos alumina	*may your divine love enlighten us,*
nos haga dignos de tu bondad.	*and make us worthy of your goodness.*
Con paso firme de buen cristiano	*With the firm step of a good christian*
hagamos grande nuestro Perú;	*may we make our Peru great;*
y unidos todos como una fuerza	*and all united in one strength*
te suplicamos nos des Tu luz.	*we beg you to give us your light.*

Even as I write the words of this hymn to the 'Lord of the Miracles', a painting that survived earthquakes and human attempts to destroy it, its plaintive chant and tinny accompanying music echo in my ears. I can see the small, devoted crowd around one of its many replicas: those chosen to carry it, walking in that distinctive sway of slaves in chains, in honour of its first followers. And I can smell incense, candles and a profusion of flowers. By verse three, I am enjoying this great Lord bowing in greeting to an altar or a statue on its path: one part of me smiling at the seemingly ludicrous sight but another part bowing too in respect for a people whose instinct it is to ritualise their faith along their own streets of sand.

As I translate the words, unable to be faithful to their full content, I myself am translated to the May procession and the Corpus Christi taking to Ballinrobe streets (if it doesn't rain!). 'Faith of Our Fathers' (dating to pre-inclusion days) and 'Sweet Heart of

Jesus' echo in my head as I can almost reach out for some honey-suckle to sweeten my path and bow in front of other altars, also decked with finest cloth, holy picture and over-flowing vase of flowers.

Prayer in Peru is not all ritual, chant and blind faith, but it is about miracles. Once when I was facilitating a group of adults preparing for sacraments, I introduced with some trepidation the miracle of the loaves and fishes, for reflection. I felt myself foolhardy in the context of such hunger but, as always, was deeply touched by the way the scriptures are alive in the stories of the poor. Each person there had had some experience related to the gospel miracle. The most memorable came from a woman who works in a *comedor*, a place of communal cooking. On the mornings, she said, when there was not enough rice, she and her companion prayed over the pot. Her friend, she explained, was not a Catholic – but each prayed to her own God! Someone always heard and they always had rice to spare.

Had I ever heard such stories before in my native land – or is it that I am more sensitive to hearing them now? I recall the woman from Ballintubber, speaking of Mass being celebrated in the roof-less Abbey without the candles ever being blown out. And I re-member stories of famine-struck homes being visited by priests who in fact had never left their beds. And then from early pend-ent crutches on a church gable in Knock to more recently aband-oned wheelchairs and stretchers, I realise that our tradition too, is one of the miraculous.

The cross and the sword came to Latin America together, some five hundred years ago. Christianity is therefore a relatively re-cent phenomenon and occurred hand-in-glove with destruction, slavery and genocide. Since its first appearance, because of the in-fluence of such people as Bartolomé de las Casas[1] in the early days and the liberation theologians of today, the cross has been re-grounded in the message of its original bearer. It has separated from structures of power and has come to give hope to the most marginalised.

Because of its short history and the violence of its imposition, Christianity in Latin America has a curious blend of the pre-Christian in its traditions. Water is the vital element of any bene-diction. Statues came to church to *escuchar las misa* – to 'hear

Mass.' There is a *Virgen de Huancayo* and a *Virgen de Guadalupe*, a *Señor de Huacho* and a *Señor de Muruhuay*; as devotees seem more aware of their place of origin than the fact that they are all faces of the one virgin and the one Lord.

As such customs jar on the missionary's psyche, they can also challenge us to re-appreciation of our own Christian adaptations, from the druidic path which underlies Tóchar Phádraig from Ballintubber to the Reek, to the Celtic Cross which encompassed pre-Christian worship of the sun. The shamrock, holy wells and holy mountains, in their turn, call us to climb to the temple of the sun in *Pachacámac*,[2] to lament the tearing apart of *Sacsahuamán* by the Spanish so they could build their churchs in *Cuzco*, and to remind the recently urbanised Peruvian of *Pachamama* – Mother Earth.

Above all, the missionary is challenged to ground her/his prayer in the fertile earth of human suffering. To witness the shaming of a person because of skin colour, to listen to a woman tell of her children's hunger, to stand by the coffin of a twelve-year-old boy who died because a simple infection was not cared for on time; all of these experiences prevent us from being neutral at prayer. A new-born baby covered in flea bites, an eight-year-old boy earning his living by selling sweets on the street, a young woman raped on the bus home and an old man bent over a rubbish dump collecting 'valuables', make us cry out with a new voice to our God, following the injunction from Lamentations 2:1a:

> Up, cry out in the night-time, in the early hours of darkness;
> Pour your heart out like water before Yahweh.
> Stretch out your hands to him for the lives of your children.

And this prayer is perhaps best prefaced like the eucharist itself, with a plea for mercy and admission of guilt.

Poetry

Perú, país querido, ¿cómo hablar de ti?
¿cómo revelar tu rostro amado,
tu tierno cuerpo torturado,
tu eterno espiritu vibrante?

> *Peru, dear country, how can we speak of you?*
> *How can we reveal your beloved face,*
> *your tender, tortured body,*
> *your eternal, vibrant spirit?* [3]

Thus begins a poem, opening a drama prepared for a Caribbean and Latin American conference of Mercy Sisters in Jamaica, July 1992, on the theme of the 500 years of evangelisation in the Americas. Had it begun, 'Mayo, dear county ...' it could perhaps have set a Mayo 5,000 commemoration scene. We're not such strangers after all. The poet, somehow, writing of home is distanced from home, as Paul Durcan shares in his memories of trying to pass out the moon with his father in 1949.[4] So, too, is the missionary never quite at home again. 'Forget your own people and your father's house,'[5] is a necessary attitude in becoming enculturated on foreign soil. The curse of being hereafter a 'stranger in two lands' is a real experience. But in this very discomfort are the makings of poetry. Only in the going away can the coming back be fruitful. As T.S. Eliot writes:

> And the end of all our exploring
> will be to arrive where we started
> and know the place for the first time.[6]

Poetry is as much about suggestion as it is about the said. The more sparingly an image is pencilled, the farther can it travel in time and space, and the more perennial a chosen symbol, the louder can it reverberate in the well of human experience. Thus it was for me when, frustrated by many a shuffling offical or recalcitrant attendant, looking with hooded eye and blank face, my mind's eye saw the likes of Slipper in the *Irish RM* and my inner ear heard the word, 'Boycott'.

The juxtapositioning of such seemingly contrasting worlds as that of Mayo and Peru makes powerful poetry write itself. Mask-spiked limestone and Andean foothills both speak the same language of harsh survival. As our ancestors heard, 'To hell or to Connaught', debate flourished in Rome as to whether the 'Indios' had souls or not. And as the cadences of Irish are sung beneath the western tongue, so too are other neglected languages hidden in the speech of Latin America, from such sources as Quechua and Aymarra.

In the same spirit as the *aisling*, Andean culture tells its story in song and dance. The *Inkarri* myth[7] describes the decapitation of the Inca Atahualpa and looks to a future time when head and body will be reunited, signifying present disorder being restored to peace. Is this not reminiscent of 'The Four Green Fields'? And do such memories not let us in a back door to understanding, bringing us home once more to re-evaluate our own heritage, letting romanticism fall away and real inspiration for a better quality of life shine forth?

Poetry is also about the expression and preservation of values. This is another challenge to the missionary. The poor can enchant us, anger us, delight us, let us down with a bang and inspire us to great heights, all in the one day. But at the end of that day, the stars that shine on us whisper, that the poor, in spite of harsh circumstances, are, '*Lán dóchais is grá*.'

I have heard women, living in straw huts without water or electricity, talk about the rich. Some people, one woman said, are so rich they have two sets of clothes. Another countered that the rich are rich because they work so hard, forgetting that she herself had been up at 4am to draw water and prepare a communal breakfast. Surely the missionary must recite a poem to such women, of human dignity and of their own worth. I remember asking a different group what I should say about them on my first trip home. 'Say that things are hard here,' they said, recalling uncontrolled inflation, disease, scarcities and empty stomachs, 'but tell them too that we will never lose hope.' How much do we need to hear that poem in unemployed Ireland? And how often did I hear a loudspeaker calling out for help because a house had fallen in, someone was sick or someone had died? Each time, the widow's mite was gathered and multiplied. All the world needs to hear that epic verse, in which every line speaks of the generosity of the poor.

Mayo/Latin America – how can we speak of you? How can we not? All I know is that prose is not enough. And the missioned poet, called for a certain time to walk the earth, needs to alternate verses between worlds. In this way, the poetry need not be confined to paper but can become a powerful force to change the face of the earth, be it sand or limestone.

Praxis

December 1991 saw a world premiere, with the potential to rock the Irish missionary in Latin America or indeed any part of the globe. On the walls of a clinic in Trojillo, Northern Peru, was written the accusation, *Irlandeses Imperialistas*, 'Irish Imperialists'. Laughable isn't it? Or is it? *Sendero Luminoso*, the 'Shining Path', a neo-maoist, terrorist group has been wreaking havoc on Peru since 1980. There is no doubt of their being an anti-life group, as they have killed, left people homeless, forced migration and damaged everything from farming co-operatives and electric pylons, to the hearts and minds of the many children they enlist into their company. Yet, one indirect good that has come from *Sendero's* cruel arm is the type of criticism it makes of all things foreign.

I have always been proud to give my nationality as *Irlandesa*, while living in Latin America. It allows me to relate to the experience of a colonised people: the planter's estates linking with the *hacienda*, famine and workhouses giving one an inherited familiarity with cholera and typhoid, and then there's the living memory of TB, still uncontrolled in my country of adoption. Sometimes, however, this identification with another oppressed people can blind us to our having learnt best from the oppressor – how to oppress others ourselves.

Sendero Luminoso makes two major criticisms of the Catholic Church and the foreigner: that we create dependency, and that we impose our own solutions on what are not our problems. While they themselves destroy any independence their own people have created, and have tried to force their own imported programme on Peru, I believe that we still need to examine our consciences with regard to the theory of their criticism.

The world is big and Ireland is a small island, but somehow as a race we have managed to spread ourselves far and wide. With some amusement at a Latin American Mercy Conference some years ago, I noticed that among the Argentinian sisters were names like Marta Barry and Annie Maguire. On another occasion in an international group, the only person who knew all the words of, 'When Irish Eyes Are Smiling', was a pure blooded indigenous woman from Belize, educated by Irish sisters, and it was Patrick Anthony, a black man from Santa Lucia, another small island, this time in the Caribbean, who was the expert on Irish step-dancing, thanks to the Irish Presentation brothers.[8]

Family names, song and dance – all neutral elements you might say. And perhaps they are. Cross-cultural exchange must be a bearer of new life. But the singer who is deaf to another's music, and the dancer who performs only to her or his own movement, can remain shuttered in a Celtic twilight, never being open to the breaking of a new dawn. When caught in a handout syndrome, when making decisions 'for' rather than 'with', when organising what we perceive as chaos into what we consider order, when rushing in for efficiency's sake rather than waiting for God's sake, the praxis of the missionary in Latin America can still look good to the admiring eye, but be lacking in cultural sensitivity and long term development plans.

When, however, we allow our memories of bog lands to slow us down to the tempo of our new-found homes; when we turn our anger, first kindled against a landlord class, to stand with the poor in their struggle for their justice; when we grapple with our own feelings of inferiority, learning how to understand and therefore forgive – perhaps then we can really stand creatively beside our new friends – respecting both them and ourselves; sharing the one breath – true conspirators! As far as that happens, *Sendero* cannot criticise us, but will be challenged by us. The poor will not be made uncomfortable by our presence but can welcome us on their own terms. We ourselves will be free to pray and write poetry, as our praxis will be in rhythm with our ideals.

Last Gifts

On my last trip home from Peru, my suitcase went astray in Cuba. I was asked to fill out a claims form in Shannon and make a general list of its contents. Exhaustion pushed an automatic button in me somewhere and I began to rhyme out: clothes, books, tapes, handcrafts … But another part of me knew that all these items were as nothing in comparison to what I also carried in my case, low on any monetary scale but high in sentimental value.

There was a rosary, each bead a white, plastic heart. Sara, the fifteen-year-old girl who gave it to me, had received it for her first communion and it was one of her few treasures. Her mother María had cried with me, the whole of one morning as I sat in the house's only chair and listened to her story. She had been raped as a young girl. Because of the shame she felt, she had not struggled or cried out. From her violation she became pregnant and gave birth to her first child, a son. María's mother had also been raped and her daughter Sara had been sexually assaulted as a child. Three generations – was it to be an unbroken cycle María pondered – fate, doom, a now unavoidable part of their family history?

As I heard María out, I recognised the story of Latin America: violation after violation, one generation shamed, the next feeling inferior and setting the scene for the third, minus identity, to be again exploited. A horrible self-fulfilling prophecy had been set in motion after so called 'discovery', half a millenium previously. Peru has had political independence since 1826 and boasts a national anthem beginning, *Sommos libres*, 'We are free'; but as is apparent in María's story as in the lowered head of the *cholo*[9] – real, longlasting freedom is far from the Latin American reality as yet.

I don't pray the rosary very much but I do pray for Sara and for all the generations of Latin America. I pray that I might see the wounds behind what can come across as stubborness, lack of initiative or apathy. I pray for the rapists, that they might act beyond their anger and learn to heal themselves rather than hurt others. And I pray for the daughters still untouched, that a new world might be theirs.

***

The first place I used to visit in Lima was a mass of straw huts, smiling children in ragged clothes, and women and men who know all about struggle. To pass in there, an open sewer had to be crossed and I always had to be careful to be gone by sundown, as there was no electricity and it would have been dangerous to have travelled home in the dark. There I found a people who could walk above life's problems, true survivors; there I made many friends, my salvation.

Naturally, I visited there again, when saying goodbye to Peru. One home that I entered had one room and a corral, enclosing place for dogs and chickens. The animal smells were heavy but the human smiles were wide. She had made some lemonade and I drank tentatively from the offered glass. Then he disappeared into the one room, only to emerge with a gift. It was a three inch statue of San Martín de Porres, complete with broom.

Was this not poetry, profound with meaning? An image of that black saint, given by a poor man, rich in generosity, to an errant creature so wrapped up in 'civilisation' as to be wary of warm hospitality. I finished the lemonade and bade my tearful farewell. But the verses of that lovely poem continue with me, urging me to give my all too.

***

Luggage I could have lost to Castro as my material memorabilia needed physical transportation, but my third treasured gift was not in my baggage. Now I write of attitudes and questions. Never again can I hear people referred to as 'black', 'coloured' or 'natives', without seeing the faces of Clotilde, Juana or Martín. Neither can I read the term 'Third World' without recognising so many different wealths of culture, so many varieties of national realities – worthy of being named – rather than being lumped together. And never can I forget that poverty is an evil we need to purge from our earth.

How I translate these awakenings into life in Mayo I have yet to see. It is one thing to live among people of various colours in Latin America but quite another to be so called forth from my racism, that I can return to my own country and meet members of the travelling culture on equal terms. I could live in peace with pre-Christian symbols in Peru – but can I also live peacefully among Christians of other tones at home, from the non-Catholic to the Catholic excluded from practice? And as a person acceptable in the higher echelons of Peruvian society by reason of my colour, and among the poor by reason of my profession, how now can I hear the cry of the poor within my own society, risking the loss of approval and status? How deep really is the praxis of my conversion, I wonder? Can my metanoia withstand the crash-landing of the missionary at place of origin?

A Final Word

Ver, juzgar, actuar is a positive spiralling rhythm on this earth. Its southern seeds can root in chasms of prayer, grow poetically through cross-cultural fertilisation and flower eventually into worthwhile praxis. Hopefully, the missionary in Latin America can be free enough to give space for this happening. And hopefully, that same missionary can have sense enough to know that the survival of that great continent does not depend solely on her or his personal contribution to its salvation.

Notes

1. Bartolomé de las Casas (1514-1566) was a Spanish Dominican who came to Latin America in 1522. At first, like the churchmen of his time, he was a slave owner. However, he was soon to undergo a total conversion and came to campaign vehemently for the rights of the indigenous. His thinking has been written about extensively by Gustavo Gutierrez in *En Busca De Los Pobres De Jesucristo* (In Search of the Poor of Jesus Christ), CEP, 1992. Gustavo Gutierrez himself is a leading liberation theologian and lives in Lima, Peru.

2. Pachacámac and Sacsahuamán are sites of Incan places of worship. Cuzco was the Incan administrative centre, the word itself meaning 'navel'. Its official spelling is now 'Qosqo'.

3.Written by Lily Ferrero, a Peruvian Mercy sister, this poem is unpublished.

4. 'Going Home to Mayo, Winter 1949', from *The Selected Paul Durcan*, 62, The Blackstaff Press, 1982.

5. Psalm 45:106

6. From *Four Quartets* by T. S. Eliot, 48, Faber and Faber, 1979 edition.

7. Reference from *Buscando Un Inca*, by Alberto Flores Galindo, 48, Editorial Horizonte, 1988.

8. For a more detailed history of Irish involvement, see *Ireland and Latin America*, Peadar Kirby, Trócaire with Gill and Macmillan, 1992.

9. The term *cholo* refers to Latin American indigenous people. It can be a derisory label but is used here with affection.

CHAPTER 14

Emigration: Tragedy or Challenge?

Padraic Brennan

1. An Ongoing Experience

Trains stop running

The scenes of tearful grief as young boys and girls left in droves from Charlestown railway station were now no more. By the early sixties, our only contact with that experience was in the reminiscences of an older generation still reliving the pain of it all. Fellow townee John Healy immortalised that chapter of our history in *No One Shouted Stop*. Home after home had closed down. The trains had run and run, carrying our youth away. In the end they ran themselves out of a job. Empty trains told their own story. There was hardly anyone left to go. The trains stopped coming. In summer even the day on the bog saving turf seemed longer. No more was the time broken by the occasional noise of a train thundering round by Ardara Hill and through the lowlands of Sonnagh – something which always gave an excuse to look up and straighten an aching back for a few minutes. The once busy station became silent and empty, overgrown with grass and weeds. The deserted crumbling station house stood as a grim reminder of a town and hinterland bled dry of its youth.

Car to Shannon

All this was history by the time I began to take much notice. For me the pain of emigration was felt in a different setting. The car to Shannon airport had replaced the train to Dublin and Cobh. The parting point for aging parents had moved from the local station to the gable wall of an old thatched or galvanised cottage. Family came on holidays that almost from day one seemed to be rushing to their end. The joy of having them home again was always tempered by the thought of another heartbreaking separation soon to follow. The fact that many of the sons and daughters were now in their forties and their parents in their seventies or eighties added a new dimension to the pain of saying goodbye. Each parting carried with it the increasing possibility that there might never be another meeting. The anguish and tears of a mother, now more than three score and ten, and the silent pain etched in the face of an equally aging father, were a grim reminder that emigration was a painful part of life for many even until their dying day.

Brief respite

The seventies gave a brief respite. Joining the EU for a time brought new prosperity to the farming community. This coupled with significant growth in the industrial sector prompted over a quarter of a million people to return to Ireland in the hope of finding a better life there. Mayo got its share of this new influx. Many young couples came back with their families to the towns and countryside of the county. To take just one example: by the mid seventies a national school in the rural parish of Killasser could boast that one third of its children were born outside Ireland. This was not untypical of what was happening in other parishes around Mayo at the time.

Old cycle returns

The 'boom times' did not last long. By 1983 personnel working with the emigrant agencies in London knew a new generation was on the move. For the first time in over a decade, young Irish faces were evident in significant numbers at the old Irish haunts round the city. Mingled among them were some of the old faces who had returned to Ireland ten or fifteen years before. They were back, their dream of 'making a go of it' at home shattered. A worsening economic situation there had squeezed them out again, leaving them with no alternative except to look for work elsewhere.

Back home, politicians played down the extent of emigration for as long as they could. To admit it would be to admit the failure of their economic policies. By the late eighties there was, however, no denying the reality. The long rising wave of emigration was in full flood. 'Kiltimagh Diaspora', an indepth survey carried out on past pupils of two Kiltimagh second level schools, showed that by the end of 1988 38% of young people in the age group 18 to 25 were now living outside Ireland.

The old cycle of emigration of the forties and fifties was back to haunt us. Yes there were certain differences. The new focal point for emigration was Knock Airport. There for many the parting kisses and tears were shared. The ease and speed of travel now and the falling cost of fares relative to earnings at work meant families had the possibility of re-uniting more frequently and quickly than before. More young people were better educated now and as a result, it was felt, better prepared for what lay ahead. Amidst the pain of parting, these factors were some consolation for families. But standing watching the farewells at the airport, on a bleak dark evening at the end of Christmas week, one sensed that the trauma and pain of saying goodbye was still basically the same as ever.

Education myth

As for education, there was an oversimplified public preception of the real situation. An awareness that we were losing many of 'the cream' of our third level graduates to overseas firms left a kind of impression that all our emigrants were now highly educated. It was often overlooked that many of our emigrating youth were still, by today's standards, early school leavers. The Kiltimagh survey showed this to be especially true of the boys who left. Of the boys from the survey sample who made their way to London, 45% were found not to have spent any more than three years in second level education.

Given that they had not the ambition to go any further with their education, most of these would likely be leaving from the weaker stream of pupils, who either through lack of ability or motivation were finding second level education particularly difficult. Not surprisingly they found life equally difficult on the streets of London. Welfare agencies working with the Irish in the city found it was the unskilled early school leavers who were most at risk and most likely to be unable to cope. It could be argued that these unskilled recent Irish emigrants are in some ways even less prepared for what faces them than were their counterparts in the forties and fifties. Then at least most of them coming off the land were no strangers to hard manual work. Today many of them hardly know what it is to hold a shovel in their hand.

Cultural Shock

At the other end of the ladder it is important not to assume that a good education necessarily makes emigration an easy experience.

Obviously it opens up better employment prospects and equips an emigrant with skills to cope better both socially and in the marketplace. But this does not prevent most new emigrants from experiencing 'cultural shock' on being thrown into a totally new cultural situation far from home. Cultural shock is something not easily defined but something deeply and often painfully felt. There is a sense of displacement and a feeling that no one cares or notices you as you move through a sea of ignoring faces. In strange surroundings, where past experiences and the familiar things of home count for nothing, it is easy to feel you have left the best part of yourself behind. Robbed of the old supports of family, friends and accustomed way of life, your sense of self worth is threatened. Loneliness can easily give way to a sense of alienation and even depression.

Needs of emigrants

At home emigration is often seen in terms of the loss to a family, the local community or the country. After the initial painful parting is over the needs of emigrants themselves can easily be forgotten. We overlook that the first weeks and months can be an especially vulnerable time for them. John Healy raised the question, how come no one tried to stop them going? I ask, who gives a damn about them once they are gone? Close family will keep in touch with letters and maybe phone calls. After that who cares? The question of emigration always seems to be translated into a question about the 'shame' and 'awfulness' of so many leaving. We seem incapable of dwelling on what happens the other side of the Atlantic Ocean or Irish Sea.

Nowhere was that more evident than in the reaction to the Kiltimagh emigration survey. The immediate focus was on what can we do to stop our community dying. Ignored was the challenge to help our emigrants live. The fact that the main emphasis in the comments at the end of the survey was on the need for greater state and church support for our emigrant services abroad was overlooked. The ongoing failure since then of successive Irish governments to increase significantly their financial support for emigration welfare services to help those most at risk, underlines that attitudes have not changed much over the years. All this is not to deny the importance or significance of the local response in Kiltimagh to the survey, of which more will be said later. It is to suggest however that the urgent need to put effort into trying to give more of our young people the opportunity to stay at home should not cause us to forget our obligations to those who are now away in another land.

2. The Wider Context

Emigration, part of human experience

Despite its attending trauma, emigration is not to be viewed as something essentially negative or as something peculiar to the Irish situation. On the contrary, it can be argued that from the beginning the phenomenon of emigration has had a natural place in human history. The Irish experience of emigration, so much a part of life in Mayo, must therefore be seen in the context of the total human experience. Because emigration is essentially a painful experience locally, it is often seen as tragic. However the pain of parting can become for many the gateway to growth, development and achievement in a new world. The history of the human race is very much a history of the movement of peoples. The God-human dialogue began with the challenge 'fill the earth and subdue it'. This implies a call to 'move out'. It presents a dynamic picture of a people challenged to reach out, explore, control and transform their God-given world.

Economic factors

This vision of humanity could not be realised if all stayed at home. The nature of the human condition ensured this would not happen. The human need for sustenance alone made it totally impractical that people would all stay in the one place. A growing community cannot indefinitely eat out of 'the one field of potatoes'. So the basic human need to find food, clothing and shelter was from the beginning a great driving force in pushing people to explore new frontiers. The jargon of today would describe this lever of human movement as 'economic necessity'.

Violence and oppression

The physical violence of war and political oppression is the second great factor in the upheaval and movement of peoples. The human conscience is scarred with the memory, and unfortunately in so many places the present reality, of the intense pain and suffering caused by this kind of violence. Most peoples can trace some part of the reason 'why they are where they are' to this kind of force.

The displacement of peoples caused by such violence may be direct, as when those lucky enough to survive are chased out by force of arms. Alternatively an oppressive regime may so control resources that whole sections of the community are so deprived and miserable that they are forced to leave. In situations like this the human violence of some in effect makes emigration an 'economic necessity' for others.

Nature of the human spirit

The third great catalyst in the movement of peoples is the nature of the human spirit itself. Given the kind of beings we are, it is part of growing up and finding our own identity that we leave the family nest. Most of us feel the need for independence and space to mature and make a life for ourselves. As soon as a child can crawl, it wants to explore the world outside of its parents' home. The process begins there. As the years go by, the world of discovery widens out to school, community and the odd short excursion further afield. By the late teens, the dreams of youth beckon the human spirit to wider horizons. Call it what you will, an instinct, an urge or a restlessness inside, there is a compulsion to 'move out and on' to a new life.

This may manifest itself as a quest for freedom or a sense of adventure that drives one to explore and hopefully master foreign places. It may be ambition and the hope of better opportunities elsewhere that tempt a break with home. For others it may express itself as a call or challenge to respond to some perceived human cause or need in another land. In one form or another there is a dynamism towards outward mobility at work in the emerging young man or woman.

Destiny of many to move

Given all these forces from the world outside and the psyche within, it was and is the destiny of many people to move from the place of their birth. These forces work together repeatedly causing new movements of peoples both within and across national boundaries. The journey may be short for some: down the road or into a nearby town or village. For others it may be further afield but of a temporary or transitory nature. In the past this could be on a

seasonal job, a trading trip or military service. More commonly today it could be on some study or training course, short term work
experience or holiday job.

Then there are others who go for a few years 'to get it out of their
system'. These are the ones who feel they might be missing something the other side of the world but quickly decide that for them
there is no place like home after all. If the opportunity is there
they will return. For many more there is no permanent home coming. They make a life for themselves as best they can in a new
world. Some are happy with their lot. Others are reluctant emigrants.

Biblical experience

The history of salvation as it unfolds in the word of God itself car-
ries in it a recurring strand of migration and emigration. Abra-
ham, the father of the chosen people, is described in the bible as 'a
wandering Aramaean'. In those nomadic times so fluid was the
movement of peoples in the world of the bible lands that the concept of having a stable homeland was but a dream of the future –
'a promised land' yet to be discovered. Peoples moved with the
seasons, fighting and jostling with each other round 'the fertile
crescent' in search of food for themselves and grass for their
flocks.

The most significant faith-formative event in the history of the
chosen people before Christ was the Exodus experience. It is
worth reflecting that this was born out of an 'emigration experience'. The great escape out of slavery in Egypt had its origins in
the movement of a people to that land centuries before in search
of food. Hunger brought them in. Oppression drove them out.
This mirrors in reverse what has happened in the west of Ireland
since the middle ages. The violence of armed forces pushed a people west often onto poor and barren land. 'To hell or to Connaught' was the order of the day. Since the famine they continue
to be driven out again, this time by 'the violence of economics'.

The church experience

Another emigration experience was at the heart of the early
spread of Christianity. Persecution of early Christians gave rise to
a 'new diaspora'. Under threat of imprisonment or death they fled
and brought the faith with them. This particular emigration event

highlights the ambiguity that can be part of the emigration experience. What began in fear, suffering and hardship and caused so much upheaval and disruption in the life of Christian communities, in the end was a powerful force in their spread and growth elsewhere, as dispersed Christians regrouped in new and often faraway places, and proceeded to evangelise those around them.

The great waves of emigration from Ireland in the last and present centuries are not without their own ambiguity. Often 'their going looked like a disaster'. There was no escaping the pain and heartbreak involved. But the story does not end there. It is true, unfortunately, that there were and are casualties who never got over the initial shock or otherwise failed to adjust in a meaningful way to life in a new land. On the positive side, however, there were many who found fulfillment and not a few who excelled themselves in making a contribution to the well being of their adopted country. Like the dispersed early Christians, the dispersed Irish have made a big impact in building up the faith community in England and the North American continent. This is apart altogether from the major contribution made by Irish missionaries who went abroad specifically to serve the spiritual and material needs of other peoples.

Emigration, a fact of life

We have looked briefly at a few of the many emigration experiences woven into salvation history. Any secular history book of significance will offer similiar instances of emigration. Indeed hardly a day goes by that does not feature new stories of emigration in some part of the world. Whether it be war or famine, the lure of riches elsewhere or the idealism of a mission call, people are always on the move. Be it by force or choice, emigration is a fact of human life all over the world.

3. Towards a response

Facing the truth

The Irish experience of emigration is therefore not exceptional. Yet we often act as though it is. We find it hard to come to terms with it as a reality. Indeed to talk about it as such is likely to be seen as treason or at best defeatist. The suggestion that emigration might continue indefinitely to be part of the Irish experience is interpreted as encouraging its acceleration. Yet I believe this must be our starting point if there is to be any kind of mature response to the emigration question. Emigration and the problems and difficulties it gives rise to will not go away simply by shouting it should not be there. It is only in facing the truth of emigration that we can hope to recognise and meet the challenge it presents both at home and abroad.

Emigration education

That truth must first be faced in the schools. At the risk of appearing to encourage an emigration mentality, my suggestion is that preparation for emigration be made an integral part of second level education. The fact is that at least a third, and in many instances more than half, of any sizeable class group in the west of Ireland are likely to find themselves at least temporary emigrants. Our youth therefore need to be well informed on the challenges, difficulties and adjustments, both psychological and emotional, that are part of the emigration experience. They need to be told also of the possible opportunities and be given clear practical guidelines on how to organise themselves in the event of deciding to emigrate. Educated thus they might later be spared a lot of unnecessary anxiety and trouble at a demanding and often painful time of transition in their lives.

Need of a better support system for emigrants

Beyond the schools we need to focus on the needs of emigrants themselves. Of its nature, emigration is painful, involving as it does separation from family and friends and the place where you feel you belong. For an island people the sea opens a chasm between us and our loved ones abroad which adds an extra edge to that pain. The ones left behind at least are on familiar home ground, still living within an accustomed life pattern. As well as the pain of parting, first time emigrants have to deal with a totally new culture and all the changes that brings.

A major concern therefore must surely be helping them to adjust to their new situation and providing them with the maximum backup support in the country to which they have gone. This means giving much greater financial support to information, advisory and counselling services for emigrant Irish people. It means also putting much more resources into the provision of temporary accommodation for those without a place to live or who might be otherwise at risk.

The task is made that bit easier in that despite the high levels of emigration most of it is still to the same few traditional places. The Kiltimagh emigration survey showed that, in keeping with past tradition, almost two thirds of all emigration in the eighties was to London or the greater London area. Proper support services in this city alone would therefore be within reach of well over half our emigrants. Among other things, it is an obvious place to establish an Irish Housing Trust to build up a bank of accommodation that would be available at reasonable cost to Irish emigrants. Initially funded out of the national budget, it should in time become self sustaining. It could be run by a board made up of government nominees and representatives from existing Irish welfare groupings already working in the city.

A handfull of cities in the USA account for another 25% of our emigrants. Adequate services here, in London and in a few pockets of Irish concentration on mainland Europe, would mean that close on 90% of all Irish emigrants would be within reach of meaningful help if needed.

The great challenge at home

The final great challenge of emigration is to try and create employment that will give more of our people the option of staying at home if they wish. Given the limited resources of the country, its geographical position *vis à vis* Europe and the rest of the world, it may be that we have to accept that recurring cycles of emigration will be part of the Irish experience well into the future. This does not stop us setting ourselves the goal of trying to provide a means of living for more of our people in Ireland.

There is for us in Mayo as elsewhere the challenge to try to consolidate what we have left and begin to expand our communities outward again. In the wake of the exodus of the fifties there was a perception that young people would not stay in a place like Mayo even if there were jobs in plenty. If nothing else, the short term boom of the seventies proved otherwise. Young and old came back in numbers, happy with the quality of life there, once they had some hope of making a living. That underlined that it is essentially a perceived lack of economic opportunity rather than social or other factors that is at the root of the recurring waves of emigration.

The word 'perceived' is used deliberately. We do not always seem to recognise the opportunities that are there, or if we do, we do not seem to have the initiative or courage to avail of them. It is not unknown for foreigners to come in and successfully develop a business idea that could have just as easily being taken up by a native. We may have one of the best educated young work forces in Europe. We can hardly say we have the most enterprising. There are of course inhibiting factors and constraints, not least financial, that militate against enterprise development. This however hardly fully explains the scarcity of enterprise initiative on the ground.

Fostering an enterprise culture

More thought needs to be given within the educational system itself to the question of fostering an 'enterprise culture'. A young work force that 'has done well' at exams is not enough. Equally we need a work force trained and geared to spot enterprise opportunities for themselves. We need to get away from the mentality that because we have qualifications and skills 'someone' owes us a job. We need more young people who can marry skills with a business idea and have the know-how, confidence, and courage to have a go at creating their own job. FÁS have been making brave efforts to develop educational modules for young people that would encourage this kind of initiative. Perhaps there is hope for the future here. However there is the difficulty that the more educated and talented, and so those who might have the best chance of successfully creating employment for themselves and others, still continue to go a largely academic route. There is need to build into both second and third level education at all levels an enterprise mentality and practical dimension.

Local enterprise companies give new hope

The emergence in Mayo in the late eighties and early nineties of local enterprise companies, whose goal is the promotion of economic development, marks a significant change in attitude and approach to Mayo's 'economic marginalisation'. It is indicative of a growing realisation that the best hope for a better future for our locality and county is dependent on our own initiative and efforts

in making the best use of local resources, skills and business opportunities. It also indicates a new recognition that, while voluntary effort is still vital, it is not on its own enough in face of the
long-term demands any worthwhile attempt at economic development will make on a community. These companies employ
fulltime executive staffs answerable to a company board and, between board meetings, to some form of steering committee.

They are integrated resource development companies (IRDs).
They act as catalysts in promoting enterprises in tourism, small
manufacturing or innovative service industries, and in the development of the natural resources of the area. They also play a part
in encouraging the development of infrastructural and amenity
facilities that would enhance the area and make it more attractive
for the economic ventures being undertaken. These companies
are funded by a combination of local fund raising, various grants
from state agencies and support from the private sector in the
form of the Enterprise Trust. The composition of the board normally has representation from each of these funding sources but
the local community has the main input.

The local enterprise companies introduce a 'bottom up' approach
to economic development, providing local communities with a
structure through which they can effectively co-ordinate local enterprise initiatives. They facilitate co-operation across parish and
local area boundaries in the exploitation of commonly shared development opportunities. They provide expertise and services to
both individuals and groups in the development of business
ideas. They are focal points helping to promote the 'enterprise
culture'.

The local enterprise companies act as an 'interface' between the
local community and state agencies such as FÁS, the IDA, Teag-
asc and the County Development Teams. Their presence, far from
duplicating the work of these agencies, has in fact made it more
effective. The companies are providing links and channels
through which the state agencies can relate to the local communities and become more involved in their development. In turn the
positive response of the state agencies to the local enterprise companies has contributed to their success to date.

It would be foolish to suggest that the problem of such high levels
of unemployment, with its attendant recurring waves of emigra-

tion, that has bedevilled Mayo and places like it, will be quickly
solved solely through the new local approach to economic development briefly described here. Such factors as the failure of the
banks to make seed capital more readily available for high risk
ventures, the disincentive to work and enterprise development inherent in the high levels of taxation presently operative in the
country, the large number of people operating out of the black
economy that partly contributes to the need for such high levels of
taxation for others, the disproportionate investment of public
funds on the east coast as opposed to the west, are among issues
that need to be addressed. Not withstanding these and other factors in the European and world economies totally outside our
control, I believe we have in the local enterprise companies of
Mayo a self-help vehicle for economic development that can make
a significant contribution to consolidating the 'remnant' of population still left in the county.

It is important that these companies be sustained and developed
further to cover the whole county. The level of community support and belief in them varies considerably from place to place. In
1989 the people of Kiltimagh put up £35,000 to launch their development company. Since then they have being contributing over
£30,000 per annum towards its ongoing operation. If Kiltimagh
can do it, any place can. As places go they do not come much
poorer. A pro rata response per head of population from every
other community in the county would raise over £1.5m annually
for development purposes. All it takes is a commitment of £2 per
week from those on a reasonable income and a little bit more from
the bigger businesses. This kind of investment, sustained over a
number of years together with the matching funds it could be
used to raise, would, if properly managed, make a major impact
on the Mayo economy. Whether this level of local funding is
achieved depends on what kind of belief and commitment there is
to developing the county among Mayo people themselves. It has
little to do with what most of us can afford but much to do with
what we are prepared to spend. More money goes out of the
county every year on lotto tickets alone than we are talking about
here.

There is need too for ongoing commitment to the 'bottom up'
strategy of the local enterprise companies at a higher level –

among the policy makers of the country. Europe strongly believes in the underlying philosophy of this approach. It is not always clear that the higher echelons of administration and government in Ireland do. One senses at times in certain quarters, a fear of losing control and lack of trust in the ability of local communities to make good use of funds put at their disposal for the purpose of building a better future for themselves. For too long, our country has been impoverished by a 'dependent mentality'. It would be tragic if now a more educated people, beginning to explore avenues through which to take responsibility for the betterment of their own locality, were hampered or thwarted by officialdom or politicians afraid to delegate. There is need for a courageous and visionary response at government level to properly managed local enterprise company initiatives in the form of backup funding and freedom to operate. It is always possible to have checking mechanisms in place to ensure that there is proper accountability for public funds used in such initiatives.

Challenge urgent and critical

The early nineties see a lull in emigration out of Mayo, more because of a recession abroad than because of any new great prosperity at home. It would however be naïve to expect that a time will not come when people will be on the move in numbers again. This, while inevitably painful for all concerned, can have positive reprecussions also, both for many of the people involved and the world at large. This must not stop us from striving to sustain and if possible increase population levels at home. The challenge to renew our local communities and re-activate some of their old vibrancy is urgent and critical. If we lose them we lose something we can never bring back. Recurring phases of emigration in future years from Mayo we can survive. The ultimate tragedy would be to end up with no one left to emigrate.

CHAPTER 15

The Talk Goes On:
Irish Culture in Europe and America

Andrew Greeley

Introduction

In November of 1992 I stood on a cliff outside of Ballycastle, nothing between me and the North Pole – from which the bitter winds were undoubtedly coming – except the Atlantic Ocean, pondering my own Irish and Mayo heritage.[1] Behind me in the mud and the rain were the Céide Fields where the first Mayo folk (who didn't know they were Mayo folk) lived five thousand years ago.

To my untutored eye, the foundations of the densely packed homes looked not unlike the abandoned stone homes of nineteenth century Mayo and even the rills in which seeds were planted looked like some of the rows I had seen in Mayo not twenty-five years ago.

But it was at least arguable that day in the Céide fields that someone with perhaps more than a touch of Celtic romanticism would think to himself, 'these people were my ancestors.'

Surely it does no harm to think so.

But if my proximate ancestors, and maybe even my remote ancestors, come from the Co Mayo, do I have any right to claim that I am a Mayo person? After all, my family (on both sides) have been in Yank-land for at least a century. Can there be any Mayo heritage or culture left after all that time? But am I not really a Yank[2] and is it not a bit of a pose, albeit a harmless one, to claim that I'm also Irish?[3]

Most Irish people give the impression that they could care less about my claim to be Irish and Mayo if it makes me happy. However, it is a claim that is not politically correct, I should think, on either side of the Atlantic. In the United States the hyphen in a hyphenated American is an equal sign, a way of dealing oneself into the America and not a way of distinguishing oneself from America. Moreover, it is part of the informal convenant which binds our diverse nation together, that everyone has the right to claim an ethnic heritage and no one is obligated to do so. Finally, if the multi-culturalists wish to exclude Irish and Irish American culture from their curricula (and they sure do), if they wish to dispense with the Book of Kells and John Scotus Eriugena and William Bulter Yeats and James Joyce and Eugene O'Neill and James T. Farrell and Seamus Heaney, well so much the worse for them.

Nonetheless a serious issue is at stake here. How much of a culture does in fact survive immigration, intermarriage, and a century of assimilation into a new society? Or to put the same issue differently: might it be that the Irish in Ireland and the Irish in America[4] have more in common with one another in certain matters than the former do with other Europeans and the latter do with other Americans?

If this be true, it does not follow that the two descendants of the Irish heritage are exactly the same, but it does follow that within the North Atlantic world, especially the English-speaking North Atlantic world, they are not entirely different either and that both have some legitimate claim on being Irish, each in their own way.

It does seem to me that such a claim is very modest indeed, but nonetheless it is one which is likely to be challenged on both sides of the moat which separates Long Island from the Blasket Islands.

Background of the research

There does seem impressionistically and anecdotally to be some similarities. Indeed in an exercise in which Professor William McCready and I once engaged we were able to make twenty-five accurate predictions (out of thirty-two attempts) about Irish Americans, based on social science research done in Ireland. However, to be certain about the similarities, one needs data from comparable survey instruments which were administered to both the Irish (and other Europeans) and Irish Americans (and other Americans). Data from the ongoing International Social Survey Program makes this comparison possible and it is on the basis of these data that I have written the present article.

Much of the research in recent years on ethnicity[5] has concentrated on ethnic intermarriage, ethnic identification, and the practice of ethnic customs − for example, Liberson and Waters (1986), Waters (1990). Alba (1990) has concluded that the ethnic groups are fading away and becoming merged in a 'Euro-American' group. While such thinking is certainly politically correct, it ignores the fundamental issue of white ethnic subcultures. Are the Jews, the Irish, and the Italians, for example, becoming like one another in values and behaviour? Are they abandoning the distinctive subcultures they have brought with them from Europe? The question is not whether they should abandon their differences but whether in fact they have abandoned them. Research on political styles (Greeley 1974, 1975) and alcohol use (Greeley, McCready and Theisen 1980) suggest that Alba is perhaps a little too hasty in homogenising these subcultures.

At a deeper level of discourse, the question is how durable are subcultures. To what extent do they survive acculturation, economic and educational success, intermarriage, and a decline in the saliency of subcultural identification? Are subcultural values and behaviours epiphenomena which are swept away by public education, university attendance, and the national mass media? Or are they based on tenacious norms which are acquired early in life and are passed on to subsequent generations equally early in life?

Moreover, should differences persist among subcultures despite assimilationist pressures, are these differences in fact residues of 'old world' culture or are they artifacts of the group's experience in the new country?

The questions first appear to be unanswerable when the subject is the established ethnic groups since systematic research did not exist on these groups at the time of their immigration to America. Perhaps the natural history of the assimilation, let us say, of Vietnamese immigrants can be traced, but it is too late to trace with rigorous data the story of the Irish or the Italians or the Scandinavians.

If, however, comparative data exist about American 'ethnics' and contemporaries in the land of origin, and if these data reveal that a knowledge of the values and behaviours of the population in the land of origin makes possible a verifiable prediction about the values and behaviours of the ethnics, then a case could be made for subcultural survival.

In such circumstances, the traits which survive would have to be quite durable since they would have resisted pressures for change in the years since immigration in both the country of origin and in the United States.

Until recently, such data have not been available. However, the International Social Survey Program (Zentralarchiv 1985 to 1991) makes possible such an exploration (Greeley 1991). Since the General Social Survey (Davis and Smith 1989) is the American vehicle for the ISSP, comparisons can be made between American 'ethnics' and their European cousins.

The Irish are a useful subject for the exploration of cultural survival. 85% of Irish Catholics[6] are third or fourth or higher order generation – 40% are fourth or higher order. Hence seven out of eight of those who identify in the General Social Survey as Irish and Catholic are the descendants of American-born parents or American-born grandparents. Most Irish Catholic families are descendants of immigrants who came before the beginning of this century. By the first decade of this century, Irish Catholic Americans had already surpassed the national average for college attendance of the college-age cohort. Irish Catholics are the best-educated and most financially successful of the gentile European ethnic groups (Greeley, 1976, 1976 bis, 1977). Their intermarriage rates are high (Hout 1991).

Moreover, the ancestors of contemporary Irish American Catholics left Ireland before many of the events which shaped that country's emergence as a nation – the Land League, the rise and fall of Parnell, the Easter 1916 Rising, the creation of the Irish Free State, the War of Independence and Civil War, the emergence of the Republic, the current strife in Northern Ireland,[7] and Ireland's membership of what is now called the European Union. One would expect that the Irish and the Irish Americans would have diverged greatly from one another in attitudes and values – save perhaps for their common adherence to Catholicism.

One therefore formulates two null hypotheses for this exercise:

1) There are no statistically significant differences between Ireland and the other modern North Atlantic nations in the ISSP.[8]

2) The American Irish will more closely resemble other Americans and the Irish will more close resemble other Europeans than the two Irish groups will resemble one another.

The diffuse research literature on Ireland, for example Arensberg and Kimbal (1965), Harris (1966), Humphreys (1966), (Messinger

(1969), Stivers (1976), Kennedy (1973), Clark (1975), McGreil (1977), and Foster (1989), tends to portray the country as archaic, rigid, fatalistic, and conservative – an agricultural, familial, and profoundly Catholic land in which ambition has been constrained by Catholic emphasis on life after death and by political and economic miseries. Hence one is led to expect, after a consideration of the ISSP items available for analysis,[9] that, should Ireland differ from the other countries in the Program, it would be on items which emphasise close family ties, suspicion of social change, opposition to new family values, and lower levels of work ethic.

One might also expect, on the basis of the literature, that there would be a high level of gregariousness among the Irish. They are often presented as a people who are good at talking, very good indeed, if not much else.

However, it is worth noting that more recent work (Ward and Greeley 1991) indicates a surprisingly high level of tolerance for diversity in Ireland. Moreover Kearney (1989) has recently suggested that it is a characteristic of the Irish mind that it is able to sustain in balance contrasting positions. 'A word,' Kearney quotes James Joyce, 'can mean two thinks.' Finally, Irish Americans have the second highest score (after Jewish women) on the NORC feminism scale. David Tracy (in classroom lectures) and Mary Maher (in personal conversation) have argued that an important characteristic of Irish culture is its playfulness – in its poetry, pub conversation, story telling, and relationship with children. Michael Hout (also in personal conversation) has suggested that Ireland is the best country in the world to be a child because Irish parents so enjoy playing with their children. Thus gregariousness and playfulness are two characteristics that one might expect to find in both the Irish and the Irish Americans if there is indeed a residual common culture.

How would such a residual common culture persist through a century in the United States? Peter Rossi, in an offhand remark several decades ago, suggested that distinctive sub-cultures are passed on unselfconsciously in the very early years of the socialisation process by which subtle but powerful expectations of the obligations of appropriate behaviours of intimate role opposites: what should a parent expect from a child, what should a child expect from a parent, an aunt, a cousin etc.

Analysis: Family Networks

The 1986 ISSP asked several questions about interaction with close family members – mother, father, brother, sister, son, and daughter. One would expect that the Irish would be more likely to live with, visit, live near, and be in frequent contact (by phone or mail) with such relatives.[10]

Since family relationships are the matrix in which personalities are shaped and heritages passed on, a similarity between the two groups in family networks would confirm that there is at least a modest cultural similarity between the two groups.

While I will try to keep this article free from extensive discussion of tables and charts, I must impose on my readers at least two tables to establish the core of my argument (pp 207-209). For my thesis of similarity to hold up, the correlations in the first row of Table 1 must indicate a statistically significant difference between the Irish and other Europeans; the correlations in the second row must not be negative (which would imply a decline with immigration); and the correlations in the third row must be positive and significant to establish a difference between the Irish and other Americans.

Thus (in the fifth row) the Irish are more likely to visit their mothers often (once a week or more) than are those from other countries (.07).[11] The Irish Americans are even more likely to visit their mothers (.07) and they are significantly different in this respect from other Americans (.06). [12]

Fourteen of the sixteen correlations in the first column are statistically significant. Only on matters of living near brothers and sisters are there no significant differences between Ireland and other countries. However, on four measures (phoning relatives) the Irish are less likely to be in contact than are others – perhaps because of the less extensive phone system and perhaps because of poverty (or a mixture of both). Thus they differ in the predicted direction from others in the sample on ten of the sixteen items.

In the second column the correlation measures the decline (or possible increase) attributable to immigration to the United States. On six of the sixteen indicators there is such a decline (minus sign) – living with relatives and visiting and living near one's father. Four of these decreases are statistically significant.

However, there are six statistically significant positive correlations in the second column, a correlation which indicates that the Irish Americans have a higher score on a variable which seems characteristically Irish – four of the six, all substantial, appearing on the subject of frequent phone contact with relatives. In some respects, it would seem, the Irish Catholic Americans are even more Irish than the Irish. Or have better phone service.

Of the twelve variables in which the Irish Americans sustain the Irish tradition, they are also statistically different from other Americans in the third row on eight measures – more likely to visit mother and father, more likely to live near all four relatives, and more likely to phone both their mothers and their sisters. The Irish are different from others in the predicted direction as noted earlier on ten of sixteen items. The Irish Americans are different from other Americans on eight of sixteen items – replacing living in the same home as their families with frequent phone calls.[13]

Moreover two out of every five respondents of Irish origins live within fifteen minutes of their mothers – whether it be in Ireland or the United States. For others, the proportion living near their mother is lower in the United States than in other countries, but for the Irish it remains the same. The same phenomenon can be observed on the subject of living near a sister – a quarter of the Irish and a quarter of the Irish Americans live within fifteen minutes of their sister. There is no significant difference between the Irish and the Irish Americans but there is a significant difference between the Irish and other Americans. The importance of the womanly parent and sibling echoes a theme of powerful, not to say matriarchal women which runs through Irish literature. The strong women do not seem to have disappeared in the USA.

The most striking differences, however, are that the European Irish are less likely to use the phone to sustain family contact than other Europeans, while the Irish Americans are more likely to use it than other Americans and than the European Irish. Nine out of ten Irish American Catholics call their mother at least once a week, six out of ten call their father, almost six out of ten call their sister, and almost four out of ten call their brother.[14] Perhaps because phones are more available and less expensive in the United States, Irish Catholic Americans use them far more often than the typical American to sustain family solidarity. They may not be as likely to live with their relatives as the Irish but they are much more likely to talk to them on the phone. The gregariousness expectation is emphatically sustained. The talk goes on.

Indeed, the Irish Americans are even more likely to talk to their parents on the phone than are the Italian Americans, a group high on family solidarity measures (Greeley 1991). 35% of Italian Americans phone their fathers at least once a week as opposed to 60% of Irish Americans. For phone calls to mothers at least once a week, the Italian proportion is 72% and the Irish 90%. These differences are marginally significant (P=.06 and .09) despite the small number of cases involved (seventy-five from each group).

Thus intense Irish family relationships do survive after a century in America, changed somewhat from the pattern currently to be observed in Ireland, diminished in some respects, which one would expect, but enhanced in other respects, which one would not expect. The null hypothesis of assimilation cannot be accepted.

Analysis: Work Attitudes

A number of items in the 1987 and 1988 ISSP surveys measure attitudes towards work, ambition and success. All the literature on Ireland would lead us to expect that the Irish would score low on these items. In fact (Table 2A) there is a positive correlation with Ireland for the opinion that one would work even if one didn't need the money and for the convictions that hard work and ability are necessary for success. Moreover on the latter two items there are statistically significant increases among the Irish Americans; they are even more likely than their Irish cousins to be convinced of the necessity of hard work and ambition. A little more than seven out of ten Irish Catholics (regardless of country) say they would work even if they didn't have to, more than other Europeans and other Americans. Moreover, while the Irish are more likely than other Europeans to endorse both hard work and ambition, the Irish Americans are even more likely to endorse such work ethic attitudes.[15] The work ethic is alive and well both in County Dublin and County Queens, County Cork and County Cook. If, as R.A. Tawney once wrote, Karl Marx was the last of the Schoolmen, so, it would seem are Irish Catholics the last of the Protestants, especially if they live in America.

Analysis: Family values and behaviour

If our expectations are confounded on how Ireland would differ from other countries in work attitudes and how the Irish Americans would differ from the Irish, they are sustained when we look at the items in the 1988 ISSP which measure attitudes and behaviour with regard to marriage and divorce (Table 2B). The Irish are significantly more likely to think that both men and women should marry without premarital experimentation and to disapprove strongly of divorce, and significantly less likely to have cohabited before marriage. On all of these items, the Irish Americans differ significantly from their Irish counterparts and indeed are like all other Americans. Family relationships may be intense among Irish Americans, but they have shed some of the values on marriage that their Irish counterparts still profess.

Analysis: Children

But not their attitudes on children (Table 2C). The Irish enthusiastically reject the notion that children interfere with parental freedom or are 'nothing but trouble'; in this respect the Irish Americans agree with them. Moreover the Irish (and the Irish Americans though to a much lesser degree) also think that a family of more than two children would be 'ideal'. On the other hand both groups, for all their enthusiasm for children, reject the notion that a childless life would be empty, the Irish Americans even more than the Irish.

Here perhaps is an example of Kearney's Irish mind at work: Children are wonderful, but you don't have to have them to be happy.

To translate these correlations into percentages, more than four out of five of the Irish (in either country) reject the notion that children interfere with parental freedom. Moreover, the Irish Americans are even more likely (by twenty percentage points) to strongly reject the idea that children are nothing but trouble and even less likely to agree (by twenty-five percentage points) that a childless life is empty. The ability to have a word ('Children') mean two thinks does not seem to have been affected by either Atlantic sea air or American prosperity.

It may be that the more prosperous Irish Americans are better able to take care of children and hence even less likely to think that they are trouble, and also have available other resources for happiness, because of their affluence, besides children. Hence they are able to afford to exaggerate somewhat the propensities of their culture with regard to these two values.

Analysis: Changing roles

Despite their conservative attitudes on marriage and divorce, the Irish are more likely to be liberal in their thinking about some of the changes in family relationships which have occurred in recent decades (Table 2D). They are more likely to reject the notions that a working mother has a negative impact on family life and on pre-school children. They are more likely to approve of two-income families. Finally they are, perhaps surprisingly, more likely to support gay marriage ceremonies.[16] On the first two of these measures the Irish Americans are even more 'liberal' than the Irish at statistically significant levels; and in none of the four is there a significant decline among Irish Americans.

Irish Americans are only marginally more supportive of working mothers than other Americans, so one could say that on three of these four values the continuation of what was a specifically Irish trait is supported by the host culture. But the issue of marriage ceremonies for gay people is something else again. On this subject both the Irish and the Irish Americans are dissidents, perhaps surprisingly dissident.

In Table 2, Ireland differs from other countries on sixteen items (first column). The Irish Americans are similar in the predicted direction on eleven items (second column), on eight of which they are also significantly different from other Americans (third column).

Discussion and Summary

The Irish, in summary, are different from others on a wide variety of measures of values and behaviour. Sometimes, as in matters of the intensity of family relationships and attitudes on marriage and divorce, they are different in the expected directions. On other matters, such as the role of children in a person's life, they are different, sometimes in the predicted direction (children are not problems) and sometimes in the opposite direction (children are not essential). Yet on other matters, such as the work ethic, they completely confound our expectations. Finally, they surprise us even more, given their conservative attitudes towards marriage, by their liberalism on the subject of working mothers and gay marriage ceremonies. Perhaps some words mean many different 'thinks'.

The Irish Americans, for their part, are less likely to live with their parents than the Irish (not unsurprisingly perhaps given their greater affluence) but are if anything more likely to live near the women in their families and notably more likely to talk to their relatives on the telephone. They have pretty much abandoned any specifically Irish position on marriage and divorce, but in other respects (in Table 2) they differ significantly from the real Irish only in their lower inclination to think a family of more than two children is desirable (and they are more likely to think this than their fellow Americans). On a number of matters, they are even more likely to endorse an Irish position than the real Irish – the importance of ability and hard work and support for working mothers, sometimes, though not always, because the host culture is supportive of such attitudes (on working mothers, but not on work). Finally, like the real Irish, the Irish Americans are tolerant (even more tolerant though not significantly so) of gay marriage ceremonies.

Irish gregariousness and playfulness seem to exist in both forms of the Irish heritage and the survival of both may well fit the model described by Professor Rossi: young Irish Americans learn very early in life that they are expected to keep in contact with their family members, particularly their mothers and sisters.

It does not follow from these findings that the Irish culture has survived completely in the United States. It merely follows that the expectation that a century of American life would eliminate most similarities between the Irish and the Irish Americans must be rejected. One can indeed use what one knows about the attitudes and behaviours of the Irish to predict attitudes and behaviours of Irish Americans. The two groups are obviously not exactly the same, but they are not completely different either – and indeed they are similar in attitudes and behaviours which pertain to the most intimate aspects of human life, marriage, family and work. The Irish Americans are perhaps not as complex as the Irish, but they are still complex and in some areas of human attitudes and behaviour almost as unpredictable. The theory that the Irish American subculture is vanishing cannot be sustained. Moreover, if it has survived almost a hundred years in this country with no sign of becoming all that different in a number of important ways from the contemporary subculture in Ireland, it is likely to enjoy considerable durability in the years to come.

Note that none of the Irish differences reported in this paper are harmful to anyone else or a threat to the unity of the social fabric so anxiously guarded by the assimilationists. The propensity of the Irish American to reach for a phone and call a relative doesn't hurt anyone else or threaten to tear the country apart. Nor does the balance between liking children on the one hand and not viewing them essential for happiness on the other. Surely the support of working mothers and gay marriage ceremonies is not an assault on the national consensus. Nor have any of these specifically Irish positions interfered with Irish educational and economic success – despite the fears of the Dillingham Commission three quarters of a century ago that the Irish predilection for alcohol would doom them forever to inferior positions in American society.[17] Subcultural differences, it ought to be emphasised though it should be obvious, do not by definition put a strain on the body politic. Some such differences do, and some do not.

If it is once established empirically that subcultures do have long-run durability and that they are not inherently a threat to consensus in a pluralistic society (positions which are held on *a priori* grounds it often seems, at least if the subcultures are white ethnic) then the question arises as to what the strategies are by which such subcultures work, most likely without any explicit intent, for their survival.

I speculate that the 'Irish' propensities described here are passed on early in life by example rather than words and so subtly that neither the transmitters nor the receivers of these cultural norms know what is happening. I also suspect that identification is more the effect than the cause of such transmission.

How do such traits survive the high intermarriage rate that Hout describes? I speculate that young people choose on the average (not altogether consciously) mates who share basic cultural traits with them. One marries, in other words, a person who does not think it at all odd to live near your mother or sister (and may do so too) and to phone a relative at least once a week. Such a choice would not be explicitly 'ethnic' but would nonetheless serve to keep alive indefinitely a subculture that is ethnic in origin.

Professor Alba[18] and his admirers (Hirschman 1991) would doubtless reply that such mechanisms are weak forces on which to pin hopes for the survival of ethnic subcultures. Such mechanisms cannot be expected to endure, they would perhaps argue, much longer. But they have it wrong: any force that sustains a subculture in this country for a hundred years cannot be all that weak. The issue, despite Alba and Hirschman, is not whether the subcultures survive even ethnic intermarriage, but how they manage to survive and flourish.

In any case, if we all eventually herded into Professor Alba's Euro-American ethnic group, one presumes that the patron saint for such a community will be a man born in England and educated in France – who then went to Ireland and drove out the snakes!

Which brings us back to the Céide Fields. Alas, there are not enough Mayo folk in the Irish ISSP, and there is no county of origin question in the American, to compare Mayo folk in Ireland with Mayo folk in America. On most of the matters discussed in this paper, those who live in the west of Ireland are even more distinctive than other areas from other Europeans, which is perhaps not a surprise.[19] However, we have no data on those whom one might call the Mayo Americans. There is then nothing which entitles me and those like me to claim a special flavour of Mayo tradition in my heritage. But one might well argue that, just as only Mayo folk can be so outrageous as to produce not one but two books about its native theology, only someone with a Mayo heritage would be so outrageous as to try to prove that the American Irish are, in some very real and not sentimental sense, still Irish.

As to whether the people who lived in the Céide fields are really our ancestors, that may be one of the interesting questions we will want to discuss in the world that is to come.

Table 1

Family Networks Among Irish and Irish Americans (r)

	Irish[20]	Irish Americans[22]	Americans[21]
Live with			
Mother	.08	-.15	
Father	.10	-.17	
Sister	.07	-.05*	
Brother	.10	-.08	
Visit Often			
Mother	.07	.07	.06
Father	.04	-.10	.06
Sister	.07	.07	.03*
Brother	.08	.11	.00*
Live Near			
Mother	.06	.02*	.12
Father	.05	-.05*	.05
Sister	.01*	.01*	.05
Brother	.01*	.01*	.06
Call Often			
Mother	-.05	.19	.09
Father	-.04	.17	.03*
Sister	-.07	.11	.06
Brother	-.04	.16	.03*

* Not Statistically Significant

Table 2
Attitudes and Values Among Irish and Irish Americans (r)

	Irish[23]	Irish Americans[25]	Americans[24]
A. Work Attitudes			
Worth Ethic	.07	-.02*	.05
Hard Work	.06	.09	.06
Ambition	.05	.19	.05
B. Marriage and Family Attitudes			
Men Should Marry	.15	-.10	
Women Should Marry	.13	-.10	
Disapproval of Divorce	.08	-.08	
Cohabited before Marriage	.10	-.12	
C. Attitudes towards Children			
Children Interfere With Freedom (Disagree)	.14	.01*	.00*
Children 'Nothing but Trouble' (Disagree)	.07	.04*	.05
Life 'Empty' Without Children (Disagree)	.09	.06*	.06
More than two children ideal	.18	-.09	

Continued opposite

	Irish	Irish Americans	Americans
D. Changing Social Roles			
Family suffers with working mother (Disagree)	.13	.10	.04*
Pre-school child suffers with working mother	.10	.09	.05
Support Gay Marriage (disagree)	.07	.05*	.05
Support two-income family	.06	-.02*	.00*

*Not Statistically Significant

References

Alba, Richard. *Ethnic Identity: The Transformation of White America.*, Yale University Press, New Haven, 1990.

Arensberg, Conrad and Solon Kimbal. *Family and Community in Ireland,* Harcourt, Brace and World, New York, 1965.

Clark, Terry N. 'The Irish Ethic and the Spirit of Patronage', *Ethnicity,* 4:344, 1975.

Davis, James A. and Smith, Tom, *General Social Surveys 1972-1989,* National Opinion Research Center, Chicago, 1989.

Foster, Roy F. *Modern Ireland,* Basic Book, New York, 1989.

Greeley, Andrew. *That Most Distressful Nation,* Quadrangle Books, Chicago, 1972.

— 1974. 'Political Participation Among Ethnic Groups in the United States', *American Journal of Sociology,* 80:170-204

— 1975. 'A Model for Ethnic Political Socialization', *American Journal of Political Science,* 19:187-206

— 1976. *Ethnicity, Denomination, and Inequality,* Sage Publications, Beverly Hills.

— 1976 bis. *Ethnicity in the United States ,* John Wiley, New York.

— 1977. 'Ethnic Minorities in the United States: Demographic Perspectives', *International of Group Tensions,* 7:64-97

— and William C. McCready and Gary Theisen. 1980. *Ethnic Drinking Subcultures,* Praeger, New York.

— 1981. *The Irish Americans: Their Rise to Wealth and Power,* Warner Books, New York.

— 1988. 'The Success and Assimilation of Irish Protestants and Irish Catholics in the United States', *Sociology and Social Research,* 4:229-236

— 1991. 'The Persistence of the Primordial: The Italian Family in Europe and America', Unpublished paper.

Harris, Rosemary. *Prejudices and Tolerance in Ulster: A study of Neighbors and 'Strangers' in a Border Community,* Manchester University Press, Manchester, 1966.

Hirschman, Charles, 'What Happened to White Ethnics?', *Contemporary Sociology,* 1991, 20:180-183

Humphreys, *The New Dubliners,* Fordham University Press, New York, 1966.

Kearney, Richard, *The Irish Mind*.

Kennedy, Robert Emmett, *The Irish: Immigration, Marriage, and Fertility*, The University of California Press, Berkeley, 1973.

Lieberson, Stanley and Waters, Mary C., 'Ethnic Groups in Flux: The Changing Ethnic Responses of American Whites', *The Annals of the American Academy of Political and Social Science*, 1986, 487:79-91

Messenger, John, *Innis Beag, Isle of Ireland*, Holt, Rinehart and Winston, New York, 1969.

MacGréil SJ, Micheál, *Prejudice and Tolerance In Ireland.*, Harper and Row, New York, 1977.

Stivers, Richard, *The Hair of the Dog: Irish Drinking and American Stereotypes.* Pennsylvania State University Press, University Park, 1976.

U.S. Department of Commerce, *Statistical Abstract of the United States: The National Data Book*, 844, United States Government Printing Office, Washington D.C., 1990.

Ward, Conor C. and Greeley, Andrew, 'Development and Tolerance: The Case of Ireland', *Éire-Ireland*, Forthcoming.

Waters, Mary C., *Ethnic Options*, The University of California Press, Berkeley, 1990.

Zentralarchiv für Empirische Sozialforschung. *Social Networks and Social Support Systems: ISSP 86 Codebook*, Der Universität zu Köln, Cologne, 1987.

— 1989. *New Family Roles: ISSP 87 Codebook*, Die Universität zu Köln, Cologne.

Notes

1. This article is based on research done in co-operation with Monsignor Conor Ward, PP, professor emeritus of Sociology at University College Dublin and Director of the Social Science Research Centre at that illustrious institution. I am grateful to Monsignor Ward (who is not from County Mayo but is a good man nonetheless) for his friendship and co-operation through our long years of research together. The original and more technical version was presented together with Monsignor Ward at the meeting of the American Sociological Association in August of 1991. Copies of that paper are available for those who wish to read a more technical presentation at NORC, 1155 East 60th St., Chicago Il. 60637.

2. It is a curious fate to be dubbed an Anglo in Arizona where I teach some of the time and a Yank when I'm in Ireland. In fact, whatever else I may be, I am neither English nor from New England. In fact I am an Irish Catholic American from the West Side of Chicago with a PhD, a Richard Daley Democrat, a Cub fan and an ardent supporter of Michael Jordan and am prepared to do (verbal) battle with anyone who denies me this identity

3. Even if my name is written down in the proper books and I have a claim on an EC passport issued at the request of the government of Ireland – for a fee, naturally.

4. I almost wrote Great Ireland, which is what Eric the Red somewhere or the other called the land beyond Greenland.

5. I use the term in this paper as distinct from race. While the term was introduced twenty years ago as applying to European ethnic groups, its usage has changed to become interchangeable with race – thus neatly excluding the possibility of research on the descendents of European immigrants. In this paper, however, the term means 'white ethnic groups'.

6. There are more Irish Protestants in the United States than there are Irish Catholics. However the former represent a much earlier and different migration and are not included therefore in this project (Greeley 1988). 4% of Irish Catholics are first generation (immigrants). 9% are second generation, 46% third generation, and 41% fourth or higher order generation. However, 80% of Irish Protestants are fourth or higher order generation.

7. The Irish data in this analysis are limited to the twenty-six

counties under the jurisdiction of the Republic of Ireland.

8. For convenience Australia is considered a North Atlantic nation.

9. The ISSP questionnaires are available from NORC, 1155 East 60th Chicago Illinois 60637.

10. Sons and daughters are excluded from this analysis because of a paucity of cases.

11. The other countries in ISSP 1986 are Australia, West Germany, the United Kingdom, the United States, Austria, Hungary and Italy. On the measures discussed in this paper, Ireland is most like Italy and least like the other English Speaking countries.

12. In the first two columns probability of errors is .01 or less. In the third column, because of the small number of cases, I am content with probabilities of 10 or less.

13. Doubtless one of the reasons the real Irish do not call home in Ireland is that there are far fewer telephones in that country. According to the US Department of Commerce (1990), there are 27 phones per 100 people in Ireland, 49 in Italy, and 76 in the United States.

14. Those who live with their parents are excluded from the base for these calculations.

15. Irish workers spend longer average hours on the job than do workers in any other EU country.

16. The Irish support for such ceremonies is stronger than of any other country in the ISSP, except the Netherlands, where the proportions are virtually the same.

17. The opposite position is taken by the Irish proverb: 'Sure, God made the creature so that the Irish wouldn't own the world.'

18. To be fair to Alba (an O'Sullivan on his mother's side) he does not deny the survival of ethnic subcultures. Quite the contrary, in a dialogue after the technical version of this paper was presented at a meeeting of the American Sociological Association in 1991, he admitted that he expected a cultural suvival, but contended that this was really not an ethnic group unless self-conscious ethnic practices and organisations also survive. He also has contended, as I understand him, that those who take the position espoused in this paper need to explain the mechanism by which an ethnic subculture persists. As to the latter, I think the dynamics described in this paper are an adquate explanation. Perhaps the difference be-

tween my position and Professor Albas is that he emphasises ethnic sub-structures in the United States while I emphasise ethnic subcultures. The extent to which these depend on one another remains to be seen.

19. I will not engage in a dicussion of whether that proves that the west is the real Ireland.

20. A positive correlation indicates Ireland correlates with behaviour.

21. A negative correlation indicates decline with immigration. An insignificant correlation indicates no difference between Irish and Irish Americans.

22. A significant positive correlation indicates Irish Americans are significantly different from other Americans.

23. A positive correlation indicates Ireland correlates with behaviour.

24. A negative correlation indicates decline with immigration.

25. A significant positive correlation indicates Irish Americans are significantly different from other Americans.

PART V

*Threats to survival
and hints of salvation*

CHAPTER 16
Context and Continuum: Europe and Mayo

Pádraig Flynn

One of the inevitabilities of a political life is that every stage and phase of it is marked by official photographs, each one showing a subtle set of changes when compared with earlier shots. Sometimes, the photographers come to your office. Sometimes, you go to their studios, where they tinker with silvered umbrellas and hold light meters close to your face, apologising for the personal invasion.

The last time, the photographer told me I could stand up and stretch my legs while she put a new roll of film in her camera. I walked over to a table filled with proofs and prints. Idly flicking, I found myself looking at a close-up of a man in his mid-fifties, shrivelled and tanned by decades of outdoor work, the eyes guarded. A man with a jutty jaw on him contradicted by a gentleness around the mouth.

My concentration on the picture pulled the photographer over to see which one I was looking at.

'Oh, yes,' she said. 'My sunset and silence man.'

'Sunset and silence?'

'Mmm. You know the Padraig Colum poem? "Sunset and silence. A man. Around him earth shattered, earth broken. Beside him two horses – a plough ..."'

She began to search on the table.

'I've always wanted to capture that moment that Colum sums up, and I was out one evening near Belmullet and saw this farmer out with a dog.'

'Not a plough?'

'No. I had to do without the two horses and the plough, but he posed without posing, if you know what I mean ...'

She was laying out two other prints beside the first.

'They're all the same shot,' she explained. 'I've just cropped them differently.'

The first one let you see every sag and scored line on the man's face. The second was much wider, so you could see the texture of big stones to one side of him, and a glimpse of sea and sunset to the other. The third shot had him centred, his wellington boots planted on his land like a statement, the dog poised, tongue hanging, and around him broken earth, bog patches, and a great swathe of scenery filled with dying sunshine.

What startled me was that the man was undiminished in the picture that held more detail. You could see a much wider context. You had the sensation that he had come a distance and might yet travel a distance. Yet within the wider context he was as simply sure of himself as he was in the close up, standing, a testimony to his life, his times and his genetic heritage.

'Could I have this?'

'Sure,' she said, 'Which?'

'All three?'

She didn't ask why, just slid them into a semi-opaque envelope and handed them to me. I would have found it difficult to explain to her quite what sense the picture sequence made to me. They made visual a concept I was becoming more clear on: that a wider context does not diminish or diffuse national or regional character, but can make it, if anything, more assertive and more relevant.

It was not always thus. In the past, there was a choice. If an individual chose to contribute on the wider stage, there was a sundering of the connection with home. It was either/or. Home might well be 'the place where, when you have to go there, they have to let you in', but even after a relatively short period outside of Ireland, when they let you in, they regard you as the returned Yank or similar, disenfranchising you with the courtesies reserved for strangers, listening to your speech to catch the flavour of another country, the phrases of a new group of friends or colleagues.

Sometimes, experience in the wider context made the place of origin progressively less relevant, as in the case of Richard Brinsley Sheridan. Sometimes, as in the case of O'Casey and Joyce, it was to provide the raw material for works completed in other lands, the memories more acid because of intervening time and distance. Sometimes, as in the case of Shaw, the place of origin became little more than a conscious quirkiness of accent, a 'bit of business' such as an actor might use to build up a character being played.

It is only in the last couple of decades that it became possible to in-
ternationalise without absence. Irish writers and publishers have
taken on the challenge and established a solid presence in the
printed word in both Europe and America, as have playwrights
and film and theatrical directors. The indications are that our visual artists will follow suit.

Increasingly, the same kind of solid presence is being created and
maintained by politicians and public servants within the EU. Not
because we are there, but because of how we do our business and
where we're from.

This solid presence could not have been envisaged when I was
born. Not only was Europe then on the brink of a war of unimag-
ined scale and horror, but, as far as Europe was concerned, Ireland – neutral – was little more than a potential strategic asset taken
out of contention and therefore irrelevant. 'Peripheral', at that
point, had a meaning that the EU has softened in the intervening
years. Not only was Ireland peripheral to Europe, but Mayo, on
the western seaboard, was less than central in Irish politics. It
would have been laughable, at that point, to envisage a situation
where a community of Europe would exist which would seek to
promote equity among all constituent nations. If the concept of a
European Commissioner had been floated at that time, it would
have been assumed that the role would demand a homogenised
persona shorn of regional characteristics and untouched by local
or county interests.

It is now becoming apparent that such an homogenised *persona*
and approach would have been less than productive, not just for
Ireland (and Mayo) but for Europe. Europe must never move beyond human scale and must never macerate away the wondrous
individual variants of culture, of credo and of character within the
community. To that end, the closeness to individuals and to local
issues which is the survival ticket of a Mayo TD, can be profoundly
useful.

During my days as a TD, and particularly in recent days as a Minister, I frequently found myself on the wrong side of a vision of
the politician as a person who should, once elected, move away
from the quotidian concerns of the individuals who had voted
him (or her) into office, in order to deal at a pure conceptual level
with legislative issues.

The word 'clientilism' was often used as a pejorative term to describe the way I (and many other rural TDs) operate. This usage seemed to me to be the rough equivalent of saying that good hoteliers would best develop their three-year business plans if they never met pesky customers. I have never bought the notion that easing the wheels of a bureaucracy on behalf of a constituent, or listening to an individual's case history of being brutalised by a law or the absence of a law, in some way tainted the thinking of politicians. Being uninterested is not the same as being disinterested.

Not only is there profound reality to Tip O'Neill's aphorism that 'all politics is local', but there is a parallel observation to be posited: all truth is specific, never general. The great truths that shape our national and international concerns are always specific to individuals and individual insights. They may later be extrapolated in generalities, but their genesis is always to be found with someone noting the significance of a singular example. So Rachel Carson's discovery of the thinning of the eggshells of birds damaged by DDT helped to create modern environmentalism. Betty Friedan's sudden sense of defeat in the face of the lifestyle she called 'The Feminine Mystique' helped to develop modern feminism. And the puzzlement of individual American doctors over an unusual configuration of ailments in their gay patients led to the identification of AIDS.

There is always a danger that a bureaucracy implicit in an entity such as the European Union will lose sight of what is local, what is individual, and become cemented by scale and inertia.

It therefore behoves Commissioners and other functionaries who are 'out in Europe' to stay tightly linked to the complex realities of where they come from, in much the same way as the painter (Fr) Jack Hanlon used to emphasise the rough texture of the canvas on which he painted, stressing that a good painter does not seek to excise all evidence of the underlying canvas, but, on the contrary, may allow it to make fleeting appearances in the final work of art.

One of the unpainted patches of my personal Mayo canvas which appeared in my European work surprised me. In the first months of my period as EU Commissioner, I began to become aware of a word. A word with which I was unfamiliar. French. But always used as a pat on the back for someone. *Connaissance*.

'What's *connaissance*?' I eventually asked an Irishman, working in
Brussels, who is a fluent French speaker. He gave that mouth-
pursed noise people give when there's no elegant direct translation.

'Knowingness?' he suggested, tentatively.

'*Knowingness*? What does 'knowingness' mean?'

There was a long silence, followed by a long, slightly exasperated
explanatory blurt.

'It means knowing where the bodies are buried. Knowing where
the skeletons are secreted. Knowing who's for you and who's agin
you. Knowing how to see round corners and duck when a custard
pie is heading your direction. Knowing who's really important
and who only thinks they're important. Knowing who can keep a
secret. Knowing who'll stand a round and who'll need to visit the
gents at that time. Knowing who'll say they'll give you their vote
and who'll actually give you their vote. Knowing when to read
the text and when to read between the lines. Knowing what a
silence means. Cop-on. Street-smarts. Cute hoorism, even.'

I thought that over. *Connaissance* was clearly a handy concept for a
mindset that serves as well in Castlebar as in Brussels. Nobody
had ever told me before that when, in the middle of a general election campaign, I would invade the home of some constituents,
roaring for cups of tea and demanding the presence of all and sundry, as opposed to those doorsteps where I stood and waited for
an invitation before making further progress, I was showing *connaissance*.

I was quite impressed with myself, retrospectively, not to say
re-inforced in my belief that operating in the wider context of the
European community may require changes in location, but it requires precisely the same skills and attitudes that the home scene
demands. Only the scale and the points of reference are different.
The challenges and the problems are the same.

Although being credited with *connaissence* is a boon to the self-
esteem, having a complete lack of pluralism attributed to one –
and to one's homeland – is rather less pleasing.

If the shadow of fear is longer than fear itself, then the shadow of
an image is assuredly longer than the reality. Accordingly, it
would happen, every now and again, in the early days of Europe,

that I would find myself being praised for expressing the most basic respect for religions other than Catholicism, in much the same way a toddler undergoing toilet training is praised when the child gets it right: 'Aren't you good, aren't you grown up?' There was an oddly patronising twin assumption that a) Ireland was an overwhelmingly Catholic country and so wouldn't have any interest in or empathy with other religions, and b) that, as a practising Catholic who made no secret of my beliefs, I was in some way likely to seek to impose pan-European Catholicism by dictat.

The message was clear: if you believed passionately in something, you were dangerous. It is one of the perverse lessons of history that we badly need to unlearn, this one. Or perhaps prove wrong by example, by illustrating that it is possible to be driven by a code, by a set of unshakable beliefs, yet not to have either the need or the intention to ram that code down other people's throats. Indubitably, the great aggressors, the global vandals of history have tended to be men who held passionate beliefs – men implacable in their terrifying certainties and in their capacity to de-humanise all who were perceived to obstruct or deny those certainties.

However, one of the great global threats of the twentieth century is not personified or driven by a messianic political leader: not only is the drug threat a faceless 'enemy within', but it is arguably an enemy within unequalled in human history.

Never before has humankind faced an enemy so seamlessly successful in its collusion with other societal tragedies, whether they be diseases like AIDS or issues like unemployment. Never before have so many of the best and brightest joined the deprived and marginalised in a commercially-manufactured hell. Never, in all of history, has there been such a seeping sense of helplessness, such a sense that any action can be subverted, any progress eroded, any campaign vitiated by the forces of evil.

Neither the drug problem nor the international problem of unemployment will be solved by passionless, rootless generalists. If these interlinked modern disasters are not to sprawn an ungovernable multiplicity of virus-like infections eating away at the essence of civilisation, they must be tackled by passionate realists. Ultimately, if what you must do is change attitudes and behaviours, then that's what you need: a passionate realist. (Not a dangerous dogmatist. The two are not the same.) The context doesn't matter. It can be religious. It can be economic. Without a passionate realist like St Paul, Christianity would never have become so structured, so massy in its distribution so quickly. Without a passionate realist like Sean Lemass, Ireland could never have moved from the depressed dependency of the fifties into the confident growth period of the sixties.

The great passionate realists are always immediately and proudly locateable in place and in background. St Paul claimed it frequently: 'I am a citizen of no mean city.' Disraeli, in nailing the (transient) anti-semitism of Daniel O'Connell in the British Houses of Parliament, claimed his racial position with acid wit and unambiguous pride.

Nobody should feel that the optimum proof that they are truly European is the minimising of one's nationality and regionality. Nor is there any such pressure in Europe. On the contrary, there is a positive relish taken, at European level, in the points of differentiation exemplified by vivid personalities. The same positive relish, curiously, is less evident in national politics, as those of us to whom the 'country and western' label has been attached can testify. The Taoiseach described that particular bit of bumper-sticker abuse as 'the Irish form of racism,' and it was no shallow description. Liberalism, in Ireland, has, in my experience, shown a capacity to categorise and sterotype its opponents in a way which is very close to racism. Since I went to Europe, taking on a portfolio which relates to issues such as racism against immigrants and others, I have occasionally been asked why I seem to have such a personal understanding of the issue. The short answer is that I have experienced it. In miniature. In non-violent form. In the words and glances and one-line snideries the convinced liberal too often uses to de-value the beliefs, the values and the language of conservatives from outside the pale. What is important is to see experience, not as something that happens to us, but as something that happens to us which can erode or enable us.

When I think of my Mayo background and my current European reality, the analogy which makes sense of it all is drawn from my family trade: drapery. The multi-coloured threads of my schooldays, my family, my friends and neighbours, my education, my knowledge of the Irish language, are all stretched firm and parallel across the weaver's frame.

Pulled across and through those fibres are the filaments of my European life: the tasks, the terminology, the scale, the scope of it.

Neither is lost in intermingling with the other. Rather, it is the contrasting tensions of the weave that gives the fabric its strength and durability.

Just as, in the photograph evoked by Colum's poem, it is the wider context of the broadest shot that gives the face of the individual most impact and character.

CHAPTER 17

Regenerating Mayo: Political Structures for Local Development

Pat Rabbitte

The 1970s were a decade of hope in Co Mayo. For the first time since the early nineteenth century, the county's population began to grow. Indeed, between 1971-79, more people settled in the county than left it, thus reversing the familiar tide of emigration that had seen the number of Mayo people actually living in Mayo drop by over one third since the foundation of the state – a telling reflection on the economics of successive governments.

However, any idea that a magic formula for economic success had been found for Mayo – or for the west of Ireland in general – was quickly shattered. Already by the end of the 1970s, the spectre of net emigration had returned. Although population growth continued in the early 1980s, it was quickly swamped by the resumption of mass emigration, and in the late 1980s the familiar pattern of population decline returned with a vengeance: by 1991 there were almost 5,000 fewer people living in the county than in 1986.

It is clear that the economic policies which appeared to work so well in the 1970s are no longer adequate for the situation facing Mayo – and the west of Ireland in general - in the 1990s. New approaches are clearly needed. And, despite the hype surrounding the huge infusion from the enlarged European Union Structural Funds over the next few years, there is little sign that the Irish government has any real grasp of the kinds of policies required to ensure sustained long-term economic development in the disadvantaged areas of rural Ireland.

From the outset, it is important to appreciate that the regeneration of Mayo cannot be seen in isolation from the rest of the country. While Mayo can undoubtedly achieve much through acting on its own initiative, the county's long-term future ultimately depends on the formulation and implementation of a national strategy of economic and social development. In other words, successful regional development requires, as an essential prerequisite, the creation of a vibrant national economic framework capable of spreading knock-on growth impulses throughout all parts of the country.

Peripheral region

Mayo is on the periphery of a country which is itself part of the European periphery. And, just as attempts to tackle Mayo's economic problems in isolation from the national context are unlikely to succeed, so the pursuit of national economic salvation must be firmly embedded in a comprehensive programme for the development of the EU's peripheral regions in general. And, generous as the EU structural funding may appear to be, it simply is not adequate for the task at hand – mainly because it is not tackling the real problems of Irish underdevelopment.

In the past, the economic problems of peripheral regions such as Mayo – and peripheral nations such as Ireland – were seen largely as a problem of inadequate local resources, capital and enterprise. The solution, therefore, was seen as lying in the injection into these regions of capital investment originating from elsewhere. Thus, Irish national and regional development policy became almost completely dependent on foreign manufacturing investment.

And, indeed, for a time this policy seemed to work. Mayo's demographic rejuvenation in the 1970s was largely the result of the introduction of several major employers of external origin such as Travenol, Asahi and Hollister. However, while these firms continue to provide a high level of good-quality employment in the county, they have not provided the basis for long-term self-sustaining growth, while the number of jobs which they provide directly is now down on that of twenty years ago.

This points to the essential weakness of the national dependence on foreign firms as the means of producing long-term development. These firms do not establish deep roots in the Irish economy. Their purchases of local goods and services are limited; because of the partial nature of the processes which they are involved in here, they carry out little original research and development work and generate few technological spin-offs; their marketing functions are largely conducted from abroad, leading to equally few spin-offs in this key area of modern economic success; and they repatriate the great bulk of their profits, which should be the lifeblood of future economic growth, but is not in the Irish case.

The upshot of all this is that the main economic benefits of foreign branch plants lies in the jobs which they directly create themselves. And, while these can be substantial in themselves, the tendency among foreign firms in Ireland has been towards long-term employment decline – even though most of these firms are doing well and expanding output vigorously. This is mainly because of the impact of new, labour-saving technology (particularly in relation to labour-intensive but repetitive assembly work, which is one of the dominant features of foreign branch plants in Ireland).

National Plan

The key to long-term economic development in Ireland, therefore, must lie in the creation of indigenously-based manufacturing and service industries, capable of securing and retaining export markets, sourcing their raw material and service requirements within Ireland, and reinvesting their profits locally, thereby generating further growth and employment creation. While there is some acknowledgement of the need for more indigenous job creation in the National Development Plan 1995-1999, there is little detail on how this is to be achieved. And there is even less evidence that the government has any grasp of how central this objective is – or should be – to the overall process of national development.

Indeed, this key issue is swamped by the Plan's effusive coverage of other issues – such as spending on roads and training for the unemployed – which, although desirable in themselves and convenient ways of spending the monies on offer from the EU, are essentially sideshows in relation to the long-term goal of sustainable long-term national economic development.

The National Plan's failure to grasp what is needed to pursue this goal realistically is further indicated by its simplistic underlying philosophy that cost minimisation (by which it means labour cost minimisation) is the key to international competitiveness. While cost competitiveness is undoubtedly important, all the indications are that, in the sophisticated high-tech international economy in which Ireland is now embedded, the real key to success is the ability to produce and deliver products of the highest quality, in whatever market niches Ireland is able to carve out a national reputation for itself.

We in Ireland have no business in trying to compete through the medium of cheaper labour. This corner of the market has already been hived off by the newly-industrialising countries of the Third World with wage rates which would never be acceptable in Ireland. Besides, after seventy years of independence, surely we should be able to offer our people more than this. We have the human resources, in the form of a young and highly-educated workforce, to make the grade in the high-quality end of the market – a sector which offers the prospect of well-paid and personally rewarding work for thousands of Irish people working at home – not the 'yellow-pack jobs' with which our foremost economic experts appear to be preoccupied.

Research and Development

We therefore need a new approach to national economic development – one which places the emphasis on the creation in Ireland of a new wave of high-tech industries with Irish roots. To achieve this we need to invest massive resources in research and development, the main source of continuous innovation which in turn is the key to economic success in the modern world. In this respect, the National Plan is a complete failure.

A recent report by the National Economic and Social Council identified the lack of a national system of innovation as the single most important cause of Ireland's relative lack of economic success compared to other small European economies, such as Finland, Sweden, Denmark, Austria and Switzerland. Repeated surveys show Ireland coming out at the bottom of the world league table of national expenditure on R & D. The most successful countries are those which spend the most on R & D, such as Japan and Germany. This is not surprising. Only five per cent of Irish manufacturing companies carry out any R & D. In fact, R & D spending by Irish firms declined by almost 10 per cent between 1988 and 1990.

The oft-quoted Culliton Report says that 'Technological competence is one of the main keys to competitive advantage' (p 55). There is no evidence of any understanding of this basic fact in the

National Plan. None of its fifteen chapters is devoted to this topic – in fact, it does not even merit a sub-heading. Technological weakness is not even included in the list of 'weaknesses of the economy' spelled out on page 24.

What is even worse, where the plan does mention R & D, it actually provides for a reduction in spending, in both absolute and relative terms, over the plan period. Thus, in the chapter on industry, spending on R & D is projected to decline from £61M to £58M between 1994 and 1997, and from 24.4 per cent of total public expenditure on industrial development in 1994 to 22.2 per cent in 1999. This is in line with the 20 per cent reduction in the national science and technology budget in 1993, and represents an unbelievably short-sighted and narrow-minded view of the role of technological development in the economic development process.

A major redirection of the state's development spending to building up our indigenous technological capacity is but one plank in the platform of national economic renewal. We also need to develop our capacity for enterprise and self-reliance – a capacity which was greatly stunted by years of colonisation and which has remained at a low level since independence. Undoubtedly a major reason for this has been the high degree of centralisation of political and bureaucratic power in this state: indeed, Ireland is even more centralised now that it was at the time of independence, and is second only to New Zealand among developed countries in the lack of power given to local and regional authorities.

Local development

Local political autonomy has a major bearing on the economic development process in at least two ways. Firstly, it facilitates the effective development of local resources – and, despite the conventional view which has dominated development policy in the past, it is now clear that even the most peripheral of regions have significant internal resources capable of being developed. Secondly, local autonomy – which, to be meaningful, must include a high degree of economic autonomy – can provide an effective medium for generating a culture of local economic self-reliance and enterprise. This, in turn, can create a well-spring from which entrepreneurs of national stature can emerge.

The EU, after many years of experimenting with the traditional 'top-down' approach of regional development, has now rejected this as a failure and has more recently begun to emphasise the alternative 'bottom-up' approach based on integrated local development. However, for this approach to succeed, appropriate structures for facilitating local development must be in place – and this is patently not the case in Ireland.

The past twenty years have seen the beginnings of a growing movement for locally-based economic development in Ireland. In Mayo, the Gaeltacht areas led the way with the formation of vibrant community development co-operatives in both the Belmullet and Tourmakeady areas. The establishment of North Connaught Farmers and Co-operative in 1972 also represented a decisive move by the farmers of both Mayo and adjoining areas to exert greater control over the development of the agricultural resources of the region. More recently, the creation of three LEADER projects covering a large part of Mayo testified to the continuing commitment to locally-based development in the county. All of which signifies that the people of the west are not prepared to allow the process of decline in the region to continue without putting up a fight.

However, the process of locally-based development will never achieve its potential without appropriate political and administrative structures which confer on localities and regions real control over their own destinies. We therefore also need new radical measures of institutional reform in order to achieve this goal.

Europe of the regions

Any serious consideration of regional survival must take account of developments as disparate as the Rio Earth Summit (Agenda 21) and the creation of the EU's Committee of the Regions. (At the time of writing, the government has failed to nominate any representatives for Ireland's nine positions on the committee.) They indicate that the day of the centralised nation state may be over and that we are moving towards new forms of political organisation based on larger conglomerates, criss-crossed by networks of smaller units.

At the same time, excessive centralisation and concentration of economic activity generate diseconomies and deteriorating living conditions. Congestion, pollution, stress, inadequate social environment and high levels of unemployment and social exclusion make urban life less attractive than it once was.

Centre and periphery are still with us but the connotations of these terms are beginning to change. Mayo may be a peripheral region in a peripheral country but this should no longer necessarily be synonymous with inevitable decline.

To take advantage of this situation, Mayo needs:

a) to capitalise on its environmental advantages and the alternative life style they offer, not just to 'stem the flow' of emigration and to release endogenous potential, but to attract new human resources to the area.

b) to base its development plans on a recognition of:

* the limited scope for further development of agriculture and the purely 'supplementary' possibilities of tourism and fishing (the shellfish subsector, aquaculture and the development of the Moy river);

* the imperative of overcoming a major block to the stimulation and attraction of development activity – poor infrastructure;

* the importance of small and medium-sized enterprises in future job creation in the manufacturing and services sectors; and

* the need for a dual strategy to address the social disadvantages of certain groups (e.g. the long-term unemployed) as well as the regional disadvantages which affect the county as a whole.

The political strategy to achieve this is based on the recognition of the pivotal role of local authorities in regional economic development and on developing structures of local government so that they are empowered to act as an engine of growth.

This could be achieved, not by Mayo in isolation, but within the context of the emergence of Europe of the Regions at EU level, i.e. as part of a more generalised movement which sees the safeguarding and reinforcement of local self-government as an important contribution to the construction of a Europe based on the principles of democracy and decentralisation of power.

The main points to be considered in this regard are:

* the application of the principle of subsidiarity – that decisions shall be taken as closely as possible to the citizen – not merely as a criterion for the exercise of powers shared between the Member

States and the Community, but as the basis for a vertical power structure progressing from Community level to local authorities and citizens;

* the protection of the sphere of autonomy of local authorities against interference from national (or regional) authorities and from adverse effects of the ever increasing transfer of parts of national sovereignty to the Community; this protection would include the right of recourse to the Court of Justice;

* the implication that respect for the principle carried with it, not merely a negative obligation of non-interference, but also a positive obligation on the part of the higher levels of power to supply the necessary resources to ensure genuine freedom of action;

* the position of local authorities as the natural interlocutors of the Commission with respect to the implementation of local development projects;

* the need to develop the co-ordinating role of the elected local authorities *vis à vis* the various bodies engaged in planning, development, enterprise creation etc;

* the potentially important role of the Committee of the Regions in the European institutions, the need to ensure its operational and budgetary independence from the Economic and Social Committee and the equitable representation of the various types of local and regional authorities which exist in each member state;

* the political potential of networks within and between regions and the radical changes they could bring to present concepts of centre and periphery and the power relations they imply.

Local government

The existing structure of local government in Ireland was designed to meet the administrative needs of a past age. It is wholly unsuited to the needs implied in regional survival. This was underlined in a report of the European Parliament Committee on Regional Policy and Regional Planning in 1990 which regretted 'the absence of a network of regional authorities within Ireland which rendered more difficult the consultation required by community legislation with regard to the preparation of the national plan.' (The same point can be made just as forcefully in relation to the current National Plan).

Tom Barrington borrows from Leninist jargon when he refers to the present structure as 'acute bureaucratic centralism'. Local government, he argues, is particularly weak and is characterised by

> a limited number of local authorities – only about a quarter of those we had at Independence; with few functions, bound hand and foot by bureaucratic rules that astonish European observers; their finances and electoral arrangements the playthings of the national parties; elected councillors treated with barely disguised contempt by both the parties and the bureaucrats; with dud promises of reform 'as a matter of great urgency' issued with cynical regularity.

This has given rise to the situation described by Charles McCarthy:

> There are, then, no local community councils or district councils springing from the need of people to provide their own local government. There are no local institutions by which people can express their views, despite the efforts of some voluntary groups of a developmental or social character. If institutions are the voice of a society, then Irish society is largely dumb.

The Danish model

Denmark provides a model of government more in tune with the requirement of regional survival. Denmark has three levels of government: communes, regional and government. All are directly elected while Copenhagen has a different administrative status.

Communes range in population size from 7,000 upwards. In West Jutland, the largest is in Aarhus which has a population of 100,000. Areas of competence are: primary education, town planning, sanitation/environmental issues in towns/villages, care of the elderly. There are 13 regions in Denmark (plus Copenhagen). They are responsible for health services, secondary education, tourism and environmental issues as they effect the countryside.

Communes and regional councils are financed through direct taxation. Danes pay approximately 50 per cent of their income on taxes – 20 per cent goes to the commune, 8-9 per cent to the region and 20 per cent to the central government.

In addition, some regional councils get a subvention from the government. The size of this is not related directly to levels of relative underdevelopment but to the composition of the population, e.g. numbers of special groups – handicapped, elderly etc. There is some reallocation of resources between councils.

The concept of stimulating economic activity through grants appears to be alien to the Danes. Regional councils can contribute to training people for employment in specific enterprises, provide sites and help with planning permission etc. A small amount of money is allocated to help local factories expand their markets abroad. They can carry out or commission investigations into development needs and so on but cannot finance economic activity.

Danish local authorities have considerable room for manoeuvre in their areas of competence within the framework of national laws.

For example, the health sector – which in West Jutland consumes 60 per cent of the Council budget – is subject to various national regulations but the Council can determine its own health policy. In the last few decades, the Council has opted for social and preventive medicine and spends relatively little on hospitals. This was as a result of a political decision that hospitals are not cost effective in raising and maintaining the standards of health in the population as a whole.

There is, therefore, room for experimentation on a local level within the framework of national laws. This is not applicable to economic development in Denmark for the reasons stated above but it could be in a context where state and local authorities do intervene to stimulate economic development.

A noteworthy feature of the Danish situation is the level of, and commitment to, participative democracy. This is difficult to illustrate in terms of institutions but it is a fundamental part of the political culture. For example, there is a basic belief that discussion is important in itself and not simply as a prelude to decision-making. There also appears to be an absence of clientilism which makes it very different from the political scene in the west of Ireland.

Conclusions

Effective local democracy is a prerequisite to creating the structures and culture within which enterprise can develop. In this respect, the revitalisation of Mayo poses similar problems and involves similar solutions to that of deprived urban areas. The main tasks are to mobilise local communities to minimise or eliminate social problems and obstructions, and to develop the social and physical infrastructure which promotes local indigenous development.

* A democratically restructured region would be better equipped to fight for a share of resources that the geographic/demographic situation would merit, and more importantly would be better equipped to decide the efficient allocation and utilisation of these resources.

* Future national plans must be based on real local input. The present 'top down' approach is destructive of local initiative and of the social infrastructure and base of local economic development.

* A national industrial strategy should provide for a significant proportion of spending on locally initiated, locally developed projects framed to fit in with the local facilities, resources, needs, and culture.

* Effective political structures require the development of a political culture where debate, transparency, and participative decision-making are the norm. Such a culture would place policy above personality and would encourage people to elect public representatives they could trust rather than 'fixers.' If local government is to be invested with greater powers (including the power to raise local taxes) then people will have to take local democracy seriously.

Likewise, a new approach to national politics is required from parties and people alike. The politics of nod and wink will cut no ice in the Europe of Maastricht. The begging bowl approach must be dispensed with if Ireland is to meet the challenge of, and avail of the opportunities in, the new European order. In any event there will be no more big handouts. In the past, such monies have been, spent 'not wisely, but too well,' and we are now paying the price.

In the final analysis, Mayo's needs will not be met by 'drawing down' billions of ECUs. Rather they will be met by creating the conditions whereby local initiative and creativity can flourish in their home ground.

Bibliography

Breathnach, Proinsias, 'Economic Change and Development: Prospects for Peripheral Regions', Conference paper, Belfast, 1993.

Mjoset, Lars, The Irish economy in a comparative institutional perspective, *NESC Report No.93*, 1992

.Barrington, T.J., 'Local Government: what is to be done?', Conference paper, Dublin, 1990.

McCarthy, Charles, *The Decade of Upheaval: Irish Trade Unions in the Nineteen Sixties*, 1973.

CHAPTER 18

Imagining God in a Saving Church

Mary G. Durkin

Introduction

The theme, *Survival or Salvation?*, when applied to the church, presents a challenge to theologians. How are we to speak about God so the church survives because its proclamation of the Good News of salvation addresses the needs of its people? This challenge is relevant for the Catholic Church, both in Mayo from where my grandparents emigrated and in Chicago where I live.

Before outlining how a theology that tells stories of God might respond to this challenge, I will elaborate on three reasons why I view the theme as a challenge.

First, the church needs to find new and creative ways of proclaiming the Good News of salvation. Survival or salvation suggest two models of church. If the institutional church concentrates its attention on a struggle for survival as an institution without taking into account the faith needs of all believers, it might survive. However, it's message will not impact the lives of the faithful with the Good News of salvation.

Second, theologians who, following Anselm's example, are seeking to understand faith by correlating the faith tradition of the church and the experiences of people in the last years of the twentieth century, need to consider how we can best assist in proclaiming the Good News.

Third, the role of religious imagination in forming a faith perspective requires a pastoral imaginative theology. The saving church needs theologians who tell stories of God.

I will then illustrate how this imaginative theology tells stories of God that speak to two common human experiences that, at times, confront people with questions of meaning.

When I search for what links the symbol of the God of the Catholic faith and the moments when people experience questions of meaning, many factors go into my interpretation. Like theologians of every age, I am limited by the circumstances of my time and place. I look to stories of the Catholic faith told and interpreted through the ages primarily by men. I examine them as a woman, an American woman, an Irish-American woman (with roots in Co Mayo), a married woman, a mother and a grandmother who lives in the latter years of the twentieth century with all the limitations as well as opportunities this self-definition implies.

Just as a book of Mayo theology might, at first glance, appear to be limited, but is not necessarily so if it speaks to experiences of those beyond Mayo, so my reflections are valuable if they spark a response from others.

Stories of church: Chicago and Mayo

Two stories, one set in Chicago and the other in the west of Ireland, illustrate how the institutional church can be a help or a hindrance as its members seek to understand their faith in a way that enriches their lives.

The Chicago Story

Recently on the South Side of Chicago, a forty-year-old father of four children, ranging in age from five to eleven years, suffered a massive heart attack. He remained in a coma for a week; but his family knew he would not live. His wife and children planned a funeral liturgy that expressed the joy of the short time they had him in their midst, their sadness at his death, and their hope in the resurrection.

When they presented their plan to the pastor, he vetoed their proposal, saying, 'I have a set formula, including the appropriate songs, that I use at all liturgies in my church. You must use this or I will not bury your husband from my church.' Fortunately, the neighbouring parish had a pastor who understood that if he ministers to people in a tender, caring way at the critical times, they will always remember those times as times of salvation. The family had its planned liturgy, but not in its own parish.

The Ireland Story

In the late 1980s, my husband and I attended a Saturday evening eucharist in a resort town in the west of Ireland (not in Co Mayo). People streamed down the street towards the church. We thought that a sign of good things to come. However, upon entering the church we discovered the men and young boys congregated in the vestibule or standing in the back of church. The women, children, and elderly knelt in the pews.

Once the Mass began, I could understand the wisdom of the men in the vestibule. The best way to describe the Mass was to say it was clerical from start to finish. A priest read the first two readings. The celebrant, his homily a mission collection plea, spoke of the need to export the kind of Catholicism the congregation experienced to all the corners of the world to which this collection would send Irish missionaries.

The congregation and the priest never interacted.

There was no handshake of peace and no music. The priests and two religious sisters distributed communion to about half the congregation. At the end of Mass (which definitely could not have been called a eucharistic celebration), the priest left via the sanctuary door, the same one through which he entered.

Later that evening we had dinner with a Quaker couple we met earlier in our trip. They asked what we thought of the liturgy. We expressed surprise at the lack of community spirit and celebration. On a previous visit we attended liturgies in Cong and Kiltimagh that had been joyful celebrations.[1]

They have a home in the resort town and knew the local church had a reputation for poor liturgies. Interestingly, these Quakers tried to assure us that it wasn't like that everywhere in Ireland. Their grandson made his first communion at a 'wonderful' liturgy in Mayo.

A surviving church or a saving church?

These are just two of innumerable stories that illustrate how Catholics in both Mayo and Chicago experience two distinct models of church. Even though Chicago is a major metropolitan area in the United States with a variety of ethnic and social groups and Mayo is largely rural with people of fairly similar backgrounds, both are microcosms of a wider clash of views on what the Catholic Church is or should be.

The theme, *Survival or Salvation?* highlights one way of viewing the challenge facing the Catholic Church today. Are we a church struggling to keep alive a hierarchical, clerical system or are we a church searching for the best way to spread the Good News of salvation, even if it means being open to new avenues for communicating this message?

A pastor who speaks of 'my church' and a parish priest who preaches about a priest and 'his' people are, at the local level, representative of the hierarchical model which holds that those in clerical positions (the pope, bishops, priests and possibly even religious sisters and brothers) know what is best for all the members of the church.

Not only the clergy are guilty of fostering this model of church. References to the church – either as a source of authority or the object of complaint – by many lay people generally are to the clerical, hierarchical structure.

A pastor who recognises the importance of ministering at times of crisis and a parish that has joyous eucharistic celebrations are representative of what I call the People of God model of church. In its ideal form this model recognises that all the faithful make up the church and all have responsibility for the church. The sense of the faithful (all the members) may represent the workings of the Holy Spirit as much as, and sometimes even more than, the proclamations of the hierarchy alone. This model also recognises the importance of listening to the experiences of the faithful when searching for ways to proclaim the Good News as both challenge and promise.

By rights, the Mayo church with its Celtic Christian roots should be comfortable with the People of God model of church. Despite the attempts to erase this heritage, I suspect that many Mayo Catholics still harbour the Celtic Christian distrust of a hierarchical church.

Even though my father and mother were a generation removed from their Mayo roots, I suspect their attitudes toward church authority can be traced to their parents' distrust of hierarchy. My parents respected priests and followed the rules of the church. Yet they also recognised church authority as human and capable of making mistakes. Father and Sister did not always know what was best. I suspect that I acquired their attitude unconsciously. Undoubtedly, this helps explain why I find the People of God model more conducive to spreading the Good News.

Theology in a saving church

The question of survival or salvation also leads to a further question about the role of theology and theologians in the church. Do we concern ourselves with the needs of a church struggling to survive or do we seek to understand how our faith speaks to the needs of a church that offers a hope of salvation? If we develop a theology that aids the latter, we will also help the church survive as the People of God. My experience leads me to believe that the people of God church needs theologians who possess the skill of a seanachaí.

For the past twenty years I have engaged in theological reflection on experiences that cause people to ask questions about the meaning of life in the common, ordinary, everyday events of their lives. I have reflected with them on issues related to sexuality, marriage, family, women, gender roles, ethnicity, neighbourhood (local community), parish, and liturgy.

I have become increasingly aware that there is a need to relate people's religious beliefs to these experiences in a way that makes them aware of the saving power of their faith. For example, what hope does the Creator/Redeemer/Spirit God of the creed offer them in times of need? What does a relationship to that God mean for the way they live their lives?

An important step in this process is uncovering images of God that have formed their religious imaginations. These are the images they acquired, most often unconsciously, by the stories of faith passed on to them when they were very young, by their parents' attitudes, and by critical experiences of their early lives. These images become the prism through which they understand their faith, at least at an unconscious level. This understanding then determines whether or not they are able to find salvation in their faith during critical times.

The next step, and the one that looks to the theologian, is to uncover new images that either supplement their positive images or replace negative ones. Stories of God growing out of these images will captivate their imaginations and help them see how their faith speaks to their experiences.

A theologian who is a seanachaí will learn to tell stories of God that will capture the attention of people of faith in much the same way that the traditional Irish storyteller did. For theology to be of service to the needs of the saving church, we need to develop a pastoral imaginative theology.[2]

Pastoral imaginative theology

Imaginative theology expands the definition of the understanding that theology seeks by recognising that the imagination plays a critical role in human understanding.

Failure to recognise this role leaves theology bereft of much of the richness of the Catholic tradition.

A pastoral imaginative theology seeks to reinterpret the revelatory and mediating power of the Catholic religious tradition using human experience as the starting point. At the same time, imaginative theology calls upon the richness of the tradition's religious and theological heritage. Imaginative theology is in constant conversation with human experience, religious heritage, and church tradition.

The many layered questions of meaning uncovered in human experience call for answers from both the heritage and the tradition. At the same time, the integration of experience, heritage and tradition supplies a new focus for evaluating particular human experiences.

A starting point for imaginative theology would be to uncover images and stories of God that shed light on the mystery we encounter in the basic experiences of human existence. These basic experiences include sexuality, family, community, work and cosmic citizenship.

People in Mayo and people in Chicago share the encounter with mystery that are intrinsic to these experiences. Given space limitations, I will address how a pastoral imaginative theology might reflect on two of these experiences in a broad sense. Other images might grow out of consideration of more specific questions encountered in different groups.

The mystery of human sexuality

The most basic, most fundamental experience we have of ourselves is as creatures with bodies, bodies that have sexuality. We are female; we are male.

Our masculinity and femininity have assured the survival of our

species. The powerful sexual drive that leads to union and pro-
creation in other animals is more pervasive in our species. We are
attracted to others not only at times when conception is possible
but at all times.

Yet our sexuality is more than sex. Masculinity and femininity
have been the main impetus for role assignments in society. Anat-
omy has been destiny for most of human history, even in those instances where we find evidence of matriarchy. At the present
time, we struggle to find how to move beyond sexual stereotyping. Our sexuality also influences how we give and receive
affection, how we model behaviour for the next generation, and
how we parent.

Taboos and myths about sexuality have been found in every culture and have been closely linked with religious understandings.
This link is no surprise since sexuality, by its very nature, is surrounded by mystery. Even today when we have vast amounts of
information about sex and sexuality, when much of the mystery
of past eras has been explained away, we still experience the surprise of sexual desire that often intrudes – sometimes positively,
sometimes negatively – into our supposedly well ordered lives.

Soap operas, television serials, romance novels, movies, all have
sexuality as an underlying theme. If the relationship between the
sexes is not portrayed, as is the case in some recent male bonding
movies, the influence of sexual stereotyping is evident.

As we make our way through life as sexual beings, we continually
discover both the joy of sex and the destructive power of sexuality. We experience the wonder and fulfillment of a relationship of
intimacy and the heartbreak and the disappointment of a broken
relationship. We have difficulty showing affection. We easily fall
into gender-stereotyping.

Because we long for the positive potential of sexuality but often
have problems achieving more than fleeting experiences of this
positive value, we find our lives as sexual beings a prime example
of the mystery of life. Why do we not do the good we long for? Indeed, why do we even long for it? What is the meaning of life for
us when we desire the good but often choose that which will keep
us from the good. Is human sexuality a good that we must learn to
use to help us achieve our goal of happiness (the good, the true,
the beautiful of philosophy)? Or is it an evil that keeps the world

in constant turmoil and shows that, ultimately, life is meaning-less?

Though some interpretations of the Christian story have consid-ered sexuality God's big mistake, and the patriarchal emphasis on the fatherhood of God has been used to affirm male superiority, there are stories of our faith that speak positively to the meaning-questions present in our experience of sexuality. At the same time, an interpretation of these stories in light of our experience of our-selves as sexual beings offers us new images of God, a God we speak of analogically.

In the creed we affirm a belief in God, the creator. The story of creation, told 'in the beginning', gives a very compact account of the creation of male and female that at the same time is rich in its potential for understanding human sexuality as sacramental.

In the second chapter of Genesis we find that God saw that it was not good for the human creature to be alone. So, God created them male and female. The man rejoiced to have someone who was bone of his bones and flesh of his flesh. The man and woman were alike, sharing the same bone and flesh. At the same time, they were different. This difference allowed them to cling together and be one flesh. In the later creation story, in the first chapter of Genesis, Yahweh finds each thing he creates, including the human, male and female, to be good.

There is more to the story. The union of male and female as one flesh is a mirror of God. Whatever it is that a man and woman must do in order to cling together as husband and wife – the love with its ups and downs – is sacramental, is revelatory of God. God is like a husband and wife at those times when they are clinging together with both the physical passion and emotional respect this requires. Better still God is like a lover – male or female. God is like a wife; God is like a husband.

Turning to the Song of Songs, we find that God is like a woman and a man in the throes of romantic love. In both Israel and the Christian tradition, the Song has stood for the relationship be-tween God and the faithful. For ancient Israel, it spoke of the rela-tionship of Yahweh and the people of Israel. In Christianity, it represented the relationship between God and the church.

Scripture scholars suggest that the Song is a collection of love songs, possibility written by women, that tells of the ups and downs of erotic romantic love. The emphasis is on the woman's role. She speaks the larger number of lines as she searches for her lover and tells of his wondrous deeds.

Thus when the gospel of John says that God is love and that those who abide in love abide in God and God in them, this love is not some abstract philosophical love. It is a love that 'no flood can quench, no torrents drown,' a love that resembles the love of romantic lovers in the first glow of a new love or the even deeper, brighter glow of a romantic love that has been renewed over and over throughout the course of a long marriage.

Relationships between the sexes are to serve as a model of this love. They are to be a revelation of the God who is love. They are to point the way for how humans are to live in union with each other because it is through this love that God reveals divine love.

An image of God suggested by this analysis is that of God as the romantic storyteller *par excellence*. However, this story, the longest story ever told, is co-authored by the people who inhabit the story, the creatures made in the divine image. So the continuing saga of a God who is love is like a romantic saga in which the characters take over the imagination of the author and contribute to the direction of the story.

The mystery of family

Another human experience that is fraught with mystery is that of the family. Every introductory sociology class learns that the family is the basic unit of society. What we learn, consciously and unconsciously, in the womb of the family shapes who we are. No matter how far we are removed from it – in time and space – its influence continues throughout our lives.

The family system approach to analysis of personality developments highlights how pervasive the family influence is, both positively and negatively. If we trace relationship patterns in family through at least three generations, we discover remarkable repetitions of behaviour by people who never knew each other. Patterns for dealing with family crisis are unconsciously passed on from generation to generation, as are family role models and spousal ways of relating as well as parent/child relationships.

In order for men and women to mature to the point where they can cling together so as to reveal God, they need the experience of themselves as lovable. They need to reach the point where they are secure enough in their own identity that they can risk intimacy. They need to have a sense of rootedness and belonging, a sense that is nurtured in family life.

Family members need a feeling of being centered if they are to learn to reach out beyond the family. People need a place where they belong, a place to come home to, a place where they are both accepted and challenged. Ideally, the traditional housewife of yore performed a centering role in the family. She created the home environment, watched over everyone, kept track of their needs, sustained them when they were in trouble and celebrated with them when they were happy.

How many wives and mothers had the luxury of performing this multidimensional role of the traditional housewife in Mayo or in immigrant Chicago communities is questionable. Still, the need for a centering place and the possibility that family can perform this role is an important consideration for personality development. Today, when the traditional housewife role is fast losing any attractiveness it might have had, family members must devise ways to assure that each member assumes responsibility for the centering role. Each member of the family needs to be a centering homemaker.

Family experiences also confront us with situations where we find ourselves wanting to do that which we cannot do, and feeling torn. We often feel a challenge to our sense of meaning in both the joys and the sorrows of family life. Family is a powerful influence on how we live the story of our lives. It is through family that we bring the past into the present and move toward the future with either a sense of hope or of despair.

Our need for centering points to the need for a larger sustaining force in our lives. We ask questions. What keeps us going? Is the force that created our world, if it is a God, one that created and then withdrew leaving us to find our own way through life's trials and tribulations? What, if anything sustains us?

Stories of our faith in both the Hebrew and Christian scriptures point to a God who lives and acts in the longest story, always allowing the story's characters the freedom to choose when and how to respond to the divine sustaining presence.

For the ancient Israelites, Yahweh is the centering force of their nation. Just as there are times when we resent what seems like the interference of a sustaining parent in our lives and want to escape from it, Israel repeatedly strayed from Yahweh but always longed to return to him. Like the traditional homemaker, Yahweh often is disappointed, hurt, angry, and critical of the Israelites. Still, they are welcomed back at the first sign that they might want to return.

The God who created everything, saw that it was good, and gave humans the freedom to choose how they would act in the ongoing saga, is always present as a focal point of the story, ready to offer suggestions about what the people should do. From this story we learn that the centering of Yahweh is that of a loving creator God who knows the ultimate goal of life is union with the divine. A centering God constantly offers us help in achieving this goal. We are never alone, even on the darkest days.

Family relationships, then, are meant to be sacramental, part of the divine story, signs of a centering God, who is somewhat like a homemaker, like a member of our family. God is like a father or mother who hugs us, centers us, when we are in need. A mother's or father's or even a sibling's hug when times are bad is but a faint hint of God welcoming back the Israelites and us, a central theme of God's story. The joy of a family celebration is a sign of the joy our co-operation in the divine story brings to the telling of the story.

Summary and Conclusion

In summary and conclusion, we have examined how the theme of survival or salvation raises a challenge for the church and for theologians. In our search for how theology might serve a saving church, we have suggested that we need a pastoral imaginative theology that speaks to the religious imagination.

As an example of how to engage in imaginative theology, we have looked at two stories of God that emerge from consideration of the 'something happens' of our experiences of sexuality and family. The sense of mystery encountered in these experiences leads us to ask what our faith says about this mystery. We asked how the creator God, who is the ultimate concern of our lives, is related to these experiences and at the same time how these experiences relate us to that God. We have discovered that our experiences as humans created in the image of God give us the capacity to mirror God, to speak about God.

God the loving romantic storytelling creator, and God the centering sustainer, are only two stories of God. As the gospel of Luke
tells us, even in the early days of the church, many people undertook to tell the events of the life of the main storyteller. This desire
to tell God's story continues. People love to hear and tell stories.
And what better story than the story of our God which is our
story, too.

The needs of people in a saving church require that theologians
make a systematic attempt to find a coherence between the various stories that together tell the story of God and the stories of
people's lives. The church in Mayo and Chicago (and other places,
as well) will be able to proclaim the Good News of salvation,
when we take seriously the need for a theology that recognises the
importance of the religious imagination.

A seanachaí telling stories of God seems an appropriate role for a
theologian from Mayo.

Notes

1. On a later trip we attended a liturgy in Mayo that, while not as
clerical as the one described here, had little in the way of congregational participation. The parish priest made repeated references
to the priest and his people as he exhorted the congregation to develop a love for the Mass by following the priest's example of preparing his sermon.

2. The term 'pastoral theology' often refers to what used to be
called moral theology. Though a pastoral imaginative theology
might result in people developing values, attitudes, and behaviours that flow from images of God, its main concern is not with
the specific issues of moral theology.

CHAPTER 19

Shall we Hope?

Enda McDonagh

Osker Schindler, of the oscar-studded film, *Schindler's List*, was an unlikely saviour. A crook in business, a womaniser and a drunk, he took on Nazi power, cunning and cruelty in saving hundreds of Jews from the gas-chambers. To-day, there are many more Schindler Jews alive in the world than there are Jews left in Poland.

The Holocaust is hardly an obvious place from which to begin a meditation on either hope or Mayo. It could seem blasphemous to compare the genocidal ambition of the Nazis and its near achievement with the admittedly crisis-ridden history of Mayo, from the 'To Hell or to Connaught' edict of Cromwell to the trauma of the famine. The intensity, scale and effectiveness of the concentration camps may have no historical parallel. Until Spielberg, no film-maker had the courage and imagination to deal directly with the horror of it. And he had the original author, Thomas Keneally, and others to filter it for him. The horrendous nature of these Nazi crimes and criminals should never be obscured. Their primary focus and victims, the Jews, must never be forgotten, particularly by western Christians. Yet there were other victims of these crimes, gypsies and homosexuals for example. And there were the collaborators of the immediate criminals, multiple, diverse and often respectable. In many ways this was the archetypal human fall, prepared over centuries by (Christian) anti-Semitism, fuelled by human insecurity and arrogance, and reflecting a moral nihilism, never far from destroying the fragile moral network which allows people to live together.

The Irish famine had some of that genocidal reach. There were however no Nazi-style conspirators, propagandists or execution-ers. The famine was first of all a natural disaster. The context was already deeply unjust. The response by the powerful was a gross human failure, if expressed more in ignoring, denying and inefficiency than in brutal intent and effective execution. Whatever the excuses, the consequences were horrific and not only in Mayo with its hunger marches and famine graves. So Mayo may be allowed its symbolic status, not only for Ireland in the eighteen forties but for all the famine-stricken countries of the nineteen nineties. 'Mayo, God help us' is of famine coinage and has much wider application to-day.

Holocaust and famine are not promising sources of hope. Diaspora had trapped the Jews. It provided the Mayos with one of their main routes of escape. (Death was the other.) Meantime the Jews have established a homeland. At what cost to themselves and their dispossessed neighbours it is still too soon to say. Mayo has experienced no parallel return, apart from a brief illusory period in the nineteen seventies. Next year in Jerusalem, for all the bitterness and the violence, has a much more plausible ring than next year in Castlebar. The state of Israel has a permanent look about it. The county of Mayo and its population look much more vulnerable.

The parallels are of course misleading. Mayo is neither by human aspiration nor divine election at the level of Israel. For all the five thousand years of habitation, the distinctiveness and destiny of Mayo have never implied such grand pretensions. A more relevant question is whether distinctiveness and destiny as a living community have run out for Mayo and its immediate Irish neighbours. Have the 'Save the West' campaigns of the last fifty years been finally exposed in all their futility? Or may Mayo still dare to hope? For what? In what sense of hope? Secular or sacred? Earthly and historical or heavenly and eschatological? Must hope for Mayo, whether prescribed by church leader or politician, be seen as the opium of church-goers and voters? If saving the west has hitherto proved impossible, should survival be now abandoned as worthless?

Coming home to death

Knock Airport is a monument to the initiative and energy of a contemporary hero of 'Saving the West', Monsignor James Horan. His own return from Lourdes to the airport in death was a further reminder of the traffic in death which had afflicted Mayo at least since famine times. Mayo has by now grown used to its people

coming home to funerals of their own, to die or just to be buried.
A childhood memory recalls, inaccurately perhaps, the last train
into Achill in 1937, bearing the bodies of the islanders burned in
the bothies in Scotland. The road home to Mayo has been so often
a death road. The airport at Knock has replaced a dozen country
railway stations in the death traffic as Mayo people come home to
bury or to be buried. New life still leaves by road, rail or air. Fresh
death brings the return. It can certainly feel like that.

In that context, a Myles na Copaleen-style fantasy might see Mayo
designated the National Cemetery of Ireland or, in more politically
correct terms, a European Regional Cemetery. Sowing and growing will naturally disappear in a 'set-aside' economy, despite the
starving millions down the airways from Knock. Plots for family
or even summer homes will no longer be able to compete in the
demand for burial sites. Picturesque locations and exhilarating
views to suit every taste – passionate Atlantic, isle-rich Clew Bay,
Nephin through the storm clouds over Lough Conn, the foot of
the Reek and the tip of Killary. Brussels supervised, OPW stew-
arded, with professional grief managers and genealogists for the
RFBI, the really foreign-born Irish, who would bring in extra
headage payments from Brussels, provided they had at least one
Irish root or otherwise eligible to play for Ireland in the World
Cup.

If the European Regional Cemetry seems too grand a project, a
province-wide Heritage Centre could be substituted. Holiday
homes, leisure parks, a meditation wilderness all might provide
relief and renewal for stressed Eastcoasters, English or Europeans. The west would be saved, preserved in asphalt and plastic,
Walt Disney in Synge song. Despair or hope would be irrelevant.
These are the agonising characteristics of real commnities, living
or dying. They have no place in the pseudo-communities of time-
out or time-warp.

Attempts, however feeble, at black humour and sarcasm have offered time-honoured solace to desperate people. Dan Berrigan
thought of them as among the few weapons of the powerless.
Mayo people retain all their other means of escape, by air, sea, rail
and road. 'All Louisburg needs is a good road out of it' – a fragment from the fifties when the 'bad' road was serviced by the
'Green Vessel' from Westport, courtesy CIE.

The logic of abandonment

An Ireland with four-fifths of its population living east of the
Shannon may be on the horizon. If that is the wish of Irish people,
who shall gainsay them? The logic of migration from the poorer
so-called periphery to the wealthier so-called centre is a worldwide phenomenon. It is not, however, simply a linear procession.
Definitions of centre and periphery are not finally fixed. Many
peripherals cannot or will not leave. A number of centrals come to
join them. And peripheries shift with shifting centres. Achill and
the Aran Islands, in their current relationships to Dublin, may
well prefigure the whole island of Ireland in its relations to Brussels, Strasbourg and Berlin. The logic of migration and abandon-
ment does not stop at the Irish Sea or the Mediterranean, as people in North Africa and Southern Europe are discovering. Walt
Disney Inc may have many more songs to sing than those of
Synge.

Cleansing by disillusion

The stripping away of illusions for people and community is
always painful and never complete. Yet it is essential to health
and recovery. Disillusionment is a cleansing as well as a painful
reality. It compels people to recognise their real probelms and
limitations, but also their real resources and possibilities. This
way lies the acceptance of personal and community responsibility
to deploy the resources and exploit the possibilities. The responsi-
bilities of others, of the outsiders with power, is not to be denied or
ignored. Acceptance of responsibility within can never be simply
isolationist or totally independent. It is a first significant step of a
continuous journey towards the re-invigoration of an ailing member of the body of Ireland and of Europe. It *is* a member of these
bodies and the key to bodily health is the health of all members.
The social and political watchword here is not dependence or independence but interdependence. Interdependence is a reciprocal
process involving mutual rights and obligations between the
members. We shall come to that.

Earthing trust

Disillusionment is born of trust betrayed and hope dashed, a frequent experience for Mayo and Co. The return of trust in a situa-

tion so painfully cleansed, must be rooted in earth and people over time. The human need to trust persists or at least survives beyond the deceits of the past and in face of the fears of the future. It may be best cultivated by starting at ground level. Without some basic trust in the earth and its fruits, human life would be impossible. Without critical caution based on experience, that trust easily betrays and destroys. Let mushrooms be our witness. Trust has to be mutual and the earth may have less reason to trust humanity in recent decades. Trust in the earth grounds human beings' trust in one another and ultimately their trust in God.

All these kinds of trust remain fragile and require protection by mutual honesty and care, at least by the human mediators of truth. In community, trust and truth are inseparable. The untruths of the past have destroyed many of the former hopes of Mayo. Those of the present and future can only do likewise. For trust to develop into hope, truth must prevail, and not just painful and ugly truth. For our delight, the truth is also the beautiful, the fit and form of the good. An incipient sense of the beauty of Mayo and its people may foster a hopeful realism, as people respond to the possibilities of the emerging good – in religious terms, of the emerging God. For that, personal, structural and religious conversion may be required.

Democracy and the reign of God

A Mayo book of theology is continually faced with the challenge of relating secular and religious sources, human politics and divine providence. The proper distinctions of religion and politics, of church and state, must not be allowed to reduce society to the secular, and religion to the private devotion. Crucial to maintaining the distinctions and fostering the relationships and dialogue of religion and politics is the reign or kingdom of God as preached and inaugurated by Jesus Christ. In summary, it means the presence and power of God in the world, creating, sustaining, healing, enabling and transforming, in promotion of the final flourishing of humankind and cosmos. Church and state are distinct instruments in the service of this flourishing, by the design of the creator God. The emergence of democracy and its further urgent developments are critical to human flourishing and divine creativity.

Trust, truth and self-government

The delicate enterprise of self-government remains at an immature stage, in need of protection and development in the most democratic countries. The call of development is two-fold: outwards to include larger regional groupings of states and eventually into some global unit; inwards in each country and political unit to ensure effective participation by sub-regions and sub-communities. In this extension and intensification of democracy, truth and trust will always be necessary and always at risk. Only in the gracious presence of the creator and faithful God can they be finally pursued, justified, and, however ambiguously, achieved.

Human rights and solidarity

Ambiguous achievement is the stuff of human history. The long history of the struggle to formulate and establish human rights, which reached its climax in the UN Declaration of 1948 and subsequent covenants, retains its own ambiguities. The worldwide protection of personal dignity, irrespective of creed, class, race or gender, announced under the Declaration, is far from perfect realisation. A more serious difficulty has been the tendency to interpret the Declaration in liberal and individualist terms so that its clear-cut social provisions, like the right to work, are simply ignored. This leaves weaker and poorer groups in society excluded and exploited by those with economic and other power. Without genuine solidarity between groups, individual civil and political rights will remain ineffectual. Deprived regions will remain in their privations. The Pauline vision of the reign of God sketches true solidarity, in which there is neither Jew nor Gentile, slave or free, male or female, but all are free, equal and one. (Letter to the Galatians 3:28) The flourishing in communion of all, aims of democracy and of the reign of God, demands attention to both human rights and solidarity.

Participation and subsidiarity

Participation in social governance is perhaps the oldest and most distinctive element in democracy. Despite the present range of participation available to people, through elections and referenda, closer and more effective participation in decision-making is necessary to sustain democracy in line with the internationalis-

ation of political authority, the independent growth of international economic power, the educational progress of people, and
modern communications. What is to be decided at the level of the
European Union, for example, how and by whom and with what
mandate from the people, must be clarified to ensure genuine participation by the people of the Union and real accountability to
them. The same requirements must be met at the level of national
government. At regional and local level in Ireland, a series of
fresh initiatives is needed to restore participation and accountability to the people from whom all political authority derives (article
6, *Bunreacht na hÉireann*). Local political authority is basic to national and international authority. The return to political fashion
of the principle of subsidiarity, that political decisions be taken at
the level of organisation of the people most closely affected, with
due regard for the broader common good, faces tough resistance
in centralised Ireland. Without implementation of that principle,
peripheral areas like Mayo have little hope and they may yet be
joined at the periphery by apparent centres like Dublin. Subsidiarity and participation require decentralisation, or better polycent-
ralisation, where the power is distributed and the single power-
centre no longer holds. In a church which regards itself as a sign
of the coming kingdom or reign of God, and which preached subsidiarity before it was fashionable, parallel and appropriate
moves to participation and subsidiarity are called for.

A Sense of Mayo, A Sense of Ireland, A Sense of ...
'You can't fool me. There's nothing west of Chapelizod,' a Dublin-
born barman in Kilburn told me years ago when I tried to explain
where Maynooth was. West of the Shannon, West of the Bann,
North of the Liffey or outside the Pale, often reflect no more than
jocose rivalry. Yet some deeper sense of our differences and even
separations, as well as our deep dependence on one another in
Ireland, our interdependence, is necessary to national health. For
Mayo to survive it needs the interest and energy of the rest of Ireland, not primarily in economic handouts, but in personal engagement and community contact, by all Irish people moving in
and out of Mayo to work and play, to rest and pray.
It could be argued that it is Mayo and its parallels which give Ireland its special status in Europe and that they have first claim on

funds arising from this status of privation and peripherality. Beyond all that, a sense of Ireland must be developed amongst all Irish people which includes a real sense of Mayo and Leitrim, of Kerry and Donegal, as well as Dublin and Waterford. Whatever about losing its claims to European funding, Ireland without its Atlantic seaboard and seaboarders would not be Ireland any more than Mayo without Dublin and Kildare would be Mayo. A sense of Ireland involves a sense of Mayo and of all the other component parts. A sense of Mayo involves a sense of kinship, participation and solidarity with all the other parts of Ireland. Only such senses of Mayo and Ireland can properly expand into European and global senses. For the Christian, the local community connects through immediate and interdependent neighbours to the furthest reaches of the one family and reign of God.

The winter name of God

The winter of 1845, the first of the great famine winters, has marked Mayo deeply and permanently with its death and departures and deaths during departures. The coffin-ships became the seabirds of destruction. That winter lingers. Intervening signs of spring have too often deceived. The sign-readers may now be too disillusioned to try distinguishing true from false. Yet true signs and their authentic readers remain gift – gift from the creator God of the still rich Mayo earth and sea and sky, and of the still rich and diverse people of historical and contemporary Mayo. The legacy of five thousand years may not be overlooked. The legacy and richness survive through the longest winter. Divine creator and human creativity are at work in the bleakest and darkest of times. Cherishing their heritage and recognising their gifts, Mayo people and their island-wide, worldwide winter companions may finally escape that long winter confinement, not only to survive but to flourish.

Hope

is the winter name of God.

Sally Dyck

APPENDIX II

West of Ireland Theology Research Association
(Cumann Taighde Diagachta Iarthar na hÉireann)

The West of Ireland Theology Research Association has emerged over a number of years through consultation between church leaders and academics. Its main objective is to develop a theological consciousness in the west of Ireland and to promote analysis and reflection in the light of the gospel on the many issues facing the west. It seeks to serve church and society in the west in an intellectual, pastoral and ecumenical way.

It has organised one international conference, 'Marginalised Societies, the Secular World and the Gospel', at University College, Galway, March 1993. The papers will be published in the first issue of the Association's Bulletin, *Diagacht/Theology*.

Membership is open to all interested in promoting the aims of the Association. Annual subscription is £10 and should be sent to:

The Treasurer,
The West of Ireland Theology Research Association
Colaiste Einde
Galway.

Members are entitled to a free copy of the Bulletin.

The Ad Hoc Organising Committee is Archbishop Joseph Cassidy (Chair), Bishop John Kirby, Professor Markus Worner, Aibhistín Ó Murchadha (Treasurer), Sr Helena O'Donoghue, Sr Kathleen McQuade, Rev Thomas Leyden, Rev Martin MacNamara (Secretary), Rev Professor Enda McDonagh (Editor, The Bulletin).